EXTREME BIRDER

EXTREME

LYNN E. BARBER

BIRDER

One Woman's Big Year

TEXAS A&M UNIVERSITY PRESS
College Station

Manufactured in China

by Everbest Printing Co.,

through FCI Print Group

First edition

This paper meets the requirements of ANSI/NISO Z39.48–1992

(Permanence of Paper).

Binding materials have been chosen for durability.

LIBRARY OF CONGRESS CATALOGING-IN-PUBLICATION DATA

Barber, Lynn E.
Extreme birder : one woman's big year / Lynn E. Barber.—1st ed.
    p. cm.
  Includes index.
  ISBN-13: 978-1-60344-261-9 (pb-flexibound : alk. paper)
  ISBN-10: 1-60344-261-8 (pb-flexibound : alk. paper)
  1. Bird watching—United States—Anecdotes.   2. Bird watching—Canada—
Anecdotes.   3. Birds—Counting—United States—Anecdotes.   4. Birds—
Counting—Canada—Anecdotes.   5. Bird watchers—Anecdotes.   I. Title.
  QL677.5.B33   2011
  598.072'347—dc22
  2010043596

CONTENTS

PREFACE

Don't cry because it is over. Smile because it happened. —DR. SEUSS

LOOKING BACK

It has been nearly a year since I completed my birding big year, the topic of this book. I still am so glad that I made the effort, and so pleased with how the year turned out. At the end of 2008, I had tallied 723 species for the year in continental North America north of Mexico. Some 35 of these species were new for me in this geographic area, 20 of which were entirely new for me.

Where does my big year fit into the world of fanatic birding? Sandy Komito saw 745 species one year (1998) and about 724 species a previous year, both of which efforts included birding in Attu (where you can add about 15 to 40 species, depending on the year, that will not be found elsewhere in the American Birding Association [ABA] area). As far as I know, no one else, with or without Attu, has seen over 715 species in one year in the ABA area. Depending on how you look at it, I am either in second place (because one person's two records have a higher total than mine), or first place in the millennium and first place anytime without doing Attu, or in third place (because Sandy's two records total more than mine).

When I began to look into who had previously done ABA big years, I was surprised that I could not find any records of women who had attempted this. Maybe women did try to find high numbers of birds in the ABA area in one year but were afraid to call it "doing a big year" or just did not let the world (or at least me) find out about it. Or maybe women just do not usually become so fanatic about birding—and have the time and money—to do a big year. In any case, to my knowledge, I appear also to hold the women's record for an ABA big year.

But the numbers, while very important to me, are not what I think about first when I think of 2008. What fills my whole being is the knowledge that doing this big year was a wonderful adventure without rival in my birding life. For a whole year I went wherever there were birds that I wanted to see, explored new and exciting areas for birds that were also new and exciting, and filled every day with birding and plans for birding, nearly nonstop, following my passion.

The year would not have been possible without the help and encouragement of many people. First, and foremost, I give my heartfelt thanks to my husband, David (who should really be called "Saint David").

Thanks to all those people at First Congregational Church in Fort Worth and at Fort Worth Audubon who did not complain too much in 2008 about my frequent absences. Thanks to Ann Hoover, whose gift of *A Big Year* inspired this big year, and to Gail Morris, who read the manuscript and improved it with her comments.

Also, thanks to Wayne Bartholomew, Benton Basham, the Beatty family, Barbara Bickel, Gene Blacklock, Buck Buchanan, Eric Carpenter, Sheridan Coffey, Scarlet and George Colley, Greg Cook, Debra Corpora, Cameron Cox, Bob Dittrick, Jon Dunn, Kim Eckert, Ted Eubanks, Tim Fennell, Jean Ferguson, Linda Ford, Tony Frank, Bert Frenz, Lena Gallitano, Greg Gillson, Ann Gilmore, Mary Gustafson, Scott Hauser, John Haynes, Gary Hodne, James Huntington, Marshall Jackson, Dan Jones, Melody Kehl, Jerri Kerr, Keith Kingdon, Mark Korducki, Aaron Lang, Tom Langshied, Paul Lehman, Ray Little, Derek Lovitch, Larry Manfredi, Jean Martin, Steve Mayes, Helen Nelson, Jennifer Owen, Brian Patteson, Jimmy Paz, Dan Peake, Father Tom Pincelli, Dave Porter, John Puschock, Dylan Radin, Martin Reid, Jamie Ritter, Bron Rorex, Chris Runk, Diana Rushing, Dan Sanders, David Sarkozi, Scott Schuette, Bob Schutsky, Debra Shearwater, Jim Sinclair, Rich Stevens, Bob Stone, Rick Timm, Ron Weeks, Jana and John Whittle, Allen Williams, Jan Wimberly, and Mimi Wolf.

And thanks to many others whose name I never knew, or who have inadvertently been left off above, who reported birds, helped me see them, and encouraged me along the way, and to all those other birders I met, or who posted a good bird sighting, whose names just got lost in my obsessive birding frenzy.

I have studied a list of all my birds,
Trying to remember who, by their words,
Helped me to put these birds on my list.
Yet I'm quite sure I may have missed
Some of you. So please forgive.
My bird-brain's small and like a sieve.

NOT ANOTHER BIG YEAR!

That's what my husband *should* have said to me when I announced that I would really like to try to do an ABA big year. And it's what my friends did say.

Those of you who have read *The Big Year* by Mark Obmascik may be thinking it, too. Obmascik's book recounts the adventures of three ABA big year birders in 1998, when the current ABA year record was set by Sandy

Komito. Komito is the only person to have done two ABA big years, and he set a record both times. His excellent account of his amazing second big year is *I Came, I Saw, I Counted* (1999). No one has equaled either of his records before or since he did his big years. In those days, one could fly into Attu, an Alaskan island hotspot for Asian birds, to increase one's ABA big year list. This is no longer possible because the Attu airstrip has been closed, and therefore, the likelihood of ever equaling Komito's highest record, or even his lower record, is very small.

Yes, perhaps I am just another person who did just another big year. As anyone who has birded knows, however, not only is every year of birding different from other years of birding but no two birding days are the same. Whether bird-filled adventure or near birdless, much of the excitement is the unpredictability of birding. What will happen? What will I see?

For me, the whole ABA big year idea really began in my mind in 2006. But I need to go back to 2002 to tell a more complete story. If you are not a birder, it may surprise you to know that seemingly normal people with the seemingly harmless hobby of bird-watching can go completely nutty over seeing more birds. In 2002, my third year in Texas, I happened to talk to a Fort Worth birder who said he always tried to get 400 bird species per year, which to me was an astounding concept. But it sounded like fun, so in 2003, I gave it a try. That year I reached 485 species in Texas, which was 5 short of the pre-2003 record. That same year Eric Carpenter, an Austin birder who actually started the year with the single-minded goal of breaking the Texas big year record, did so by having a list of 505 species. In 2004, Howard Laidlaw, a birder from the Houston area, topped that with 511 species.

My Texas big year was in 2005, a year I enjoyed birding so much that I didn't want it to end. But it did end, and I had a record-breaking 522 species due to the combination of an astounding influx of birds into Texas, way too many hours spent on birding, and 90,000 miles of driving! In the void that followed, I wrote up my adventures and then went back to more and more birding.

In 2006, right after I finished my Texas big year, my birding friend Ann Hoover gave me a copy of Obmascik's book to celebrate. Of course, I knew that this book existed and had even handled it a few times in a bookstore, but I had deliberately put it back and decided *not* to buy it. It was too risky. Reading something like that might give me the harebrained idea of doing an ABA big year myself. But now I owned the book, and it sat on my bookshelf. Whenever I saw Ann, she would say, "So how do you like the book?"

and I had to admit that I had not started it. I was afraid to, with good reason, it turned out. The minute I started reading about what the three men did in 1998, I wanted to try it myself. What exhilaration there would be. Such a quest. Nonstop birding.

But reality intruded. We could not afford for me to fly all over the country, including flying to Alaska more than once, with the additional motel, rental car, and gas costs. My minimal guess at the likely costs was in the range of about $65,000, not including food. We still owed on our credit cards for my 2005 Texas big year. If I did an ABA big year, I knew I would have to do it to my best ability, not some half effort. No, I just could not do another big year, and certainly not an ABA big year.

Time passed. One day in mid-2007, my husband casually asked me when I thought we should get a second mortgage. I looked at him blankly and then realized that he meant, yes, do another big year, and we would figure out how to deal with the costs somehow. When I finally grasped this concept, and got the green light, I never looked back.

In what follows I have tried to convey what happened during my ABA big year in 2008—my worry times, which were many; my ecstatic times, of which there were even more; and the dull times (not too many); and some of the planning, scheming, and finagling to try to see birds that did not always cooperate. As I wrote the first draft of this late in 2008, I still did not want it to end, in spite of my extreme tiredness and indebtedness, and my need to catch up with my nonbirding life and all the things that I had put off during the year.

What Is An ABA Big Year?

I am a fanatic, obsessed birder and have great difficulty abstaining from birding for even short periods. Even birders who are less than fanatic often want to do more than just go out to look at birds. Sometimes they like to challenge themselves, for example, to see how many bird species they can find in a particular geographic area within a particular time period. This type of effort is known as doing a "big day" or a "big year" in that geographic area.

While there are many ways that a fanatic birder can do extreme birding, doing a state big year or an ABA big year (a big year done in the "ABA area") is thought by many to be pretty close to the most far-gone, fanatic thing that a birder can do. The ABA area is defined by the American Birding Association as including the 49 states of the continental United States, Canada, the French islands of St. Pierre et Miquelon, and adjacent waters to a distance of

200 miles from land or half the distance to a neighboring country, whichever is less. The ABA area does *not* include Mexico, Hawaii, Bermuda, the Bahamas, or Greenland.

Although there are ABA "rules" for when and which birds may be counted, birders may choose to ignore the rules because there is no enforcement mechanism other than the threat that other birders will disapprove of one's tactics or results, think poorly of the noncompliant birder, and ignore the birder's claimed sightings and totals. For those who strive and claim to follow the ABA rules, there also is no reward for obeying the rules, or even for getting a big list while following the rules (or not), other than a feeling of accomplishment, and perhaps the approval of others.

Although there are those who disapprove of counting birds, listing birds, or doing a big year as being undignified, worthless, or ridiculous, or all three, for me, doing a big year both times has been wonderfully exciting, rewarding, educational, and challenging. Even as my list increased in number, and as "just one more" became my fervent prayer, doing a big year became even more motivational and exhilarating. As the year drew to a close, each new bird added to the list seemed a greater and greater miracle.

It's hard to explain the lure of the bird chase to someone who has never experienced it. Each new day and each new year of birding are an empty canvas. You can change the paint and the hoped-for result, but unlike brushes, birds often do not behave as you wish and cannot be controlled. Birds can fly unpredictably or decide to vanish. Alternatively, when all goes well, they can sing and announce their presence to you, or even better, give you a view.

The result of a bird chase depends to some extent on the birder's cleverness and knowledge in finding the birds, but sometimes depends much more on perseverance and time spent, and often on luck. A successful result of a chase requires not only that the bird be present but also that the birder gets to where the bird is and finds it. Sometimes the likelihood of success can be increased by employing birding guides, friends, or audio bird attractors such as recorded bird songs or owl calls on an iPod or tape. It is well known that use of taped bird calls should be limited or avoided depending on the circumstances. Sometimes such use violates park or sanctuary regulations. The ABA has rules against use of taped bird calls under various circumstances, such as during breeding season or when the bird being sought is a rarity. To help in a bird chase, perhaps a little ESP, magic, or other incantations can be employed—there is no rule against those.

How Does One Plan A Big Year?

The short answer to the question of how one plans a big year is "with diffi-culty." It's sort of like herding cats, or in this case, birds. The essence of it is that for birds that spend very little time in the chosen area of the big year (e.g., the ABA area), special effort must be made to find them within their narrow win-dow of presence. In the extreme case, for very rare birds, if possible, everything must be dropped to allow for the chase for the rare bird before it disappears. Between these special efforts, it is important to find the more common birds, which requires tailored travel to go where they are likely to be found.

Ideally for someone doing a big year, it is best if the birder's life has no demands other than birding and if the person is totally flexible and available. Unfortunately, for the bottom line of the bird count, most birders need to have some life in addition to birding, and even more unfortunately, prior birding plans themselves often limit what other birding can be done. For example, plane reservations for my Alaskan trips needed to be made in advance, to take advantage of special fare discounts, and such reservations were not easily changed if I wanted to chase an unexpected rare bird elsewhere. There often was a financial penalty for changes and last-minute plans.

All of the above advice on doing an ABA big year assumes that the big year birder has knowledge of when, where, and how to find all the possible birds and can somehow orchestrate trip scheduling to maximize the number of bird species seen and not miss too many species on each trip (which would require additional trips to "mop up" missed species or result in a lower bird count). It's very easy to focus on finding rarities and to forget to plan for and take time to look for the more common birds.

Of course, it is important not to wait until the big year starts to plan it. Most states have rare bird alerts (RBAs). Observers report sightings of rare or unusual birds, which are posted on Internet sites. There are also bird-finding books for many states. Long before my big year began, I spent many hours studying bird books, particularly the range maps of the birds, perusing the state rare bird alert postings, and checking the state guidebooks to see where were good spots and what were good times of the year to find particular bird species. I put Post-it notes on a 2008 calendar to try to block in time periods to plan my trips in the most bird-maximizing way, moving the notes around as new information made me realize that I needed to be someplace else then or needed to be in a particular place earlier or later in the year. I studied other big year reports that were available, as well as bird tour company Web sites, to see when other more experienced people thought it was wise to travel to particular areas or to find particular bird species. I consulted friends and a few tour guides. And I read a lot.

One part of planning and doing a big year is working out whether it's going to be a solo or a group effort. Because I did not know anyone else who was ready, willing, and able to do an ABA big year when I did, much of my birding was alone. I do have quite a few women friends who had expressed interest in joining me on some of my trips, so I periodically e-mailed my schedule to them to see if they wished to accompany me. The result was that on many of my longer out-of-state trips, I had one or two good birding friends to share the birding fun and the costs of rooms, car rental, and gasoline—all of which I greatly appreciated.

Then, there is the matter of dollars, many of which are required for any big year. The more fanatic the plans, the more likely there will be increased cost. Some effort can be made to stay at cheap motels, eat frugally, and take advantage of cheap airfares and car rentals. But if you are going to go out and bird all over the ABA area, it will cost a lot of money. Closely associated with all that travel is the regrettable use of fossil fuels if you are going to cover the entire ABA area as much as is required to have a chance at the largest number of bird species (unless you bicycle it entirely, which of course, is very laudable but does not allow for seeing as many birds as my more costly effort).

You try to plan a big year while remaining flexible, but the unexpected appearance or disappearance of birds, and life itself, sometimes just gets in the way, so you do the best you can, over and over.

A Bit Of Background

Before I get into the details about my ABA big year, I need to mention some background information to help you understand the parts of my life that are not directly related to doing a birding big year.

First, I am not a professional birder, but instead have an unrelated career that has many demands. Although I have been birding since age seven and have an undergraduate degree in zoology from the University of Wisconsin, my advanced training was first in bacteriology and then in law. After working as a research microbiologist and professor for about eight years, I went to Duke Law School. I am now in solo practice as a patent attorney in Fort Worth. I have many wonderful and interesting clients, for whom I file patent applications and work to obtain patent protection. Because I do not have any staff and because patent law has many deadlines, it is important that my clients are able to find me and that I have time to work on client matters and am not gone from my office too long. Juggling critical client needs and out-of-town birding trips was a major part of a big year. I checked e-mails and phone messages as regularly as possible and often took my laptop computer and client work with me on the road.

Second, while I have lived in Wisconsin, Alaska, Oregon, North Carolina, and Texas (since 2000), there is much of North America where I have not birded. Without extensive planning, and lots of consulting of the Internet, including state bird listservs (weekly Internet reports of bird rarities for each state), and gathering information from bird books, friends, acquaintances, and total strangers, it would not have been possible to do a "satisfactory" big year.

Third, I have an exceptionally wonderful and understanding husband, Dave. His passion is not birding but weather. During the years that I was a microbiology professor, he was a meteorology professor, but he, like I, also changed careers and is now a church pastor (United Church of Christ). His love of watching the weather, including programming his computer to do more and more complicated and dramatic weather-related analysis and forecasting, probably helps him understand my birding fanaticism. Whatever the reason, I am grateful.

Finally, perhaps you are wondering just why I undertook this big year (or perhaps you have written it off as unexplainable obsessiveness). Although it is difficult to self-analyze, I think that my overall objective was a hard-to-define combination of just loving to bird and needing an excuse to do it nearly nonstop for a full year, the need to compete and see how well I could do, particularly against men, and the opportunity such a year provided to take pictures of birds and have adventures about which I could give talks, and maybe, about which I could write a book. [Note: Unless otherwise indicated, I took all the photos and made all the paintings in this book.] During my big year, when I was asked what my goal was, my first answer was usually "to get 650 species" (my secret goal of 700 being almost unimaginable, as it takes years and much work for "normal" birders to get 700 on their life list). Then I would add that my goal was also to "break the women's record" for an ABA year, since I had never heard of a woman who had tried this seriously. As far as I could tell, this goal required getting over 522 species, the number I reached in Texas in 2005, which of course is in the ABA area. After I reached 700 species in October, my answer to the question of my goal was always "just one more."

ABA CHECKLIST AND CHECKLIST CODES

The American Birding Association has a list of all of the birds that have ever been documented in the ABA area, which can be found at http://www.aba.org. This is the list that an ABA big year birder studies, drools over, rejoices over, and weeps over.

For the less than absolutely fanatic birder, it may be surprising to learn that each of the bird species that has ever been observed in the ABA area has been assigned a code that is intended to correspond to the likelihood of the bird appearing in the ABA area. When planning a big year, it is very useful to pay attention to these codes to determine which birds are most worthy of spending extra effort to find. The ABA codes may be briefly summarized as follows: Code 1 and Code 2: regular breeding species and visitors to the ABA area, with Code 1 birds being more widespread and usually more numerous and Code 2 birds having a more restricted area, being in lower densities, or more secretive; Code 3: rare birds that occur annually in the ABA area in very low numbers, including visitors and rare breeding residents; Code 4: casual birds, not recorded annually in the ABA area, but with six or more total records, including three or more in the past 30 years; Code 5: accidental birds, recorded in the ABA area five or fewer times, or fewer than three times in the past 30 years; and Code 6: birds that cannot be found, due to being extinct or extirpated from the ABA area, or all are in captivity or releases are not yet naturally reestablished.

Unfortunately, although these codes generally reflect reality, the process of finding birds is made more difficult by the fact that birds do not know their groupings and do not always behave predictably. In fact, they often behave as if they are deliberately trying to ruin the system. Why else would a normally common sparrow (or gull or warbler or . . .) suddenly become difficult to find?

Even if you know that a bird is uncommon or common, that does not get you to the bird. No bird is common everywhere, and some quite rare birds can be very common in a restricted locale. But if, in addition to noting a species' ABA Code, you bird often enough, you begin to get a good idea of whether a particular bird that is sought will be difficult to find. A big year birder must "get" all, or as many as possible of the Code 1, 2, and 3 birds as soon as possible, so that when a Code 4 and Code 5 bird shows up, the big year birder can spare the time to chase it. Chasing Code 6 birds is not a normal part of a big year birder's plans (unless the big year birder is convinced that a bird formerly classified as extinct, such as the Ivory-billed Woodpecker, really still exists somewhere).

At least that's the theory on which I worked. No matter how hard I tried, however, I could not figure out a way to get some of the birds that I really should have found. For example, in my ABA big year, I never found a Connecticut Warbler, which does not normally migrate through Texas (my home state). When they were singing on their northern breeding territories, I was in Alaska, north of where Connecticut Warblers breed. When I returned to the lower 48 in July, Connecticut Warblers were silently lurking in the north woods raising their broods. I missed them in fall, too, because I did not know where to position myself in their southward path along the East Coast of the United States, and I did not have time to just sit somewhere and wait for one of them to pass by. Even if I had tried to intercept them during their southern migration, I might still have missed Connecticut Warblers for the year, but I will never know. I was off doing other bird chasing.

A breakdown of my sightings in 2008 indicates (to the best of my counting ability) that in 2008 in the ABA area my list included 492 of the 492 Code 1 birds; 167 of the 170 Code 2 birds; 41 of the 71 Code 3 birds; 16 of the 92 Code 4 birds; and 7 of the 115 Code 5 birds. No Code 6 birds.

EXTREME BIRDER

JANUARY

I Can't Believe I'm Actually Doing It!

NEW BIRD SPECIES SEEN THIS MONTH: 333
TOTAL BIRD SPECIES BY THE END OF THE MONTH: 333
PLACES BIRDED: Texas, Minnesota, New Mexico, Arizona, California

JANUARY 1

I am in Rockport, Texas. Soon I will leave with Debra Corpora, a birder friend at whose house in Rockport my husband and I stayed over the Christmas holidays. I will join the "shrikes," four women birders from the Rockport area, to do a big day and in the process begin my ABA big year. I understand that the primary reason for their name is something to do with shrikes having good eyesight.

I have been looking over reports from the North American Rare Bird Alert (NARBA) and agonizing over whether I should chase the reported Barnacle Geese (eastern United States; status uncertain), Smew (California), Brambling (California), Northern Jacana (Arizona), or Ivory Gull (northeastern Canada).

I am torn between planning (having a reserved plane, motel, and car, with attendant problems with cancellation) and spontaneity (being able to chase, but usually at a higher cost for last-minute reservations). For now, I'm sticking to planning trips in advance.

JANUARY 2

Last night, after only one day of big year birding, I was too tired to write. Not a good sign. Our day was great but cold for Texas (45–55 degrees) and windy. The five of us shrikes birded the Rockport and Port Aransas areas, plus Hazel Bazemore Park at the edge of Corpus Christi, a hotspot that has a great assortment of local birds and often a rarity. Despite sparrows being kept down by the howling winds, we were all enthusiastic and good-spirited.

At the end of the day, which began with a fly-across-the road-right-ahead-of-us Common Loon, we tried for Great Horned Owls and Common

Sandhill Cranes are one of my favorite birds, and I was glad to see them on the first day of my big year.

Pauraques, missing both. We wound up with 101 species, mostly winter Texans. Highlights for me included a very cinnamon-colored male Cinnamon Teal, spectacular Roseate Spoonbills, fly-over Sandhill Cranes, a Peregrine Falcon at its usual winter perch on a water tower, a White-tailed Hawk working the grass-covered area south of Port Aransas, Common Terns and Sanderlings along the Port Aransas beach, a noisy Great Kiskadee, and a stunning Vermilion Flycatcher.

Today Debra, who is an avid birder retired from the education field, and I drove to the Valley (Lower Rio Grande Valley of Texas). Originally we were going to go to the King Ranch, which offers bird tours of its widespread birdy brush, woodland, and agricultural habitats, but the target Masked Ducks have not been reported in a while.

After getting to the Valley, Debra and I first went to Sabal Palm Audubon Center in Brownsville to look for a reported Dusky-capped Flycatcher. It was so windy though that we would not have been able to hear it if it had called. We did hear what we thought was the flycatcher, but it was too indistinct. We went to the University of Texas campus at Brownsville and immediately found our goal, Green Parakeets, which are routinely found there.

Sanderlings are common shorebirds along the Texas coast.

Green Parakeets have become established in a number of places in the Lower Rio Grande Valley of Texas. These were seen in Brownsville.

We are in our second room for the night at a not-to-be-recommended motel in Brownsville. The first room had no hot water, and this room has no heat, and it is supposed to get down to the 40s tonight. Debra's off to see the poor desk clerk, who can't leave her post, to get a set of keys for a third room. (The third room was fine.)

JANUARY 3

I'm writing while waiting for the wireless service to start working here in my room in McAllen. It's important for me to be able to check regularly on rare bird reports from across the ABA area to help me plan where to bird on future days and to post my daily bird sightings on my Web site so that I do not get too far behind.

Today, we started again at Sabal Palm but were luckier with the Dusky-capped Flycatcher. Not only did we hear its distinctive mournful call but we saw it right over our heads.

We went to Progresso Lakes, a rural Valley subdivision, where despite much looking we were unable to find a reported Golden-crowned Warbler. Then we were back to Frontera Audubon in Weslaco, where we added a Rose-breasted Grosbeak and skulking Ovenbird. Anzalduas County Park (Hidalgo County), one of my favorite Valley birding sites, was also nice, as it was a calm day. We wandered beneath the live oaks and found a Northern Beardless-Tyrannulet.

Our final stop today was Bentsen–Rio Grande Valley State Park, but we found few birds. As we waited for dark and the park's evening owl walk/drive, almost immediately we saw and heard Common Pauraques, and after dark, we heard Great Horned Owls. We did not see or hear any small owls.

A Dusky-capped Flycatcher was a very welcome find on January 3 at Sabal Palm Audubon Center, Brownsville, Texas.

The original plan had been to go to Salineño tomorrow, but now that drive seems too long. Instead, we plan to bird at Bentsen again in the morning and maybe Santa Ana National Wildlife Refuge afterward.

JANUARY 4

I'm back in Rockport, my first expedition for my 2008 big year finished. I have 162 species for the year, three more than at this time in 2005 for my Texas big year. One of the reasons that I love Texas so much is that it is relatively easy to find considerably over 100 species in a day in the coastal area or the Valley. It just takes knowledge of where to go to find the birds and a nonstop determination to find them.

We ended this trip because we were tired and there are no species for us to look for in the Lower Valley. I still need to look for birds in the Salineño area, with its Muscovy Ducks and Red-billed Pigeons, and its drier habitats with other still-needed Valley birds. Tomorrow morning, Debra and I are going to Aransas National Wildlife Refuge (NWR) for Whooping Cranes and whatever else we can find before I go back home to Fort Worth.

JANUARY 5

It was a very foggy morning at Aransas NWR, and we were lucky to get a view of a single Whooping Crane. On the way to the refuge, we saw three Wild Turkeys high in a tree along the road, displaying as if it were Thanksgiving and being watched by an interested Red-tailed Hawk perched just above them. At the refuge I also added Wilson's Snipe probing the mud with its beak, a darting-by Gray Catbird, and a calling Clapper Rail. On the drive out, a beautiful, sunny mild day, we saw a Ferruginous Hawk on a pole. In the unclaimed fields across the highway from Goose Island State Park, we found two Le Conte's Sparrows and two Grasshopper Sparrows as we tramped across the uneven grassy terrain.

We then returned to Rockport. Late this afternoon, my husband and I went to my usual birding sites in Port Aransas (Birding Center and Paradise Pond), and I added Cedar Waxwings and an American Robin to bring my year total to 172 species. That tied my 2005 Texas total as of January 5.

Grasshopper Sparrows were singing near Goose Island State Park, Texas, on January 5.

JANUARY 8

On my way home from Rockport on January 6, I went by way of the plowed fields around Granger to look for wintering Mountain Plover and longspurs, without success. It was very windy, but I did see five other new birds (Eastern Bluebird, American Crow, Pine Warbler, Carolina Chickadee, and Vesper Sparrow).

I began the day yesterday in Fort Worth by sighting three Short-eared Owls, with their distinctive wavering hunting flight silhouetted over the fields in the predawn light. Within four hours I had 15 new species, all fairly common for North Texas in winter: Harris's, White-throated, Field, and Fox Sparrows all lurking in the roadside bushes, Red-bellied and Downy Woodpeckers and Blue Jays in my yard, noisy Northern Flickers, a shy Hermit Thrush, a scolding Bewick's Wren, a Brown Creeper working the tree trunks, and many Horned Grebes on Lake Benbrook.

Today, Dave and I got up very early for me to go to the Dallas–Fort Worth (DFW) airport for my "owl trip" to Minnesota with Jerri Kerr, a birding friend from Plano, Texas, who wanted to add northern birds to her life list. I've been close to panic all morning. I have client deadlines and little time between when I return from the Minnesota trip and leave again for California.

I look forward to the northland and owls, and hopefully getting photos of them. Yesterday, birders reported an Ivory Gull in Duluth, but I have heard that it is gone. On the plane I plan to study the printout from the Minnesota rare bird alert and the Minnesota maps.

Meanwhile, from my e-mails, I learned that four Masked Ducks have been found on the King Ranch. Some years no Masked Ducks are found in the United States at all, so I need to try to see one before they disappear. I cannot get to the Texas coast before January 24 or thereabouts. The biggest problem (other than money) in a big year is not being able to be two (or more) places at once.

On the flight I reviewed Kim Eckert's book, *A Birder's Guide to Minnesota*, and tried to ignore the bumpiness on the plane. I made a goal bird list for Kim, who will be helping us on our first full day in Minnesota. First on my list—owls, especially Northern Hawk Owl and Great Gray Owl—and in addition, Gray Partridge, Ruffed, Spruce, and Sharp-tailed Grouse, Northern Goshawk, Gyrfalcon, American Three-toed and Black-backed Woodpeckers, Black-capped and Boreal Chickadees, Bohemian Waxwings, both crossbills, both redpolls, and Pine and Evening Grosbeaks.

Today in Duluth the skies were gray with low clouds, but birding conditions were fine, about 35 degrees and slightly windy. Unfortunately, we found none of the rarities. I saw six new species for the year: a hunting Rough-legged Hawk, Bald Eagle, Pileated Woodpecker, Common Raven, Black-capped Chickadee, and Red-breasted Nuthatch. All but the chickadees are found in Texas, but it's good to get them now.

Tomorrow, Kim Eckert is meeting us at our motel and we're off to Sax-Zim Bog, the vast Minnesota winter birding mecca. I hope we get at least a few of the specialties.

JANUARY 9

It was a great day. In the morning we drove to the Sax-Zim Bog and looked for a number of birds, finding most of them, except the Great Gray

Owl. Unless the snow, which is coming down now, is too deep, we'll try for it tomorrow.

After lots of slow icy road trolling, we found a distant perched Northern Hawk Owl, both Common and Hoary Redpolls (essentially stripeless, white with a pale rosy flush), many Pine Grosbeaks mostly at feeders and loads of Evening Grosbeaks (gorgeous deep pinks and golden-yellows, respectively), Gray Jays on the roadsides, and one Black-backed and one American Three-toed Woodpecker nearly across the road from each other. At a home in Duluth, we waited in the cold for hours and eventually saw a reported wintering Varied Thrush, as well as a Boreal Chickadee amid a flock of Black-capped Chickadees in the trees.

We looked at Lake Superior, adding Red-breasted and Common Mergansers and a Glaucous Gull. Then we took a quick trip to Superior, Wisconsin, where Snowy Owls had been reported. No luck there. Kim's cell phone rang, and he learned of a Snowy Owl near the federal prison in Duluth. It was almost dark when we got back to the prison area, and all we could see at first was no-parking signs. When we spotted the Snowy Owl on top of a post, we did a quick stop (not parking) to look at it and get a few photographs.

At dinner tonight we pumped Kim for more information for tomorrow's birding, all plans subject to a reality check if it snows too hard. The forecast is for 1–2 inches, but it's hard to know how bad that will make the roads.

JANUARY 10

Another great day. Jerri and I began with a drive west of Duluth to near Tamarack where Kim had said that Sharp-tailed Grouse have a lek (an assembly area where the males display in their courtship and breeding ritual). We saw a total of about 11 grouse at two lek areas. Two of the males were dancing around, tails up and bowed wings down. Then they would stop and sit in the snow facing each other about 10 inches apart, seeming to be either glaring at each other or thinking, "Now what?" Or maybe panting from the exertion. They were definitely in the cute category. I did not notice anything but displaying, posturing birds, but it is possible that an unseen female or two were around to inspire their performances.

After receiving a call from Kim saying that no Bohemian Waxwings had been seen yesterday at an area we had been thinking of checking out, we went west to a couple of other sites in Deerwood and Crosby. At first we found no waxwings. All of a sudden Jerri spotted a flock of birds in a tree.

Unfortunately, and unexpectedly, they were Cedar Waxwings, rare during the winter this far north but not needed by us Texans. We were very disappointed, but as we were driving back through Deerwood, a little starlinglike flock went over. We followed as best we could through the neighborhoods, through stop signs (stopping perfunctorily), to two little crabapple trees where we saw a flock of Bohemian Waxwings perched. We went onward after seeing Dark-eyed Juncos, Common Redpolls, and Red Crossbills in Deerwood.

We drove to Sax-Zim Bog to try again for Great Gray Owls. Because it was snowing, I was worried more than ever about the icy and/or snow-packed roads and deep roadside ditches. We moved slowly and steadily on, going back and forth primarily on Nichols Lake Road, where the owls were supposed to be, and scanning the snow-covered branches for big, dark lumps. No owls, but we did find two Northern Shrikes. Then we slowly traversed McDavitt Road, where we had a surprise—a perched Black-billed Magpie.

Another surprise came at 4:20, when it was getting rather dim out. A huge perched Great Gray Owl right along the roadside allowed us to drive quite close to it, and when it flew, it only went a couple of trees down and perched again. Then we saw a second one, also perched, allowing us to see both of them at the same time. With much lingering elation, we made our way back in the slippery dark to Duluth and supper at a place featuring walleye and wild rice. Thanks to the early winter darkness, we had time to savor a change from fast food.

Tomorrow is our last day here, and then I need to cram in client work for a couple of days. I'm at 222 species, still behind my 2005 level for Texas only, but I think I'll get ahead when I go on my California trip, assuming I can get through my work.

JANUARY 11

We're sitting on a plane at the Minneapolis–St. Paul airport while the plane is de-iced. A fine spray from a mobile, long-armed truck is splattering on the snow-covered wings.

Today was another great day, even though we got only two new birds for my year. The best thing was finding White-winged Crossbills. We had driven to Two Harbors north of Duluth, and after what seemed like hours of driving a few spruce-lined streets over and over where the crossbills had been reported, we heard them (unmistakably), but they flew off without our seeing anything more than silhouettes. We agonized over whether to keep looking and whether

Two Great Gray Owls were the highlight of the trip to Sax-Zim Bog in northern Minnesota (January 10).

to count them, and decided that their sounds being identical to those on the tape, their shape and size being correct, their being in a flock, and their being in the right neighborhood made it certain that they were White-winged Crossbills. Still, we were not happy about counting them and wanted a better view (known commonly in birding circles as "BVD," or better view desired).

We left to head to the airport along a scenic road, passing spruce trees with dustings of new snow and glimpses of the lake. When we came to a sign for Stoney Point, I remembered hearing that crossbills had been seen there before, so we turned in. We had gone only about a half mile toward the lake when we heard an unmistakable crossbill sound; then we saw a small flock of crossbills with bold white wing bars. The crossbills were hanging upside down in the spruce trees and flitting about, causing great rejoicing and high-fiving within the car. We continued south, past Duluth to Minneapolis–St. Paul for about a half hour seeking farmland and partridges. There was little of the former and none of the latter, and it was time to head back to the airport.

I spent some time trying to figure out where to go on my upcoming trip to Morro Bay, California, via New Mexico and Arizona, and making many lists of things to do, for both my big year and for my life, such as it is, outside my big year.

JANUARY 14

I have been driving for over four hours heading west from Fort Worth toward California. It's a cold day, 57 degrees, with pale blue skies and scattered cirruslike clouds. I am desperately trying to amuse myself. Every now and then a Red-tailed Hawk peps me up. I'm hoping for anything new. Yesterday was the first day of this year without a new bird. Today, all I can hope for is some stray between now and bedtime, probably near El Paso. I'm now at 277 miles for the day and 226 species for the year.

On a side note, this morning before I left home, for the second morning in a row, there were two female Rufous Hummingbirds at our house, instead of the usual one (which we call "Rufie" and about which I have posted much on the Texas bird listserv, Texbirds). For one tense moment, they actually sat at the same feeder, but of course, on opposite sides.

JANUARY 15

Yesterday I stopped at Monahans State Park where I saw very few birds. I did manage to pish up (make squeaking sounds to attract) a skulking Crissal Thrasher and a winter-plumage Lark Bunting with black surrounding its beak. I also saw a Curve-billed Thrasher by the visitor center.

Today my first stop was Rio Bosque Wetlands Park in El Paso, where Long-eared Owls have been seen this winter. It was an amazing day. My big hunt for the Long-eared Owls was looking bleak. Everywhere I saw droppings and cast-off owl feathers hanging on the scraggly brush and on the grass, but no owls. I climbed over prickly branches and ducked under overhanging branches, peering intently at each and every shrub and sapling. For a while I wandered in and out of the brush and around the outside of the brushy area, hoping to see movement or to spook a bird out. Nothing. Then I went down in the gulch beyond the trees. Still nothing. I explored the other side of the trail. No owls, but an unidentified quail shot up and away. Then I went down into the gulch and thought I heard a slight rustling sound. A Long-eared Owl was staring at me from its perch about 6 feet off the ground. Then I saw another, and another, some flying off a short distance, others hopping in the branches, and others staying put for a while and then leaving. There were probably 10–12 owls. I quickly took some pictures through the branches and then backed away and stood still. Gradually, the owls returned to their brushy area.

On my way out I found some Gambel's Quail, little curved topknots bobbing as they scurried away. At the wetlands park near the entrance along a little puddled area were a singing Marsh Wren, Lincoln's Sparrow, Song Sparrow, and a Black Phoebe perched on a low branch over a puddle.

A wintering flock of Long-eared Owls was seen at Rio Bosque park in El Paso on the drive west (January 15).

This Burrowing Owl in El Paso ducked down low in an attempt not to be seen (January 15).

On the drive out of the park, I noticed long pipes about a foot in diameter on the ground, and I started looking for Burrowing Owls peering out. I did not find any owls by the pipes, but in a little depression about 40 feet back from the road in the dirt, I noticed a round lump that was a Burrowing Owl. I got out of the car and cautiously approached the lump, taking repeated pictures. The owl never left but slowly flattened itself to the earth as I approached to within about 13 feet before backing away.

I drove west toward Tucson and then south to Madera Canyon. Because I was not sure where in southeast Arizona to go, the trip was planned to be unplanned, and I did not have any room reservations for the night. I called Santa Rita Lodge, booked a last-minute room, and arrived there just at dusk. Since my arrival at the lodge, I have been doing paperwork for my big year and eagerly awaiting tomorrow. I can't go online here because there are no phones and no wireless access in the cabins.

Tomorrow is supposed to be cold and windy. My goal birds are the reported Aztec Thrush and the Crescent-chested Warbler.

JANUARY 16

Today began with much huffing and puffing up Old Baldy trail in Madera Canyon. I could feel my lungs, sadly underutilized lately, begging for air, but I kept plugging along. When I reached the draw where the Aztec Thrush had been seen, three birders were staring at the thrush. I had to scramble up the rocky hill area toward them, go beneath the overhanging branches of the tree where the bird was perched, and then pull myself into a place where I could sit and look back toward the tree. Amazingly, my loud passage beneath it did not rattle or flush the thrush, as it was busy alternately eating berries off the tree and chasing away Hermit Thrushes that also wanted some berries. The Aztec Thrush was my first "lifer" of the year (a bird that I had never seen before).

I hung around listening for chips that might signify a mixed flock possibly including the Crescent-chested Warbler, but no such luck. I had to leave anyway before the predicted Santa Ana winds hit the desert and made driving difficult, or worse, closed the passes to California.

My first lifer of the year—an Aztec Thrush at Madera Canyon, Arizona, on January 16.

After getting lost in Tucson, I gave up on the idea of trying to find Catalina State Park where a Rufous-backed Robin was being seen. Hopefully I will find one later this year. I headed north to Casa Grande, following the directions to a golf course and pond where a Northern Jacana, a rarity in the United States, had been recently reported. This bird had apparently been present on the golf course for months, or maybe years, but the golfers had not recognized it as a rarity until recently. I walked across a wasteland of dirt piles and puddles, where I could stare across to the golf course. As soon as I saw a pond with coots nibbling grass on the edge, I looked through my binoculars and saw the Northern Jacana among the coots.

Two for four in Arizona, I hopped in my car and sped west. The winds picked up periodically, but I made good time, arriving at the California border about dark. I am scheduled to attend a birding festival in Morro Bay, with many field trips and local bird experts. Tomorrow I'll check on birding areas between here and there, and if it isn't too windy, I might find something.

JANUARY 17

I'm in Morro Bay. It was a great day, but I had to start it by nervously creeping to and through Los Angeles. Somehow I switched over to autopilot while totally conscious and functional. I emerged north of the city and wound my way through untold suburbs. Every time I attempted to bird at a site mentioned in my California birding guides, I got lost trying to return to my northward route. I did see some new year birds, bringing my total to 259 species. Today's new birds were a tame Surf Scoter on the ocean inlets, California Quail flocks, Western, California, and Heermann's Gulls, Western Scrub-Jay, Barn Swallow, talkative Chestnut-backed Chickadees, drab Oak Titmice, Townsend's Warbler, California Towhee, and ground-feeding Golden-crowned Sparrows. The chickadee has a distinctive three-note attention-grabbing call that I could not figure out until I finally saw the birds.

JANUARY 18

I'm at 278 species now. Another great day on the Morro Bay "big day" field trip with 19 new species for me. At first we nearly froze, with an amazingly fierce cold wind. On a lovely bluff walk we looked down on cormorants, shorebirds, and many Surf Scoters, and gradually the sun warmed up the world and we began to thaw. The afternoon was warmer and pleasant.

This Barn Owl was hiding in a palm tree in Morro Bay, California (January 18).

Today I added Brant, Canada Goose, Greater Scaup and Long-tailed Duck, Western Grebe, both of the lower-48 western cormorants (Pelagic and Brandt's), Black Oystercatcher out on the ocean-washed rocks, Marbled Godwit, Whimbrel, Surfbird and Black Turnstone seen as we walked along the ocean overlooks, a few more gulls (Thayer's, Glaucous-winged, and Mew), a Barn Owl hiding up in a palm tree, a glowing Red-breasted Sapsucker unaware that it just could not hide its color in the park trees, fence-sitting Western Bluebirds, and singing Western Meadowlarks.

Tomorrow is the first pelagic trip of many that I expect to take this year. Pelagic trips go out on the ocean, where there are many birds that rarely or never come within sight of land in the ABA area but are still countable if within the area. I look forward to the birds and vow it will be a good trip, without seasickness.

JANUARY 19

I did the pelagic trip and felt great. I woke up this morning with the tune and words of a calming meditative song going through my head, and I actually calmed down as I faced the trip. I also took all my normal pre-pelagic precautions of eating nonfat food, getting much sleep, wearing the Scopolamine patch, and taking anti-seasickness pills. While there were quite heavy swells, I felt fine, though a bit drugged. I did it all, and I stood tall and did not get seasick.

I added 11 new bird species to my year list. It was surely wonderful to see hundreds of Rhinoceros Auklets, plus Common Murres, Marbled Murrelets, many Black-vented, Sooty, and Pink-footed Shearwaters, Northern Fulmars (mostly dark), Pacific Loons, Black-legged Kittiwakes, and a Pomarine Jaeger, all birds difficult at best to see from land.

For tomorrow, I changed my field trip and am going to the Carrizo Plain, where today they saw a few California specialty birds that I'm hoping to spot, especially Yellow-billed Magpie and Tricolored Blackbird.

JANUARY 20

I reached 300 species today for the year. I'm still amazed at having this many species with 10 days still left in January.

The Carrizo Plain area is broad and open and just a bit like West Texas, except not too far away is an ocean. Number 300 for the year was Cackling Goose. Other new birds seen today mostly from the road as we drove were Golden Eagle, Prairie Falcon, Mountain Plover (a small flock wandering about an abandoned yard and on the dirt road), Band-tailed Pigeon (a large flock perched in a park for the evening), Lewis's Woodpecker, many Yellow-billed Magpies, Bushtits, Mountain Bluebirds, Sage Sparrows, and Tricolored Blackbirds.

Although I have a few days until I'm back in Texas, I need to figure out if I can find time to try for the Masked Ducks in Southeast Texas and for Purple Finches in North Texas. Maybe I should go to Georgia for the Green-breasted Mango that's been there since November. There's much to think of and do elsewhere, and here I am in California.

JANUARY 21

Today in Ventura, California, I added three birds to my year list. I added, and no longer need to worry about, a lovely male Eurasian Wigeon amid the American Wigeons on South Bay Road in Morro Bay.

At Montaña de Oro State Park, I heard many Wrentits and then saw two of them in the campground along an overgrown edge. The last new bird of the day was a Hutton's Vireo at the Santa Barbara Botanic Garden. I had hoped for Nuttall's Woodpecker, but it was not to be. The botanic garden was a very birdy place in the afternoon.

Tomorrow I should get a lifer—if the weather holds and the Island Scrub-Jay doesn't go extinct before then.

JANUARY 22

This was repeatedly a day of "plan B." As I headed over to the Channel Islands Island Packer building in Ventura this morning, it began to rain and continued nonstop. The rain was forecast to continue, and there is no shelter on Santa Cruz Island. I decided to cancel my trip and instead head east to the Salton Sea. All went fine after I got away from the Los Angeles area and its traffic, but I could not find any Yellow-footed Gulls at the sea. I did see Ring-billed, California, and Bonaparte's Gulls.

About 4:00 I decided to head to Arizona. Once I got into Arizona, I learned of a reported Ruff southwest of Phoenix. Since it was dark, I decided to stay as close as possible to the Ruff location to try for it tomorrow. Unfortunately, it was very difficult to find a motel room. When I found motels, they were very expensive ($159 and up) and all were smoking rooms. Finally, I found a room I almost could afford in Goodyear about 20 miles from Phoenix.

This was the second day of 2008 without new birds. There will be many more such days.

JANUARY 23

It was a good day, but I was not sure about it at first. My first goal was to find the reported Ruff. It had been hanging out with yellowlegs in flooded fields, but I could not find any yellowlegs. If there were any flooded fields, they were too far from the road for me to see them. I did see some very distant Great Egrets, probably in the wet areas that I could not find.

I headed east to Tucson to try again to find Catalina State Park and the Rufous-backed Robin that was still reported as being there. For a while it looked like another drubbing, but I decided to wait it out and keep looking.

Finally on the return trip to Texas from California, I was able to see the Rufous-backed Robin in Tucson's Catalina State Park (January 23).

Although it was not around when I got to the park, it had been seen a couple of hours earlier. There were many birds scratching in the leaves or sitting in the bushes—Canyon and Spotted Towhees, White-crowned Sparrows, Curve-billed Thrashers, Pyrrhuloxias, and Northern Cardinals, but no robin. After hours of searching the area, I found the Rufous-backed Robin in the tree it reportedly favored. It gobbled up some berries and then flew down to a branch a few inches above the ground and sat motionless. Maybe it had been there all along. I got some pictures of it munching.

Since it was only midafternoon, I decided to drive the 70 miles to San Rafael Grasslands to look for Baird's Sparrows. It was a lovely drive but very windy, and I did not see any sparrows. There were a couple of Chestnut-collared Longspurs.

I am in Tucson and will go to Madera Canyon again tomorrow. Ideally, I'll find the Crescent-chested Warbler, but even if I don't, maybe I will add other birds. After that I may try the grasslands before heading east. I'm concerned about the weather. It's possible that my Sandia Crest trip will be snowed or iced out.

I'm at 310 species.

JANUARY 24

It was an excellent morning at Madera. At first it looked like I would have to settle for Cassin's Finch as my only new bird of the day. I trekked upward past the unoccupied Aztec Thrush site. Neither the Crescent-chested Warbler nor the thrush had been reported the last couple of days. Before I turned around and started back down the mountain, I told a couple of other hikers about my big year quest and that I was looking for the warbler but had not found it. I was halfway down the trail when one of them came running down telling me that the warbler had been rediscovered. I knew that I had to turn around and go back up, but I had little hope that it would still be around by the time I got there—surely at least 25 minutes away even if I hurried as fast as I could. I struggled mightily to go up fast, huffing and puffing along. The path seemed to lengthen ahead of me. As I came around each bend, I prayed to see people gathered watching the warbler, but there was no one. Finally, I came upon three men all looking in slightly different directions. Not a good sign. Suddenly one of them saw it again, but all I saw was a yellowish blur. The bird was gone, disappearing in the brush. I obsessed—was a blur countable since I knew what the bird was, even though I saw nothing but the blur? I knew the answer was "no," but still, maybe?

It took much hunting and hiking, but this Crescent-chested Warbler was seen in Madera Canyon on January 24.

The two remaining men went up the path looking down the slope. The bird had been fraternizing with juncos. I looked at each junco I saw, and then, there it was—the Crescent-chested Warbler. I called out to the others that I had found it, and they, as well as others who arrived soon, saw the lovely little warbler ignoring us all in its search for breakfast.

I was happy and headed back down the mountain again. At Santa Rita Lodge I found three Pine Siskins before resuming my trek eastward. I ended up in Las Cruces tonight.

JANUARY 25

The day began with a beautiful mountain drive, interspersed with cloudy, foggy patches, as I drove to Albuquerque and Sandia. About 10:30, I arrived at Albuquerque and then wound my way up the slushy, icy road to the visitor center at Sandia Crest. A light covering of something red had been spread on the snow and ice in a very spotty attempt to keep cars from sliding down the mountain. It mostly seemed to be pretty safe, but I drove slowly anyway. The trees got whiter and whiter the higher I got, with those at the top covered with rime ice. I was the only tourist there for a while and immediately saw all three rosy-finches (Black, Gray-crowned, Brown-capped), plus perky Mountain Chickadees and

All three rosy-finches winter at Sandia Crest, New Mexico, including this Gray-crowned Rosy-Finch.

A Mountain Chickadee hopping on the snow at Sandia Crest, New Mexico (January 25).

flashy Steller's Jays, all feeding on seed thrown on the snowy deck. After I took many pictures through the window of the visitor center and had a cup of hot chocolate and a muffin (such a tough birding life), I left and inched back down to the highway. I managed to stay awake on the drive to Texas, becoming more alert as the shadows lengthened and the prospect of roadside pheasants at dusk neared. In northwest Texas, I saw three or four Ring-necked Pheasants on the roadside. Before finding a motel in Dalhart, I went to Lake Rita Blanca and amid the puddle ducks and geese found two Wood Ducks. I'm at 320 species.

JANUARY 27

Yesterday was a long day. As usual I was at a site north of Dalhart before dawn to look for American Tree Sparrows. I waited in the car as the eastern sky went from pitch black (but moonlit) to pale pink to even pinker. Periodically I turned off the car to listen, but it was about 20 degrees and I could not sit too long with the engine off with the window rolled down so I could listen for sparrows.

Finally, I did hear some little chips, and eventually it was light enough to get out and tromp around the long grasses. Both my pishing and my canvassing the area on foot resulted in just a few White-crowned Sparrows.

Wearily I got back in the car, realizing that I would have to drum up a tree sparrow somewhere else. Then, on a lark, not having tried it with tree sparrows before, I played the American Tree Sparrow song. There was an instant response, with three perched up, flying in closer. [Note: On this occasion, as always, I tried to adhere to the ABA guidelines, only playing the song as briefly as possible, after concluding that these nonendangered birds would not be harmed by hearing a brief song of one of their own kind singing.]

Unfortunately, that was the last new bird of the day. I wandered the Panhandle heading homeward, getting very tired of driving by the time I reached Childress. I was absolutely wild with boredom by the time I reached home with 526 miles for the day and 321 species for the month.

Masked Ducks wintered at the King Ranch on the coast of Texas. This was one of six seen on January 30.

JANUARY 30

I drove south yesterday, fighting a nasty crosswind with gusts to 40 miles per hour. After 440 miles and fruitlessly exploring windblown Granger fields for longspurs, I got to Kingsville.

This morning I joined the half-day King Ranch tour, the goal being Masked Duck. We saw five Masked Ducks together, dozing and then diving, and later a single one in another pond. What great birds for my big year list.

I got another six species for the year on the King Ranch (Fulvous Whistling-Duck, Green Heron, Solitary Sandpiper, Common Ground-Dove, a lone Sprague's Pipit, and Bronzed Cowbird), and two more (Yellow-crowned Night-Heron and Black Skimmer) in Port Aransas.

I'm happy to be at 330 birds. The striking views of the Masked Ducks captured in my pictures and emblazoned in my brain will give me sweet dreams tonight.

JANUARY 31

I birded at a Houston home today, adding the reported Calliope and Allen's Hummingbirds, and later Tree Swallows. I'm partway home tonight, expecting to arrive tomorrow morning.

Three hundred and thirty-three.
It's a magical number it seems to me.
Anyone else with sufficient obsessing
Could have done the same without
    even stressing.
I'm sure I'm nuts, but that's not new.
This is just something I have to do.

FEBRUARY

Elaenia, Dovekie, and Bananaquit

NEW BIRD SPECIES SEEN THIS MONTH: 67
TOTAL BIRD SPECIES BY THE END OF THE MONTH: 400
PLACES BIRDED: Texas, North Carolina, Florida, Pennsylvania, New Jersey, New York, Oregon

FEBRUARY 5

Birding has slowed down. Client matters are being given priority, although I did sneak in a bit of birding this month.

On February 1 in the late morning, I went down to Johnson County's Buddy Stewart Park (Texas) for Rusty Blackbirds. Although good habitat puddles were plentiful as in previous years, at first I could not find any blackbirds, except a few Red-winged Blackbirds. I tromped around the whole place and twice drove slowly through the park. Finally, near a big flock of White-winged Doves on the ground were four Rusty Blackbirds.

After that, I wandered about looking for sapsuckers or kinglets but found nothing more. On the way home on Goforth Road in southeastern Parker County, just past a pond in a deeply wooded area, I found a Yellow-bellied Sapsucker. I had two year birds in February so far. That night I tried for woodcocks at a Fort Worth wintering spot but heard no peenting sounds (woodcock's distinctive call during displays).

The next morning, I tried for woodcocks at another Fort Worth spot, but again, I heard nothing. A calling Barred Owl, new for the year, was a nice consolation prize. That night I went to the first site and was able to see a skulking Brown Thrasher in the brush. Just before it was completely dark, I drove back up the road and was delighted to hear an American Woodcock peenting off in the woods not far away. I could hear the woodcock fly high into the air a couple of times. Two times a woodcock flew low over me, silhouetted distinctively, its very long bill sticking out from its plump body.

I refrained from birding again until this morning but then went to

An Eastern Screech-Owl peers out of a tree in Fort Worth on February 5.

Memorial Oaks Park in Fort Worth to look for an Eastern Screech-Owl. I quietly approached a broken-off tree that has a hole where I had seen an Eastern Screech-Owl a couple of years ago. Again, I saw an owl sitting up in the hole. After I took a picture, the owl disappeared back into the hole. I wandered off and then came back; the owl was looking out and again disappeared as it heard me approaching. I crept toward the tree and waited. After about 10 minutes, the owl reappeared, but just long enough to peer out at me and allow me to get some more pictures.

The Eastern Screech-Owl brought my year total to 339 species.

FEBRUARY 6

Today was a good birding day. I went to Hagerman National Wildlife Refuge on the Oklahoma-Texas border. After a little searching, I came upon a birdy area with many American Goldfinches, some Dark-eyed Juncos, and

This Red-headed Woodpecker was seen at Hagerman National Wildlife Refuge on February 6.

six Purple Finches, which were new for the year. I was just about to leave the wooded area when a Red-headed Woodpecker called and flew toward me through the deciduous trees. Number 341.

FEBRUARY 10

At about 4:00 yesterday afternoon, I was grocery shopping in Fort Worth, planning to drive south to the Lower Rio Grande Valley today for some general bird hunting, but my plans were changed. When I was halfway down the cereal aisle, the first call came from Mary Gustafson (a Texas Valley expert birder), who told me about a Blue Bunting seen at Sabal Palm Grove Sanctuary, and then another call came from Ann Hoover (Fort Worth birding friend) telling me that some kind of elaenia (thought to be a Yellow-bellied Elaenia) had been found at South Padre Island (SPI), at Scarlet Colley's bird-friendly site on Sheepshead Street. Scarlet is a bird lover and dolphin lover who provides food and water for birds at a few sites on the island. I pushed my cart down the grocery aisles, not seeing the groceries as I tried to figure out whether to chase the elaenia and the Blue Bunting. I would have to leave as soon as possible. Any kind of elaenia would be a new year bird. I raced home, made a very quick supper, finalized some client work, and packed. I was able to leave home by 7:11.

I drove and drove, through thankfully low traffic in Austin and San Antonio. Nothing interesting was on the radio, and I had no good CDs aboard. It was dark and boring outside, but my brain was in overdrive mode and I was wide awake, grappling with the possible miracle of an elaenia for my big year. Saturday night turned into Sunday morning without my noticing as I drove glassy-eyed through the darkness.

When I arrived at SPI, I could not decide what to do, since it was still dark and I could not bird and I was so tired. I provisioned myself at an open gas station. I then half slept in the car until dawn when another car with friends arrived at the bird site. Even before it was light, we drifted toward the rail fence that separates the lot from the street, trying to see into the dark bushes. We waited for the elaenia (species at that time not yet certain) to show up,

One of the most amazing birds to come to the United States in 2008 was this White-crested Elaenia at South Padre Island, Texas, on February 10.

peering pointlessly into the dark brush beyond the fence. Almost as soon as we could see anything in the thick growth (about 7:05), the insect-catching elaenia appeared. The bird, with an easily observable, very white streak on the top of its head, acted like a constantly moving kinglet.

After watching the elaenia for about an hour, the four of us went over to Sabal Palm Audubon Center south of Brownsville for the Blue Bunting, but we were not so lucky. Neither the bunting nor the elaenia stayed around for much more than a day. It was very good that we had raced down there when we did. The elaenia was ultimately identified as a White-crested Elaenia, a North American record, clearly one of the most unexpected birds of my big year.

Today, in the Valley I also added Buff-bellied Hummingbird, Purple Martin, and Ferruginous Pygmy-Owl to my list.

FEBRUARY 11

Although I missed some birds that I wanted, today turned out to be pretty good. I added both Hooded and Audubon's Orioles. Then, instead of finding a seedeater at San Ygnacio, where they are regularly seen, I unexpectedly

Audubon's Orioles are regular at orange feeders in South Texas. This one was at Salineño.

found an early Wood Thrush under the saplings. At 6:15 P.M., after waiting for hours, I saw five Red-billed Pigeons flying off to the right at the river's edge at Salineño. Unfortunately, even after spending much time looking for the seedeaters at the "usual" spots, behind the Zapata Library and at San Ygnacio, I did not find any and will need to return to look for them.

FEBRUARY 14

I drive along a forgettable Texas road very early in the morning, my mind lost in nothing. I glance up from the white lines stretching ahead into the darkness and see from my compass that I am going north. For a short moment I wonder where I am and what my northern desti-nation is. Of course it comes back to me. I'm heading toward what I hope is birds.

Why are my poems so oft about driving,
Instead of the birds for which I am striving?
Because the driving is often so boring,
I need to do something to keep me from snoring.
And because when I'm birding, my thoughts do not stray
To plans for the future, or things far away.
And so, the doggerel flows out of my pen,
And the miles are traversed, 'til I'm home again

I just learned that a Eurasian Kestrel and an Arctic Loon are in California. I can't go there now. This has happened before and will happen again—birds are found that I want to see and cannot go see anytime soon. I'll be on the East Coast until February 25 and then in northern Oregon until March 5. But it can work out. A Bananaquit (from the Caribbean) has been reported in Fort Lauderdale, Florida, and I'll be there on Monday February 18.

FEBRUARY 15

Yesterday I drove over 600 miles, going from McAllen to Fort Worth via Houston to look for, and find, a Lesser Black-backed Gull, thanks to informa-tion from Martin Reid, an expert San Antonio birder. I also had my zillionth try for longspurs east of Austin, but no luck.

I met my birding friend Ann Hoover at Raleigh-Durham today. We prob-ably will not get any new birds until we get near or at the coast. My North Carolina birding friend, Lena Gallitano, gave us information on places where we might find some of our goal birds. On the way to the Outer Banks, we saw the ever-present Great Black-backed Gulls on the bridges. Following Lena's pointers, we found Great Cormorant and Purple Sandpiper just south of the

This Purple Sandpiper was feeding on the algae-covered rocks on Pea Island, North Carolina (February 15).

Oriental Inlet bridge and found an American Oystercatcher, which I had somehow missed in Texas so far. We saw Northern Gannets over the ocean. American Black Ducks were almost common waddling through the roadside grass. It was fun birding, but hanging over my head was the knowledge that small-craft advisories were out for the next day, with 5–7-foot waves predicted.

I'm at 359 species for the year.

FEBRUARY 18

On February 16, the North Carolina pelagic trip did go out. The waves were just 5–7 feet once we got out on the ocean. After bouncing and heaving up and down modestly, things then escalated substantially, with waves 9–10 feet high. Brian Patteson, the boat owner and captain, handled things masterfully and usually warned us in advance when he shifted direction so we could go to a place on the boat less likely to be washed over with spray. I wore rubber boots and complete raingear, but my rain pants leaked badly, and I got very wet and cold.

The good news is that I did not get seasick. The multitudes of Northern Gannets held my attention, and my early feelings of seasickness passed without any outward signs. The birding was quite good. New birds for the year were Red-throated Loon (about 10), Razorbills (about 15), Red Phalaropes (about 13), Manx Shearwaters (distant but visible as shearwaters with light underparts, about 3), and most wonderfully, Dovekie (3, one very close in flight, a lifer).

At the end of the day, Ann and I staggered happily off the boat, ripped off our Scopolamine patches, and went over to Buxton Woods for a walk. We were pleased to be able to eat well at a seafood restaurant, especially Ann, who had fasted all day.

On Sunday, February 17, we got up at a rational time, finished our packing, and set out to see if we could add year birds for me and lifers for her. The Eastern Towhees at Pea Island were both. The approximately 100 Tundra Swans on both North and South ponds and the 3 Palm Warblers in Wanchese were year birds for me. We were unable to find any Sharp-tailed Sparrows of either species, probably because it was quite windy. We also were not able to find a Fish Crow. It looked for a while as if we would be crowless, but a little flock of crows materialized in Wanchese, cawing, unfortunately, like American Crows. If there was a Fish Crow among them, it was silent.

We also tried for Henslow's Sparrows before dark at the Voice of America

Northern Gannets were common on the North Carolina pelagic trip on February 16.

I was delighted to finally locate the Bananaquit in Fort Lauderdale, Florida, on February 18.

site along U.S. 17 where they reside, but the grass was mowed too short, and it looked like the appropriate habitat was gone. We heard a few chirps and saw a few low-flitting birds, but the birds that we saw well were not Henslow's Sparrows.

We turned toward Raleigh and my friend Lena's house, where we had a very pleasant dinner and birdy conversation. This morning we hung around to watch the three Baltimore Orioles and the other birds in her yard. Now it's time to figure out what I'm going to do in Florida, where the plane should be landing soon.

FEBRUARY 19

Yesterday I picked up my rental car in Florida, and instead of heading south to my Homestead motel, I drove north to Fort Lauderdale for the Bananaquit that had been reported on North South Lake, a place I thought I had located on Mapquest. Unfortunately, there appeared to be streets of all possible variations on that name, such as South South Lake, South North Lake, and my first two tries were not where the bird had been reported. A kindly gentleman, who had come out of his house to see what I was up to as I stood in front of his house looking uncertainly around me, told me, literally, where to go. When I arrived at the correct street, confirmed by the sight of another person with binoculars, the two of us walked toward a distant bottle-brush tree, a location where the Bananaquit had been reported. The other birder saw something dark in the tree that was the Bananaquit. We saw it well and stayed awhile until the bird dove across the street.

Today, Larry Manfredi, a Florida guide, came by my motel about 6:30 in the morning and took me to an area of Greater Miami called Pinecrest to look for some Miami specialties, all of which we found. The new birds for that part of the trip were Fish Crow (finally), a couple of White-crowned Pigeons perched on power lines, Red-whiskered Bulbuls, a Spot-breasted Oriole, a female Painted Bunting, and a little colony of White-winged Parakeets in a grove of palms hidden in an office building outer alcove. We then drove to the Everglades, adding a distant Snail Kite, Purple Gallinule, a high-flying Short-tailed Hawk, Wood Storks probing the canals, and Glossy Ibis to my year list. After lunch, we drove to a nearby area called Pembroke Estates

Limpkins are a Florida snail-eating specialty (February 19).

to search for Limpkins eating lakeside snails and found one slowly working the edge of a lake.

We ended our birding for the day in Larry's backyard, where we found a Shiny Cowbird coming to the feeders with Red-winged Blackbirds and a Brown-headed Cowbird. The Shiny Cowbird, while not generally a welcome bird because it lays its eggs in other birds' nests, was new for my year. Larry also had a wintering Dickcissel in his yard and a couple of Ruby-throated Hummingbird females, allowing me to end the day at 385 bird species for the year.

FEBRUARY 21

I have had almost two "wasted" days, because the warblers I saw yesterday in the Everglades will surely be at Sabine Woods and High Island in Texas in spring. I'm too tired to plan where I need to go to maximize my chances at rare birds. Of course, there's no guarantee that I could have found either a Smooth-billed Ani (yesterday) or a Florida Scrub-Jay (today) even if I had driven farther and planned better. I will be back.

The plane drones on through clouds of gray;
My mind is blank and far away.
A bit of bumping brings it back,
And then it's on another tack.
We're headed north to cold and snow;
I'm not sure that I want to go.
This big year thing has got me tired;
My motivation's 'bout expired.

FEBRUARY 22

I have been in East Brunswick, New Jersey, since last night. Every now and then during this big year, I have thought, "I hope I get a little, harmless, gentle adventure in my big year. Something to write about that doesn't hurt or injure me or anyone else and doesn't entirely deplete all our financial assets." My unbelievable mixed-up drive here last night, going round and round the Philadelphia airport, was terribly frustrating and tiring but definitely not worth elevating to an "adventure."

Maybe this snowstorm is a little adventure. This morning when I looked out very early, the world was covered with about 2 inches of snow. It had been forecast but not so early. I thought I would be able to sneak in a trip to Montauk before it got too bad. As it was, I stayed all day in my Motel 6 room, watching the snow fall, fretting, and then settling in to do some client work. I changed my reservations to stay here tonight, too. I decided that the weather was too nasty for me to go on the New Jersey pelagic. I hope to go to New York tomorrow and do land birding.

FEBRUARY 24

Yesterday, the wild-goose chase began after the enforced layover. Early in the morning, but not too early because I was worried about icy streets, I headed north toward New York. In less than 20 miles, I was on my way across various bridges to Long Island. After asking a gruff woman toll-booth attendant for directions, launching into my description of where I wanted to go, I was interrupted by her yelling out, "Bell Parkway, take Bell Parkway." As far as I could tell no such parkway exists, and I realized she must have meant "Belt Parkway," or so I hoped, because that's what I took. Eventually I knew it was the correct road, and slowly, through little town after little town, I drove east. Mile after mile, it hit me why it was called Long Island. It got prettier, the road passing through lovely pine "barrens" that did not look barren at all, with periodic tantalizing views of the water.

Finally, I reached Montauk, where rare geese were being regularly reported, both a Pink-footed and a Barnacle Goose, often together. I carefully checked the Ditch Plains pond and the Theodore Roosevelt County Park area where these geese had been seen, but I found nothing but Mallards, Canada

Black Scoters and many other ducks were seen in the ocean off Long Island, New York, on February 24.

Geese, domestic geese, and a Northern Pintail. Out in the ocean at the end of Long Island many sea-ducks were bobbing in the waves quite close to shore, among which I identified Black and White-winged Scoters and King and Common Eiders.

About 2:30 I decided to give up on the Montauk geese and try for the Pink-footed Goose that had been seen at Stony Brook mill pond, nearly two hours away, though in the same county. When I arrived at Stony Brook, I found about 20 Canada Geese, some Hooded Mergansers, and a few Mute Swans. One report had said that the Pink-footed Goose arrived one day at 5:30 P.M. It was about 4:30 when I got there, so I drove around checking out other goose-filled water vistas. As I parked the car back at the mill pond, I realized that the number of geese had increased, and more were arriving. Two other birders had also arrived, and the three of us walked across the crunchy park snow toward the geese. The geese were totally oblivious of us and greeted each other noisily. Then I saw it, the Pink-footed Goose mingling with all the other geese. The other two birders were pals from Ohio and knew Dan Sanders (big year birder of 2007) and Greg Miller (one of the three big year birders covered in *The Big Year*). As it got dark, we all took off, they to check out Montauk the next day. I headed west, having decided that I could try for a Barnacle Goose at Califon if I went west in New Jersey that night.

All day long on February 23, my throat was getting sorer and sorer, and I felt more and more miserable as I searched in vain for a motel somewhere near or on the way to Califon. Eventually I found a place to stay directly south of it.

Cheerily but sickly, I headed north this morning, carefully navigating the snow-covered roads. The roads did not strictly correspond to the maps and were rarely labeled, or they were labeled with a different label than on the map. I remembered that the Ohio birders had said that the Barnacle Goose was at the Raritan River, so I looked for something that might indicate a river. I passed through Cokesbury and at a completely unmarked intersection headed left, which appeared to go down into a valley, maybe a river valley? I guessed correctly,

I've driven myself, I know it's true,
But there's so much that I need to do.
Really, it's all in my head,
When everything is done and said.
Yet it's as if an outside hand,
Something I just don't understand
Has hold of me and won't let go
Is keeping me from going slow,
Is dragging me, is pushing, pulling.
It's not as if that I'm not willing,
But somehow, I must pause enough
To do the usual mundane stuff,
To breathe, relax, regroup, repair,
And then find birds without despair.

and there it was, a bridge, a river, and lots of geese, all but one being Canada Geese, and one Barnacle Goose, mostly dozing as were the others. Every now and then it lifted its head, with its lovely white face and preened. I took pictures, and then I hit the highway.

FEBRUARY 27

Debra Corpora and I are headed west from DFW to Oregon, Washington, and British Columbia. My cold, or whatever it is, still is. I'm supposed to be planning this trip but just can't make myself wade through the text of the Washington and Oregon information. We'll just look out at the ocean and stop at parks. I will do the probably rainy pelagic trip (90 percent chance of rain), and we'll go up to British Columbia for the Sky Lark and Northwestern Crow. Debra has not decided yet whether she will go on the pelagic trip because she is terribly susceptible to seasickness.

We are flying over snow-capped mountains, high enough that the trees do not come all the way up the mountains. There are vast stretches of mountains off to the northwest—Rockies, I assume. A few lenticular clouds float off to the right, and the mountains are becoming the whole view.

FEBRUARY 29

Our drive from Portland two days ago was pleasant and gorgeous, but no new birds. It was great to see the Oregon coast again, after 30 years since we last lived in Oregon. Yesterday we birded the Newport area. The day was nice, but because of my cold, it was nice in a foggy sort of way. At Devil's Punch Bowl, a spectacular ocean rock formation, we saw Harlequin Ducks. Then at Beverly Beach State Park, we had a mixed flock of Golden-crowned Kinglets, Yellow-rumped Warblers, and Chestnut-backed Chickadees. We scanned the ocean and backwater expanses, finding White-winged and Surf Scoters, Common Loons, Common Goldeneyes, Red-breasted Mergansers, and Buffleheads. Amid many Surf Scoters was a couple of Pigeon Guillemots, and nearby, a Red-necked Grebe.

Today, Debra and I drove south to Florence and took a lovely drive along Sweet Creek (near Mapleton) with the goal of finding an American Dipper. The trail periodically went over a stream and around boulders. The sound of the rushing water obscured nearly all other sounds, but a couple of times,

On February 29, I explored the Oregon coast.

we heard what I'm sure was a dipper. Then Debra stopped, having heard something, and we saw movement across the stream. Two bobbing American Dippers were lurking under a branchy rock ledge at the far side of the stream. Periodically they would duck out of sight, and then they were visible again. It was not their normal behavior of hunting on rocks that I remembered, but they were indeed dippers. And they were number 400 for the year, on the last day of February.

March Madness and More

NEW BIRD SPECIES SEEN THIS MONTH: 52
TOTAL BIRD SPECIES BY THE END OF THE MONTH: 452
PLACES BIRDED: Oregon, Washington, British Columbia, Texas,
Oklahoma, Kansas, Nebraska, Arkansas, Georgia

MARCH 2

Yesterday, Debra drove me over to the Newport historic waterfront in the desultory rain spurts. People were gathered about with binoculars and packs and coolers, mostly under an overhanging awning. I went into the office to check in and was told that the captain had canceled the trip due to high winds (and waves, I think). I had psyched myself to do this trip, but I was secretly relieved. I went out to the others, who were gathered to see what was going on.

Now what? Debra and I started asking for ideas of local places to bird, or of particular birds to chase. We learned where a Trumpeter Swan had been seen and were about to go there when the captain appeared and said the

Black-footed Albatrosses were my favorites on the Oregon pelagic trip on March 1.

weather had shifted again and the trip was on. We all (except Debra) boarded his boat. Before we left the sheltered harbor area, it was quite calm, but out on the ocean, it was rougher. Oddly enough, it was not the waves but the wind and the periodic rain that were worst, but I did not get sick.

It was a good day for birds. I saw three year birds on the ocean—Black-footed Albatross, Laysan Albatross, and Cassin's Auklets, plus many Common Murres and Rhinoceros Auklets, and lots of Northern Fulmars, fighting over chum on a line that the crew put out. Birders often throw fish parts and fish oil behind a pelagic boat, causing many seabirds to follow the boat.

My main problem was that I still had a cold, and I was doped up on cold meds as well as the Scopolamine patch, and felt pretty loggy. Fortunately, I was dressed warm enough. I sat like a bump on a log as the birds flew by and around the boat, but when the first Laysan Albatross came close to the boat, I did get up. I had been worried about getting my camera wet, especially with salt spray coming over the boat, but the captain managed to maneuver around quite a few storm systems out over the ocean, and we got very little rain after the first couple of hours.

Northern Fulmars were the most common on the March 1 Oregon pelagic trip.

This Barrow's Goldeneye was one of many in the Hood Canal area of Washington on March 2.

When we got into port and docked, I looked for Debra. When I found her, she said with some urgency, "Do you think we have time, and do you have the energy, to go to see the Trumpeter Swan before dark?" She had located it earlier in the day. She drove as fast as possible to somewhere south of Newport to a farm pond, where the swan had been staying. It was still there and visible in the half light, a glowing white swan in the near darkness. I had four new birds for the year on the first day of March.

Today, we drove east to Olympia, Washington, and west to Port Angeles. It was very rainy and foggy in Oregon, but as we got into Washington, the fog cleared. When we reached the Hood Canal area, we were able to see many Barrow's Goldeneyes, as well as some year birds for Debra.

We had dinner in Port Angeles tonight. I'm at 405 species so far and hope to add at least 2 tomorrow.

MARCH 4

I added four new species yesterday, but none today. Yesterday, in a little drizzly rain, Debra and I drove to the ferry dock in Port Angeles about 6:30 A.M. We had morose thoughts of standing on a fast-moving, rainy deck trying to see "pelagic" birds. It took us awhile to find where cars were supposed to line up for the ferry.

We got our tickets and drove into the bowels of a huge ferry, the *Coho*. Before passenger cars were allowed on, six or seven semi-trucks and trailers pulled on, which were swallowed up in the beast. The huge parking deck was

The melodious chorus of Sky Larks was our main goal on Vancouver Island, British Columbia (March 4).

below the various lounges and concession/store areas. We were not allowed on the car deck during passage, so we grabbed our binoculars, cameras, and coats and went up the stairs. To our surprise, the forward observation area had huge clean glass windows, and we could see down into the water along the front sides of the ferry without going outside. The rain had let up, and we had good visibility. It was quite calm, and even before the ferry started moving, we both saw an Ancient Murrelet well.

About 9:45, we arrived in Victoria, Vancouver Island, and saw our first (and many more) Northwestern Crows, hopping about on buildings, lawns, and branches and flying across the sky.

Debra had already seen Sky Larks on a previous trip, but it had been fall when they were not displaying. Sky Larks were introduced on Vancouver Island many years ago, and the remnants of the established population are countable under the ABA rules. After driving north, we stopped first at Martindale Flats, a site where the larks have traditionally been found. It was still raining, but I think we could have seen or heard Sky Larks at our many stops if they had been there. The fields were mostly muddy and flat, but we saw nothing except Mallards and Killdeer. We headed farther north to the "daffodil fields" (currently without visible daffodils), another reportedly favorite spot for the remaining Sky Larks. I pulled off the road, rolled down the windows since the rain had almost stopped, and heard unfamiliar sounds. Somewhere, notes were raining down and around. It had to be a Sky Lark. We got out and looked and waited. In a couple of minutes, the singing ceased. I looked around and saw a small brown bird, 20 feet away from me, levitating upward, starting to warble its little heart out—a Sky Lark. It kept going upward, upward, until we lost track of it. We saw other Sky Larks all around, going up and down, for a total of seven or eight, a bird species having a song exceedingly more glamorous than its appearance.

We tried without success to find a reported Northern Goshawk at Horth Hill Regional Park, which itself was hard to find. It was misty but bright, a very out-of-the-world experience. The sunlight was indirectly lighting the hanging moss and lichen-coated branches. Everything seemed to shimmer and glow from within. Little musical sounds came from beneath the wet brush, which I'm sure were primarily Winter Wrens, but a nonbirder might have thought it was faerie orchestras. We walked for about half an hour, but except for some finchy-siskin sounds high above and the wrens, there was no evidence of bird life. As the trail started to get more complicated, we decided to turn around and work our way out before we got lost and missed our ferry. We drove back toward the ferry landing and then waited, as very slowly, an unbelievable number of trucks drove onto the ferry—maneuvering a right-angle turn in a very small space.

Our ferry trip back across the Strait of Juan de Fuca was much more bouncy than the first trip. Every now and then, the ferry hit a big wave with a thud and would tip back and forth, side to side. We were glad to get off, but we had to wait in our cars in the enclosed belly, sandwiched between semis for what seemed like weeks, before the door opened and they let us drive out.

Not having had enough birding, we drove at dusk to Ediz Hook, Washington. By the light of the now-set sun, we saw Barrow's Goldeneyes and Gadwalls, a couple of turnstones (unknown species), and a little scuttling flock of Western Sandpipers. Satisfied, we returned to our hotel.

Today we drove south to the Portland airport, giving ourselves 45 minutes at the John Wayne Marina, which had many Pigeon Guillemots, Barrow's Goldeneyes, Horned Grebes, at least one Pacific Loon and Common Loon, Red-breasted and Hooded Mergansers, a few Marbled Murrelets, Surf Scoters, and Pine Siskins. We then hustled south, turned in the rental car, and are now sitting at the Portland airport.

Now I have more multiday trip ideas than there are days in March, plus some quicky trips. What made me think I could do a big year? I have so many birds to see, and they aren't staked down. I desperately need to get to Arizona again to try for the harder-to-find species and not leave it to the last minute. I already can sense that some of the grouse and owls are likely to be difficult for me to get this year.

MARCH 6

It's a rainy day in Fort Worth. It's supposed to snow, and I can see some sort of particles coming down periodically. Having dealt with client matters of importance yesterday, I packed up the car with scope, warm clothes, and rain gear and hurried over to White Rock Lake in Dallas, where a Little Gull has been reported (those not familiar with North Texas may be surprised to learn that Dallas is over 50 miles from where I live in Fort Worth). As soon as I got to the east side of the lake, I spotted Bonaparte's Gulls, with which the Little Gull had been seen earlier, and pulled into a parking space. Upon lifting up my binoculars, I saw the black rounded underwings of a Little Gull. Over the next half hour, the bird alternately was obvious, hanging in the same general area surrounded by Bonaparte's Gulls, or vanished completely. The Little Gull is number 410 for the year.

MARCH 8

I spent the day at home doing miscellaneous chores and avoiding real work. It's odd—I need to plan more of my big year, but I don't like to make plans. I need to schedule various pelagic trips, but every time I schedule something, it means I will not be able to chase something spontaneously. I am pushed and pulled in too many directions.

MARCH 11

I'm driving to Nebraska, chasing a bird, probably a nongoose, wild-goose chase. Every now and then a Common Crane, not native to the United States, is reported somewhere in the Midwest as part of a huge flock of native Sandhill Cranes. A few days ago, one was found in Nebraska. It may still be around. At least I'll get close to my fill of Sandhill Cranes.

My crane crusade is done—no Common Crane. I gave it my best. On March 11 until dark and the next day most of the time between dawn and 12:30, I cruised the country roads, stopping whenever I saw cranes, which was in nearly every field, looking for a crane with black and white, not mostly gray on its head and upper neck. The problems: most (95 percent) of the cranes' heads were down, and many (about half) of the cranes were too far from the road to see even with a scope, and I could see tens of thousands of cranes. But I tried. It was wonderful seeing and hearing so many cranes. Every now and then the sky was full of cranes going this way and that, often silhouetted so that a black head would not show. Sometimes, in between the cranes, and star-sprinkling the sky, were geese—Canada, White-fronted, Snow—little Vs, long strands, individuals. I never saw anyone else out there with binoculars or a scope.

The good news is that after an hour of crane looking on March 12, I zipped off to north of Grand Island to look for Greater Prairie-Chickens at a site I learned about from the Internet. Almost exactly where I was supposed to, I saw one male Greater Prairie-Chicken, or at least his full head, neck, orange puffed-out gular, and "shoulders" as he craned (no pun) his neck above the grass. A new bird anyway—number 411.

I then headed south. It just had gotten too windy to set up the scope on the cranes. My goal was Smith's Longspur at the Stuttgart, Arkansas, airport. I'm embarrassed to say that I didn't know if they had already migrated, but they are "sparrows" and hopefully don't migrate early, although I suspected that this is a bit late for them. I saw one Smith's Longspur at the airport. I saw the distinctive tail and behavior, apparently a very late, but not unheard of, sighting.

Today I went from Tyler, Texas, where I had stayed overnight, up to Tyler State Park, where I heard and had great views of Brown-headed Nuthatches.

Jana Whittle found a Fork-tailed Flycatcher in Sabine Pass, Texas. She e-mailed and called me yesterday, and her husband, John, called this morning. They are both active in the Golden Triangle Audubon Society on the upper Texas coast.

This is one of multiple Fork-tailed Flycatchers that came to Texas in 2008. This one was at Sabine Pass on March 16.

Thinking about my big year as I drove to Sabine Pass, I concluded that it's going to take about 20 miracles for me to see 700 species this year. I went through the bird book yesterday and listed what was still possible, and got to 682, which includes a fair number of very optimistic, hopeful assumptions about birds that I may not see and leaves no room for missing anything. I did not include Fork-tailed Flycatcher in my year wish list. I crossed my fingers (which is hard to do when driving and when writing, which of course is a no-no). I had planned to head to the Valley today and then up to Sabine Woods, so I was just reversing the order. I wore my Scissor-tailed Flycatcher earrings today—I haven't seen these birds yet this year either.

I *did* see the Fork-tailed Flycatcher at Sabine Pass. I was afraid I had missed it, as the winds were very strong when I arrived at Pilot Road in Sabine Pass. Two people who were at the site had seen the flycatcher some 20 minutes earlier, and then it had vanished. Its habit was to stay low in the leeward side of the salt cedar or other bushes, which was on the far side of these bushes, so the bird was difficult or impossible to see much of the time unless it was flying or at the nearest bushes. About 20 minutes after I arrived, we saw the flycatcher, perched about 3–4 feet off the ground on the back of the nearest salt cedar, but only visible if we walked down next to the salt cedar. For a while, it flitted about or sat quietly, and then disappeared again. I saw it on and off from about 3:35 to 5:00.

When the Fork-tailed Flycatcher seemed to be gone, I left and went to Sabine Woods, a refuge owned by the Texas Ornithological Society. I did not find much at the woods or at the willows down the road, two prime spots for spring migrants. It was just too windy and too early in the season.

MARCH 17

It was even windier today, and therefore I abandoned my plans to revisit Sabine Woods and drove to Anahuac National Wildlife Refuge. At the Yellow Rail Prairie, I was able to see a couple of Seaside Sparrows, sitting on low perches in the marsh. Other than that, I found few birds.

I went on to Boy Scout Woods in High Island (owned by Houston Audubon Society), which was also quiet, and checked out Bolivar, a coastal area good for shorebirds. I drove fairly slowly, scanning the pastures, looking for

A Wilson's Plover grabs a bite at Bolivar, Texas, on March 17.

Nelson's Sharp-tailed Sparrows abound but are hard to find at Bolivar (March 17).

American Golden-Plovers, two of which I found standing between cow pies, which dot the fields.

Bolivar had no Red Knots, one of the species that I seem to have difficulty finding in Texas, especially when I'm doing some kind of big year. On my walk out to the beach at very high tide, I found two Wilson's Plovers, many Piping Plovers, and Short-billed Dowitchers, and during my return walk back through the grasses that grow above the tide line, I spooked up two Nelson's Sharp-tailed Sparrows. I ended the day with 420 birds for the year.

MARCH 18

Today was an amazing day. It started mildly enough with only Sandwich Terns to add to my list at the Port Aransas beach. I saw a few warblers (Northern Parula, Yellow-rumped, and Palm) at the Birding Center and Paradise Pond in Port Aransas. I headed to the Valley with thoughts of going to South Padre Island. I got about 10 miles out the highway toward Port Isabel on the coast and realized that the wind was rocking the car so much I could hardly drive. It was probably not a good idea to go across the high bridge to SPI nor was it much fun to try to bird out on the island in that wind.

Therefore, I decided to reverse direction and headed inland to avoid the windy island. But where should I go? Suddenly, I remembered Allen Williams's wonder yard (a private yard in Pharr, Texas, landscaped to attract birds and open to birders) and decided to give him a call to ask whether he still allowed birders to visit. He said it was interesting that I had called because he had just seen what he believed to be a White-throated Thrush in his yard, then called a White-throated Robin. Birds' names are sometimes changed due to new scientific information. The American Ornithological Union (AOU) evaluates reports and observations of birds, including genetic information. As a result, species are sometimes renamed, reclassified, and/or regrouped, resulting in species being "lumped" together or being split apart into newly defined species.

This White-throated Thrush was a rare visitor in Pharr, Texas (March 18).

Excitedly, I quizzed him about the robin and told him I was on my way. I arrived at his house about 45 minutes later and began to bird. I wandered to the back premises and then came back. He said he had just seen it again in a mulberry tree near his pond. Within 15 minutes, the White-throated Thrush was back, hanging on the end of the mulberry branches, munching berries. Periodically it flew back into the bushes but generally reappeared quite quickly.

I briefly saw a shy Clay-colored Thrush, but it did not come out of the underbrush very much. Before I left, a Chuck-will's-widow flew into a tree in the back of the yard, and Allen pointed it out to me. I took one more spin around the back of his yard before I left, and a small flock of Red-crowned Parrots flew over me. I had four new species for the day.

MARCH 19

Today was much less eventful, really not eventful at all. I did much looking for Muscovy Ducks at Salineño and seedeaters at Zapata, San Ygnacio, and Laredo. Nothing. Then I drove back toward the Lower Valley. My earlier thoughts of staying in Laredo changed when I could not find a motel. I could not even find any rooms in McAllen or surrounds. Good old Spring Break. I thought of just heading north but found a room in Rio Grande City.

MARCH 21

Yesterday I added a few birds to my year list. I began the day at Bentsen State Park, where I parked and began to walk to the hawk tower (counterclockwise on the main road). Being up on such a tower allows birders to have an unobstructed view of the sky so they can spot migrating hawks flying past. It was a nice walk, and I was feeling good, but except for a few toots from a Ferruginous Pygmy-Owl and the screams of a Gray Hawk, it was pretty still. Not too long after my arrival at the tower, I got my year Swainson's Hawk. The main raptor activity, however, was Turkey Vultures, a couple of thousand, mostly distant to one side or the other of the tower.

Midmorning, I saw a Brown-crested Flycatcher. Altamira Orioles were around much of the time, as were Yellow-rumped Warblers and a Nashville

Warbler. The winds were very light and the morning pleasant, but that was it. Midday I walked out to the park entrance, completing the 3-mile loop, and drove to South Padre Island.

I persevered and got to the Convention Center where I saw a single cooperative Clay-colored Sparrow flitting near the ground, up and down, from a bush, and one Lincoln's Sparrow. Out on the flats at the Convention Center were the usual zillion Laughing Gulls, terns, Sanderlings, and waders, plus a couple of Snowy Plovers and Roseate Spoonbills.

I fought my way back through traffic and off South Padre Island and headed north to Debra's house in Rockport. At Debra's urging, and after having obsessed for months, I finally decided to go to Georgia to try for the Green-breasted Mango, which has been there since November.

I'm now trying to get home but am stuck in a huge traffic jam near Waco. Today was a "down" day. Lately the days are usually either very good or very boring. Today was the latter. No sign of a Golden-cheeked Warbler or a Black-capped Vireo at Balcones Canyonlands north of Austin this afternoon, and it took forever to get there. I did see some very cute Cliff Swallows at the bridge coming out of Tivoli, north of Rockport. I'm at 430 species. There is probably no chance of anything new until Georgia on Monday. Depending on whether I see the mango and whether I can find any birdy habitat, I could see some new birds there.

MARCH 23

I began Easter bound for Atlanta and then Dublin, Georgia, where the Green-breasted Mango was hopefully still being seen. The mango did not disappoint me. About 10 minutes after I arrived at the Jackson backyard in Dublin this afternoon, Marshall Jackson and the mango appeared. It's a gorgeous bird, though still evidencing a bit of molting. The bird came back to the feeders two additional times while I was there (5:50 to 6:50), feeding at a little feeder to the back and side of the yard. I'm planning to go back early tomorrow when the sun should better illuminate the mango's favorite feeder, but I did get a good photo today. After that I plan to go toward the coast and try to get some more Georgia birds for my ABA big year list.

The Green-breasted Mango stayed around Dublin, Georgia, for months—long enough for me to get there on March 23.

MARCH 24

I got up early today because I could not sleep thinking about the wonderful mango. I need to tell the full story. I knew about the mango in November 2007. It was too soon to go, and I just knew it would not stay into 2008. But January arrived—it was still there. I looked up airfares—big. I calculated the number of miles to drive it—too many. I decided not to do it. And the bird would leave; I was sure. February arrived—the bird was still there. But it would certainly leave. So I did nothing. March arrived. The bird was still there. But it would certainly leave. Then I did some different calculations on birds needed to reach my 2008 goal. I needed the mango. I needed everything. The mango was still there. I checked on airfare for an immediate flight—astronomical (about $1,200). Then one day in mid-March it hit me. Maybe I could get to Dublin on frequent flyer miles. If the bird stayed . . . I called American Airlines. I called Dave. I obsessed. I called American Airlines again and

> Slightly scimitrical bill
> Body of pulsating green
> Throat of a hue, so stunning and true
> The purplist that I've ever seen.
> Body and wings that are big
> Tail that is coppery and bold
> A most welcome sight, in strong brassy flight,
> A miracle to behold.

found that, of course, I couldn't use my frequent flyer miles on just any flight, especially on any immediate flight. The earliest possible flight was on Easter. I would need to skip church. I called Dave again. And then I did it; I reserved a frequent flyer flight for Easter noon, to return two days later. Two days for me to will the mango to stay put. I waited. I flew. I picked up my rental car, trembling with haste and worry. I drove and drove and found Dublin and the Jackson home. I stood in the yard—still trembling with anticipation and wrestling with self-loathing for having waited too long. But in a mere 10 minutes, the bird arrived.

MARCH 25

After seeing the mango one more time this morning, I raced off to the Georgia coast to the historic place where Saltmarsh Sharp-tailed Sparrows are supposed to be. Unfortunately, I had neglected to notice from my Internet perusal that the site is closed on Mondays. On to Jekyll Island, but I found no new birds of any kind. The wind did not help.

I drove to Okefenokee National Wildlife Refuge, where I found few birds. I finally did hear the up-high-in-the-trees talking of a Red-cockaded Woodpecker, and later back near the same spot (an "upland trail") I saw two of them and wasn't skunked for the day.

I also added a Great Crested Flycatcher and a Prothonotary Warbler, both audio only (but I knew I would, and I did, see both of these birds later in the year).

At home this morning, I fed my wintering Rufous Hummingbird and after packing the car, headed south. My ultimate destination was Rockport by way of the Austin area. I had to try again for the two Hill Country specialties.

Once again I went to Shin Oak deck at Balcones Canyonlands. Soon after I arrived, I started hearing a Black-capped Vireo, distinctly different from the multiple-calling White-eyed Vireos, and eventually I saw it briefly as it flew to a bush and disappeared.

Other birders there had just come from Warbler Vista, where I had never been and where they had seen multiple Golden-cheeked Warblers. I decided to go there next. I parked in the parking lot, grabbed my camera, and took the trail. I hadn't been in the cedars more than three minutes when I heard a chip and saw two "Golden-faced" Warblers—I call them that because all of a sudden I was suspicious that I might be seeing Black-throated Green Warblers. I just might be remembering incorrectly what Golden-cheeked Warblers looked like (I usually see them only once, at best, per year). I quickly snapped two pictures and raced back to the car to check out the bird book to be sure of what I had. They were Golden-cheeks. Within 10 minutes of my arrival at Warbler Vista, I was on my way to Rockport. No time to study the gorgeous birds. What a great place—I'll have to come back to visit again.

It was an uneventful drive with a bit of rain, and I arrived in Rockport about 10 minutes after Debra did. We sped in my car to Port Aransas to check the warbler scene. We had not been at Paradise Pond too long when we saw a Louisiana Waterthrush, my main goal. We also spotted a Prothonotary Warbler—spectacular, golden, flittingly poking about in the mud— multiple Yellow-rumped Warblers, a Black-and-white Warbler, and a Nashville Warbler.

We had lunch and then went back to Rockport. When I checked my e-mails, I noticed that a Northern Pygmy-Owl had been found in Big Bend. I will be in Big Bend on April 3. Maybe I'll get this one—I'll surely try. With a bit of luck I could get four small owls on that trip, the Northern Pygmy, Elf, Western-Screech, and Flammulated (if I camp on top at Boot Springs, which I need to do).

MARCH 29

Today, very early, I drove to Indianola, Texas, where the Texas Ornithological Society (TOS) Magic Ridge Sanctuary is located, in the middle of nowhere. Ron Weeks (TOS president) had scheduled a field trip there, starting at 6:30, before the Magic Ridge dedication in Port Lavaca. Early on, I heard my big year Sedge Wren. We wandered down the road, periodically being summoned back to Brent Ortego's bird-banding table to see the wonders he had found (five or six warblers, none of which we saw while birding among the thick bushes). Then, about 8:10, we started hearing two Black Rails calling, apparently to each other. Ron gave them a little jolt of taped Black Rail, and they moved, invisibly, to within 6–8 feet of us. But nothing could bring them out where we could see them.

My year Eastern Kingbird showed up at Magic Ridge, too. I think all of the East Texas Eastern Kingbirds must be migrating together, because I saw them everywhere I went for the next three days.

After the dedication, Ron led some more birding, wandering the fields looking for shorebirds in wet fields, but there were few wet fields. We found a low area with a shallow pond and wet areas, with many yellowlegs and Blue-winged Teal, a few American Wigeons, and a couple of Pectoral Sandpipers. I ended the day at 441 species for the year.

MARCH 30

I got up about 4:45 and drove to Anahuac National Wildlife Refuge for the first of the season Yellow Rail walk led by David Sarkozi that began at 7:00 A.M. David, a past president of TOS, volunteers at Anahuac NWR and leads multiple Yellow Rail walks there each year. Yellow Rails are difficult to find when they winter in these marshes but can sometimes be caused to fly a short distance by dragging a weighted rope across the grass. Thank goodness we saw one on the morning walk. Rushing over, across, and around the sedge hills and tussocks, often through deep puddles, is hard and frightening. I kept worrying about falling and drowning my camera and missing the rail. Prior to the rail walk, we saw two American Bitterns standing by the road, doing their bittern thing, standing stock still, beaks pointed skyward. We also saw a Least Bittern.

Least Bitterns are one of my favorite species on the Texas coast.

I had originally planned to go to Bolivar for terns and shorebirds, but Sabine Woods was sending out beckoning signals to me, so I drove there. Unfortunately, the few warblers that had arrived the day before seemed to be gone. I found a couple of Orchard Orioles and a very odd female Hooded Warbler with a black eye line at Sabine Woods.

MARCH 31

I spent the night in Groves, planning to bird at Sabine Woods this morning and eventually head home. It rained and thundered all night, and when I got out to Sabine Pass, water was everywhere. At Sabine Woods, there were no birds. I quickly went to McFadden Wildlife Refuge, envisioning lots of rails flooded out of the marshes and wandering the road. A bit less dramatically, but very welcome, were two King Rails together, hugging the edge of the marsh on the cut grass.

About 9:00 today, I realized that I needed to go to Bolivar and Rollover Pass for terns. At Rollover Pass I saw many terns on the Gulf, but they were not black, or very little. Finally I saw one Black Tern, my goal. I crossed back over the road to the bay where the sandbars were covered with birds, mostly Laughing Gulls and Black Skimmers. To my delight, a few Least Terns were sitting on the sand (I saw more at Bolivar later), and a couple of little peeps with black legs and stubbed-off, modest bills, my first Semipalmated Sandpipers of the year.

I continued on to Bolivar, my goals being Baird's Sandpiper and Red Knots. While Baird's continued to elude me, I finally found two Red Knots. Although I couldn't drive near them because they were beyond barricade posts, I was able to walk quite close to get a few photos.

Today, as I barreled along in Ellis County scanning the grassy agricultural fields on both sides, looking for bug-eyed Upland Sandpipers, suddenly, I saw them—three bug-eyed heads looking at me from a lawn along the road. Thankfully there was a side road, and I was able to drive back along the highway to get closer for a few photos.

And that is it for the first quarter of the year. I had a total of 452 species— short of Komito's number of species by this time, but not bad. My problem now is that the focus knob on my Brunton binoculars has quit focusing. What is it about big years and Brunton focus wheels? At least there's a lifetime guarantee on the binoculars.

Upland Sandpipers finished the month of March for me.

APRIL

Neither Snow nor Sleet Can Keep Spring Away

NEW BIRD SPECIES SEEN THIS MONTH: 84
TOTAL BIRD SPECIES BY THE END OF THE MONTH: 536
PLACES BIRDED: Texas, New Mexico, Colorado, Florida

APRIL 2

I'm driving west toward Big
Bend National Park, about 550
miles from Fort Worth. I need to
get there to get a camping permit
before the Panther Junction visitor center closes. If I get a permit,
I will brave the forecast heavy
winds, hike to Boot Springs and
camp, and try to get a Flammulated Owl. It's early in the season,
but the owls should be there. Of
course, there are a lot of other
new bird possibilities for the year
in Big Bend. If I get there too
late, I'll have to revise my plan.

APRIL 3

Here I am, sitting on my
orange air mattress at the BC-1
campsite in Big Bend, up in the
Boot Springs area. I was in doubt
much of the way as to whether
I'd make it up the mountain. It

A big year quest is just like gambling—
You pays your money and then get rambling.
You takes your chances, and bet on winning,
But you also know, from the beginning,
That you might just never get what you're after,
Or maybe the day will end with laughter.
The birds will show, or they'll disappear,
The clouds will rain, or perhaps they'll clear.
You might get lucky, or lose the hand,
In spite of all you've done and planned.
You keep on trying; you keep obsessing,
You pray for yet another blessing.
The dice are thrown, the wheel is turning,
You hold your breath; are pulled by yearning.
You can't escape it, despite the cost,
Despite the hours of sleep you've lost.
The joker's you, but you're not knowing,
With blinders on, you keep on going.
Although you're doing something mad
You do know that your heart is glad.
Yet big year birding's so much more,
It's peering out an open door
To see the beauty, hear the sound,
It's such a wondrous world around.

is such a relentlessly steep climb, especially difficult with a heavy pack. The weather is lovely, no strong winds as of yet, just pleasant breezes alternating with absolute stillness.

Yesterday was windy but not bad. My first new bird of the day was Cassin's Sparrow—a couple of them singing south of Monahans. Once I arrived at the Big Bend headquarters, about nine hours after I left Fort Worth, I got my permit for the campsite. Mark Flippo (Big Bend ornithologist) told me that the Common Black-Hawks were being seen, so I headed to Rio Grande Village where they have nested for years, with a brief stop at Dugout Wells, where an Ash-throated Flycatcher greeted me, the first of a few new birds for the day.

At Rio Grande Village, I immediately went to the known Common Black-Hawk site, a small grove of large cottonwoods. With very little scanning, I located a Common Black-Hawk perched about 20 feet up in the one of the "usual" trees. I took a few pictures and then was surprised to realize that there was a second one perched about 10 feet from the first. By backing off on the lens magnification, I could get them both in the same picture. I could see nest materials in the tree, but it might have been a previous year's nest.

I wandered around the Rio Grande Village campground after a picnic supper. Then, since darkness and possible owls were taking so long to arrive, I drove into the amphitheater parking area and packed my big pack for today in the light of day. As dusk approached, I drove over to the Boquillas Canyon trail, hoping to hear and/or see Poorwills. It was very dark, and they should have been there, but maybe the wind kept them away or kept them silent. I did hear a Rock Wren while I waited for dark. After that I drove around the campground, hoping to hear owls, but nothing again, probably due to the wind. I drove to Chisos Basin, arriving about 10:00 P.M. I washed up in the restroom there and crawled into the back of my car (the back seats were removed, giving me almost enough room to sleep unbent). I had not reserved a room or tent space, and there were no vacancies in the park. I slept amazingly well even though it was quite cramped with all my gear.

This morning I reluctantly prepared for today's hike up the Pinnacles trail. Every single time, including today, that I have hiked this trail, especially with an overnight pack, I vowed that it would be my last time. I decided that today I would not rush, since I felt wobbly and breathless. My first target was the Northern Pygmy-Owl that had been reported a couple of miles up the trail. Although I heard a couple of distant toots, I decided that the sound was too little, too far away, and too uncertain to be counted.

I continued my plodding and huffing and puffing, stopping a bit to rest, hearing a Colima Warbler close to the top and another at the top, 4.5 miles and some 25 switchbacks later. If it hadn't been for the lure of a Flammulated Owl, tonight's goal, plus Colima Warbler and Blue-throated Hummingbird, which I hoped had arrived from the south, I probably would have quit and turned around. I persevered, and even put up my tent right away when I got to the campsite, rather than resting. The sky is clear, but the weather can change quickly in the mountains.

After relaxing briefly, I tromped over to Boot Springs. Almost immediately I heard a warbler sing and surmised, correctly as it turned out, that it was a Painted Redstart. I did not hear any Blue-throated Hummingbirds in their usual spot at the beginning of Boot Springs. After I had walked up the drainage for a while, there was a male Blue-throated Hummingbird nearly hidden in the shade of a large conifer even though perched out in the open, constantly giving his metallic call and moving his head back and forth as he called.

I returned to my tent. Since about 3:00, I have been sitting at my campsite, completing basic birding records, and then writing.

APRIL 4

Yesterday evening about 6:00 P.M., I wandered to Boot Springs again, to rest and to wait for owl time. There was a pack of park workers staying at the building at Boot Springs, likely to interfere with my plans to quietly listen at a picnic table as I had in 2005. Instead, I went down toward the springs. Suddenly, at 6:45, when it was still half light, there were two low Flammulated Owl–type hoots. They seemed to come from across the Boot Springs gulch, up the hill, in the conifers. Then there was silence. I waited. About 7:00, the sound started up again, usually a few sets of hoots followed by total silence and then repeated. About 7:22, it quit, and I did not hear it again. The bird was either gone or otherwise engaged. By now it was very dark in the canyon.

When there were no further bird sounds, I decided to wait (and sleep) in my tent, the lure of which was very strong. I was very tired. As I approached my tent, a Western Screech-Owl started calling (unstimulated by any iPod or tape playing) and called very briefly nearby. I crawled in the tent, and that was it for my consciousness. Although I awoke periodically throughout the night due to cold, cold, cold, and very hard ground, I never heard any Whip-poor-will (too early in the year) or the screech-owl again. I did hear a distant Flammulated Owl calling.

This morning I packed up my tent quickly, wanting to get down the trail fast to try one more time for the Northern Pygmy-Owl, but no luck on that. I did add a Rufous-crowned Sparrow foraging in the flats above Chisos Basin in an area where I have seen them before. A surprising addition, at least for Big Bend (for me), was a lovely male Phainopepla, black with white on the wings, perched up on a snag and then flying out to flycatch and away.

When I got down the mountain, I collapsed at the car, very relieved to shed my pack about four hours after I had started down. I never do the trail very fast, even downward, when I have my pack on.

I decided to try to check in at Chisos Basin to see if I could get a room key early. It was not possible, so I decided to go birding by car. Once my pack was off, and I had drunk a needed power drink, I felt pretty good.

At Sam Nail Ranch, an old homestead area with a few trees and a some-times functional windmill, the Bell's Vireos were in for their breeding season and were their usual noisy selves. Otherwise, it was pretty quiet. The trees were just beginning to leaf out. No water was visible below the windmill even though the wind was blowing. I continued on to Cottonwood Campground, my main goal being Lucy's Warbler. On the way, driving in sort of a daze, I suddenly saw a dark spot in an ocotillo and thought "oriole." I did a U-turn and saw a gorgeous Scott's Oriole.

Onward to Cottonwood Campground, where I drove around the area past the few campers, and then parked at a shady campsite near the gate. A beautiful Gray Hawk was hanging about the large trees, at first carrying some rat-sized prey. My first Black-chinned Hummingbird of the year was bouncing about in the high branches, twittering. I walked over to the north side fence-row trees, and in almost the same place as in previous years was a Lucy's Warbler, absolutely plain gray until I saw its very rusty rump. My goal was accomplished, but of course there is no rest for the big year birder.

I drove down to Santa Elena Canyon and back to Sam Nail, but the birds all seemed to be taking a siesta. I decided to go back to the Basin, get my key, and shower as the best uses of the bird downtime. About 6:00, I bought some cheese at the store and headed to Dugout Wells for Elf Owl. There were a couple of people there also owling. About 8:45 a couple of Elf Owls started vocalizing and continued intermittently until I left at about 9:30.

Gray Hawks nest each year in Big Bend National Park, Texas (April 4).

I went back to the Basin for a bed-sleep at Chisos Lodge for the first time in three days. In spite of aching muscles and a cold room (outdoor temperature of 45 degrees), I slept pretty well.

APRIL 5

I got up at 6:00 and decided to go check out the Elf Owls again, because I can never get too much of owls. When I got to Dugout Wells, the owls were in full chorus, particularly loud near the parking area. I saw a Common Poorwill just before I turned off the road at Dugout Wells.

I then headed out to the Blue Creek trail, where Gray Vireos nest in the scrub past the building. It was a crispy clear morning (42 degrees) with very light or no wind. Feeling almost featherlight without a backpack, I started up the trail. Almost immediately, I found a Green-tailed Towhee. After reaching the building, I heard and then saw two Black-tailed Gnatcatchers, shortly before I lost the trail. After casting about in vain for anything that remotely resembled a trail, I just struck off up one of the washes, figuring I'd find my way out eventually. I headed up gradually. Eventually I reached a place where grass and brush blocked my way and stopped to listen. In the distance I could hear what sounded like a Gray Vireo. I bushwhacked through the brush and found another wash and proceeded upward some more. I got very close to the singing Gray Vireo but never saw it.

After the Gray Vireo stopped singing, I decided to head back. Although I knew that I should be able to find my way out, I was quite nervous about it. I hadn't gone very far when I found the trail near a big boulder. I figured out that on the way up I had turned a small bend around the boulder and had not looked in the direction of the trail and therefore had not seen it.

The temperature was still pleasant, but birds were quieting down, except for a very raucous pair of Cactus Wrens up toward the trailhead. One of them went into a nest, and it sounded like there were squawking young ones inside.

A Zone-tailed Hawk cruises near Fort Davis, Texas (April 5).

I began my journey home, making a couple more stops before leaving the park. Very near Sam Nail Ranch, I saw some swallows and got out of the car. They were Violet-green Swallows with the white extending almost all of the way across their rumps.

I also checked every single vulture along the way to see if it perhaps was a Zone-tailed Hawk. Zone-tails, typical prey-hunting hawks, look much like Turkey Vultures from a distance, with similar blackish silhouettes and flight behaviors. Their similarity to carrion-eating Turkey Vultures allows them to hide within a Turkey Vulture flock so that potential small prey animals (and birders) do not notice them. Observant birders, however, can tell the difference by noting the white tail stripe on the Zone-tail and the yellow beak and feet.

About 11:30 I was out of Big Bend. I was mainly looking for kingbirds (Cassin's and Western) and Zone-tailed Hawks. No luck on the former. They must not be in yet, because when they are, they are everywhere. About 3 miles north of Fort Davis, one of what appeared to be Turkey Vultures turned out to be a Zone-tailed Hawk. I was pretty sure even before I raised my binoculars, as it looked blacker, smoother somehow than a vulture.

> The meaning of each day is rarely found in words.
> The essence of each day is wrapped up in its birds.
> Their being and their songs, their beauty and their flight,
> Days spent with birds. Days filled with light.

APRIL 10

The last three days have been slow and stressful. Tuesday night (April 8) I went out to Lipscomb County in the Texas Panhandle where Lesser Prairie-Chickens have leks. I looked and I listened. Finally, distantly, through the scope I saw two of them, head to head, posing. I blinked while I adjusted the scope, and I lost them, never to be seen again.

As I headed south from Lipscomb the next day to pick up my road west, I was immersed in a wild hail/snow/rainstorm. It quickly accumulated on the road, and even though the road was flat, I was worried about skidding. Little did I know how mild it was compared to what was to come in Colorado. Gradually I got out of the worst of it, but it rained most of the way across Texas and into New Mexico. Then I heard the Colorado highway reports on the radio—snow, snow, snow all across Colorado, especially where I was headed, to Gunnison.

As I got closer to my destination, the forecasts seemed to indicate that I might get to Gunnison, or close, before the snow got too bad. I drove like mad as I had all day, noting kestrels, redtails, and magpies as I flew by. I arrived at Waunita Hot Springs, the location of the Gunnison Sage-Grouse lek, 20 miles from Gunnison, about 4:20, before the snow. It was cold and windy as I joined others who were also checking out the blind before the morning watch. No grouse were around at midday of course, but among the Mountain Bluebirds, American Robins, and Dark-eyed Juncos was a Sage Thrasher.

I had assumed I would see Gunnison Sage-Grouse at their lek today. After agonizing my way over the increasingly snowy road from Gunnison to Waunita Hot Springs, and waiting silently for about three hours in my car in the cold through the gray, lightly snowy, windy dawn without anything but fly-by ducks and a Bald Eagle, I along with the others there learned that the deep snow must have kept the grouse away, and there were not going to be any grouse sightings that day.

Mountain Bluebirds were common along the fences near Gunnison, Colorado (April 10).

Not having much choice but to continue on my chosen itinerary, I headed west to my reserved motel in Craig. I was almost immediately slowed by nasty roads with more snow coming down and blowing around. The road was icy I'm sure, but I tried to go slow enough so I couldn't feel it and didn't have to brake. Then luckily I came up behind a snow plow that was putting down sand. I settled in to patiently follow it. It made me feel safe, even though there were lots of places in the road that were packed with ice and snow that the plow did not clear.

Slowly I got to Grand Junction after some more treacherous pass areas and then headed northeast. I planned to take a short detour to look for owls that had been reported near and past the Powderhorn Ski area, but the snow was coming down, the road was wet, the temperature was dropping to 31 degrees, and the road was steep. It was gray and cloudy, and I chickened out (appropriately enough) and turned around.

Mostly the roads were okay to Craig, with only a bit of snow. I stopped at a large water "pond" near the Colorado River where I could see some white specks. I was hoping to redeem the day with a Franklin's Gull and was glad to find two of them among the Ring-billed Gulls and Bonaparte's Gulls. I've had three new birds for the trip, at 480 species for the year.

APRIL 11

I slept in because when my alarm originally went off, it was snowing furiously and I could not bear to face it. About 7:00, I headed north of Craig. I was going to a Greater Sage-Grouse lek, but the icy road was closed because of an accident. I went northwest (plan B) up to Cedar Mountain. The park was unplowed and inaccessible, but I drove very slowly along the highway looking and listening. There was a loud "jay sound" to the east over some cedars, and I briefly saw two Pinyon Jays as they dove into the cedars, just as another two jays flew off and over the hill. I then drove to Hayden, intending to check out the Greater Sage-Grouse leks north of there, but the snow got deeper and deeper, so I turned around.

I gave up—I had no more ideas of where to look—and headed to Walden where I was scheduled to stay that night. I was early, so I decided to randomly explore. On the drive in I had found CR26, a roadside site for Greater Sage-Grouse, which was sort of plowed but looked uncertain for driving. In my extra time, I decided to walk in with my scope to see if I could find a stray Greater Sage-Grouse. No luck on that, and the wind picked up and it started to snow.

Greater Sage-Grouse were buffeted by the wind in snowy Colorado (April 12).

I drove north from Walden until the road was too icy, then back through and south. About 10–12 miles south of Walden, I noticed dark bird blobs ahead among some stunted sage—and the blobs turned out to be Greater Sage-Grouse. Some 22 Greater Sage-Grouse were hunkered down, all facing into the wind, most of them sitting behind individual sage clumps, weathering it out. After I took many pictures and rejoiced greatly, I drove farther south and found 10 more. I turned around when the road got too icy near a sad, dying birdless fir forest. I checked in at Walden, and contrary to my usual fast-food custom, went out to eat a Mexican special at the nearby bowling alley.

APRIL 12

Again, I got up later than I had intended, having forgotten how early things become visible when it's snowy, and drove to Coalmont and CR26. I was uncertain about driving that road, but it was 2 degrees, and walking in seemed to be out of the question, especially in the wind. A car was coming out as I drove in. The passengers told me that there were no displaying birds, just a single male up the road. I drove in and saw the one bird and turned around. As I headed out, I saw the other car stopped, its lights flashing, and I noticed that there was a Greater Sage-Grouse crossing the road 15 feet in front of the car. About 12 more grouse were in the snow coming up onto the road, probably to get out of the deep snow in which it was difficult for them to walk. All of them started walking up the road toward me and then came alongside me, just off the road, and I could take pictures without shooting through the front window. The grouse were mostly picking at the vegetation. One sort of puffed up and looked like he wanted to display, but he appeared to change his mind. The grouse never even seemed to notice as our cars drove out to look for more birds.

I stopped by Loveland Pass, where blowing snow was everywhere and every parking lot was full of skiers. There was nowhere to stop and look for White-tailed Ptarmigan, so I headed to Denver and then back to Gunnison. I needed to try once more for Gunnison Sage-Grouse.

Distant Gunnison Sage-Grouse, finally on the second try at Waunita Hot Springs near Gunnison, Colorado.

APRIL 13

I began the day at the Gunnison Sage-Grouse lek. I never did get a good count, but there was a very welcome group of them, with at least 15 of each sex, including displaying males and casually strolling females spread out across the "field." All of them were quite distant, but the males' "attitudes," if not their detailed feather patterns, can be seen from the photos. They all left by 7:40, which was good, as I was about frozen (18 degrees). I headed west for the Black Canyon of the Gunnison, which is supposed to be a good spot for Dusky Grouse, but most of the park was closed due to the waist-deep snow, and I couldn't go exploring. I did see a Clark's Nutcracker, however, perched in a tree on the drive into the park. I plan to go back to Loveland tomorrow and then home. Texas now has flamingos and a Ruff—hopefully they will all stay, but I'm not sure I have time to look for them before I go to Florida later this month.

APRIL 14

I had no luck this morning at Loveland Pass from 7:00 to 9:30, and I swear I looked at every rock. Lots of little ptarmigan-sized blobs, but none moved, and they mostly were too far away for me to see what they were. Since then, I've been driving and am now in the Texas Panhandle. In Springer, New Mexico, I saw two Western Kingbirds. I'll be in Dalhart, Texas, soon, and then on to Childress. If the Ruff is still in Austin, I need to figure out a way to fit in a quick trip there soon.

I am trying to figure out my future birding schedule as I drive. This last week (hopefully limited to this last week), the joy disappeared from my big year. In the midst of spectacular mountain scenery, sterling white mountains, and a few nice birds, all I could think about was the birds that I was missing in Colorado, the time I was losing navigating the icy roads, and the need for more birds. I'm definitely *not* doing as well as I had assumed I would. Of course, there are eight-plus months left, but every bird I miss now requires me to go out later and search for *and find* it.

APRIL 17

I am in Florida where I'll bird with my North Carolina friend Lena. As mentioned earlier, a Ruff was at Hornsby Bend in Austin, Texas, while I was

A Florida Scrub-Jay looks down at us at Juno Dunes Natural Area, Florida, on April 17.

in Colorado. When I got to Childress, Texas, on April 14, I called my friend
Debra in Rockport to see if she had heard any Ruff updates (no); then I called
Eric Carpenter, who runs the Austin Rare Bird Alert. The last report had
been on the morning of April 13. I decided to stay in Childress and then head
home the next day. About 10:00 P.M., however, Eric called me back and said
that the Ruff had been seen in the early afternoon. I changed my plans and
started driving south toward Austin the next morning at 3:15 A.M.

I arrived at Hornsby Bend about 10:30, raring to find the Ruff. There was
no one there when I arrived, but a few people showed up soon. We were all
very careful to stay in approved sites, and we all saw the fairly distant Ruff
(actually a young Reeve, the female). No photography by me though because
the bird was too far away.

I then looked around to see what else was at Hornsby Bend: lots of peeps
(little shorebirds of the *Calidris* genus primarily), including quite a few
Baird's Sandpipers, which were new for my year. On the drive out at about
11:30, I saw first a lovely, breeding-plumage female Wilson's Phalarope and
then realized that there was a flock of about 10 of them. I added three new

birds that day (April 15). I was glad that we did taxes early this year for once and I did not have to race home for that.

Today, Lena and I immediately headed out to Fort Lauderdale to try for the Smooth-billed Ani, but there were none to be found. I'm probably not going to get them in my big year, as they seem to be gone or nearly gone from the state and very, very secretive.

We were finally able to find the Florida Scrub-Jay at Juno Dunes Natural Area north of Fort Lauderdale. There were two of them, found near the parking lot where we had left the car only after we had walked through the entire area. We did get to see many Gray Catbirds, an Eastern Towhee, a Common Yellowthroat, and a Palm Warbler.

APRIL 18

We went to Ding Darling National Wildlife Refuge today but learned that the wildlife drive is closed on Fridays. We were able to walk a couple of trails though and had a chance at a Mangrove Cuckoo at one, where we were told that some bird folks were "legally" playing tapes to find the cuckoos for research purposes. No sign of the cuckoos or the researchers though. Before that we saw a Common Nighthawk and two river otters.

This Osprey nest was at Sanibel Island, Florida (April 18).

After fish sandwiches on Sanibel Island we drove down to the lighthouse. We were not planning to stay long, but a nest of Ospreys with a "mama" and three nearly grown young kept our cameras busy. We also saw two Magnificent Frigatebirds and a Gray Kingbird.

We drove toward Corkscrew Swamp, stopped in Fort Myers for gas, bought soft drinks, got back in the car, and it would not start. At all. The car was dead. I called the car rental agency and told them that we needed a new car fast, as I envisioned losing birding time sitting at the gas station. Eventually, the tow truck bearing a replacement arrived. About 4:15, we headed once again for Corkscrew. We paid our entry fee and started out on the boardwalk. Almost immediately, we saw the first of many Swallow-tailed Kites for the trip, but that was the only new year bird there. The once wet mangrove swamps were bone dry.

The Corkscrew closing time was fast approaching, so we hastened along the boardwalk. Two people ahead of us were motioning us to come and see something down along the boardwalk. As we approached, we could see that there was a struggling Red-shouldered Hawk on the ground. We couldn't tell if it had caught something to eat or was itself caught and couldn't get away. We realized that we needed to contact the rangers so someone could try to

Gray Kingbirds are easy to find in south Florida (April 18).

Graceful Swallow-tailed Kites were seen at many places in south Florida (April 18).

extricate the hawk. All of a sudden the hawk gave a couple of mighty flaps, and we could see that it was holding a very large snake. The hawk would not let go, but we could not wait around until the fight was won or lost. We wished the hawk well, knowing that if the hawk made it without dropping the snake, the hawk was going to be a very fat, stuffed bird for a couple of days.

APRIL 19

Back at Corkscrew Swamp today, we identified the waterthrush that we had seen briefly yesterday as a Northern Waterthrush. In a little flock with American Redstarts and a Northern Parula, we also saw a Red-eyed Vireo. We checked the vireo for whiskers to see if we could turn it into a Black-whiskered Vireo, but could not.

In the late morning, we left Corkscrew Swamp and headed down to the Miccosukee area. A ranger told us of a place down the highway to the east that was good for Snail Kites, and we found one there. We then drove back west and walked the short Tree Snail Hammock trail, which was rather slow (as expected) because it was in the middle of the afternoon. We reached a small bridge where another car was parked and a man with binoculars was standing, looking at a Black-crowned Night-Heron, not a new year bird, but

This is the first of many male Black-throated Blue Warblers that we saw (April 19).

very photogenic. As we glanced around the cypress swamp on both sides of the road, we could hear a Prothonotary Warbler. Lena found a Black-throated Blue Warbler, which I was delighted to see was a male, difficult to find in Texas. We took many photos of it in the dark, dappled leaves and then continued our drive onward.

APRIL 20

About midday, we went to the Everglades. There was not much action, but we ran into three people who told us that there was a good birding place known as "Lucky Hammock" just north of the park. We went back to our car and went looking for Lucky Hammock, which was a great birding place—lots of Blackpoll and Cape May Warblers, plus at least one Indigo Bunting. The main highlight of Lucky Hammock, however, was a full-size juvenile Barred Owl sitting on one of the branches. We took many pictures of it. As dusk approached, we heard a calling Barred Owl and, not long afterward, saw an adult Barred Owl fly into a nearby tree. The young owl cried pitifully, but the adult just sat quietly and then flew off, eliciting more cries from the baby. The young one tried to hop and fly to another branch in the direction the adult had gone but did not appear to be able to fly. We left the owls to sort it out and headed for our motel in Florida City at the edge of the Keys.

APRIL 21

We drove toward Key West, stopping at a few places that were reported to be good birding areas. Our first stop was Dagny Johnson Key Largo Hammock Botanical State Park. Nearly immediately we heard a slow-talking vireo

A young Barred Owl sat in the middle of a tree full of warblers at Lucky Hammock, Florida (April 20).

and saw a Black-whiskered Vireo after a bit of looking. It was number 500 for my year. There were warblers there, too, but none new for the year, so we continued on down the Keys.

Our next bird-producing spot was the Key West Botanical Garden Tropical Forest, where we added a Blue Grosbeak and saw more warblers, Gray Kingbirds, and a Western Kingbird. Then we hastened to the marina in Key West, getting lost on the way. We found the MV *Playmate*, the boat scheduled to take us (Lena, me, eight other participants, Larry Manfredi, the guide, and his crew) to the Dry Tortugas, a place one can sometimes find Caribbean rarities. We were given a brief talk about the boat and then were on our own after loading our luggage on board, so long as we were back on the boat by 3:30 A.M., when it would be close to setting sail.

I put on the Scopolamine patch, took Dramamine, and clambered up to my top bunk in a cabin the size of a small bathroom, with 8 square feet of floor space (less than 2 feet wide). Lights out, I tried to sleep in the gently rocking boat. No sooner had I shut my eyes than my heart started pounding, and I could not get a breath. All I could think of was getting out of that tight space. I maneuvered in my bunk to get down with a minimum of disturbance to Lena who was trying to sleep in the bottom bunk, and I went ashore. It seemed a good time to go over to the shore bathroom. I returned to the boat, crawled over Lena's stuff, and assumed the position, only one position being possible in the narrow bunk. Again, panic in such a tight enclosure. I repeated getting down and out, walked around a bit, and returned to the boat while mumbling calming words, vowing to stay in the bunk this time. And I did. I was too tired to do anything but sleep.

APRIL 22

My long-delayed sleep was very deep, and I slept through the boat starting up. I woke up to the smell of coffee in the dining room and the voice of Lena and others who were already up. By the time I got on deck, they had seen a few birds, all of which reappeared later, so I had not missed anything.

I got my first year bird of the voyage before 8 A.M., the first of many today, a Brown Noddy. Shortly thereafter, three Audubon's Shearwaters (not usually seen there) flew by, landed on the water, and were pursued by the boat, photographed, and flew away. Numerous Bridled and Sooty Terns, Masked Boobies, plus four Brown Boobies, flew by, some quite close to the boat. At

We saw numerous Masked Boobies on our boat trip to the Dry Tortugas, Florida (April 22).

Hospital Key some hours later, we saw the Masked Booby colony sitting on a desolate, nearly unvegetated sandbar in the middle of nowhere, part of Dry Tortugas National Park.

We went to Garden Key, where the remains of the nineteenth-century Fort Jefferson often shelter birds that fly in from the ocean. Our boat approached some old iron and cement pilings where many Brown Noddies were perched and flying about. Our goal was a Black Noddy, two of which were regularly being seen at this location. We all looked over each piling and each bird, and Larry finally located one of the Black Noddies amid the Brown and then worked to get all of us to see it. Eventually we all saw the Black Noddy, and I got some photos.

After lunch we birded on land at Garden Key. There was a good assortment of warblers, *all* of which I had already seen for the year (American Redstart, Northern Parula, Ovenbird, Northern Waterthrush, and Hooded, Black-throated Blue, Blackpoll, Wilson's, Cape May, and Prairie Warblers), but I did add a fly-over, well-seen Bobolink, a couple of long-tailed Yellow-billed Cuckoos, and a couple of Swainson's Thrushes, most of which were at

Two Brown Boobies watched our boat go by on our way to the Dry Tortugas, Florida (April 22).

the little, nearly not functioning, drip area where the fresh water was attracting small birds.

Each of us got to take a boat ride to the nesting Keys nearby, one of which had mostly Brown Noddies and Sooty Terns, and one with mostly nesting frigatebirds. On the latter island, a Red-footed Booby had been seen on the previous trip, but we could not find it again despite three or more trips over and constant telescope scanning from Garden Key. I did add a low-flying Bank Swallow.

APRIL 25

Yesterday after early-morning searching, we left the Fort to return to Key West. On the way, the most interesting sighting was an American Coot, not usually there. A little after 5:00 P.M., we were birding on land again at Key West Botanical Garden, where a Yellow-green Vireo had been seen the day before, but we could not find it. We did see a Worm-eating Warbler, which was great, and was my most recent addition to my year list (none today). We stayed in Key Largo overnight.

Today Lena and I birded the Key Largo Botanical Garden again. We had eight species of warblers, but none of them were new. I hope there will be some in Texas next week for the Birding Classic.

The plane is bumpily making its way down to DFW. I have spent the entire trip making a new list of birds that are still possible, and it's looking better than my previous calculating. Maybe I'm more optimistic (less realistic?), but it seems *almost* possible to reach 700. I have not counted any Asian strays that are not regularly seen in Alaska. Hopefully I'll get some of them on Adak, the Pribilofs, Gambell, Nome, or Barrow in Alaska. I'm rather excited but have a lurking fear that my addition was wrong. I made a list of people/guides to contact, reservations to make, and birds to try to get in each place.

APRIL 29

I arrived home safely and did chores and client work nonstop. On Sunday, April 27, I climbed into Dave's car (mine had a very worrisome sound, like a flat tire without any visible signs) and headed to Houston. Our team gathered with our leader, Tony Frank, and we headed southeast to scout for the Classic competition.

The Great Texas Birding Classic begins today. This is a competition to count birds in a specified Texas coastal area, and this is the second year I will be on one of the teams. Two of my teammates are Sheridan Coffey and David Sarkozi. For years, Sheridan was in charge of the Texas Rare Bird Alert, and David, in addition to being the Anahuac NWR Yellow Rail guide, as mentioned earlier, owns Texbirds, the listserv where people can report birds seen in Texas.

When we were doing scouting for the Classic, we saw a Brown Pelican flying near Choke Canyon, a long way from its Gulf home. Among the birds in the Calliham unit of Choke Canyon State Park were Franklin's Gulls and Bank Swallows (both new for Texas for the year). Also, there was one Yellow-headed Blackbird and the first of many Bullock's Orioles.

We stayed overnight at the Bass Inn near Three Rivers and the next morning went back to explore the park some more. In the half light, two of us saw a couple of Chuck-will's-widows and a Great Horned Owl, and I heard (and briefly saw) my first Yellow-breasted Chat of the year. When we all got back together, we walked down Emperor Run trail to listen for Bell's Vireo (not heard), but we did see and hear a Least Flycatcher. We went to Live Oak

County where we saw a little flock of Northern Bobwhite, heard Cassin's and Black-throated Sparrows, and had a single Yellow-headed Blackbird in a flock (not seen on the Classic itself). We wandered through Bee, San Patricio, Jim Wells, and Nueces counties, seeing the expected birds and a few warblers, and then east of Riviera to a large pond where we saw quite a few shorebirds (Stilt, Pectoral, Baird's, and Spotted Sandpipers, American Avocet, Black-bellied Plover, as well as a new-for-the-year White-rumped Sandpiper), a Rose-breasted Grosbeak, Northern Waterthrush, and Black Tern.

We checked out La Sal del Rey on our way to the Valley, for our first view of a Lesser Nighthawk (a year bird) and more of the same birds we had already seen. On April 28, we went to Starr County Park in the Valley, and David whistled a Ferruginous Pygmy-Owl call to spook out little birds, and a Ferruginous Pygmy-Owl answered. That caused us to put the park on the list of places to go for the Classic. Unfortunately, when we went back for the Classic itself, there was no response to David's whistles. We had to look for it elsewhere.

We started today, the first day of the Classic, by hearing and then seeing a Tropical Kingbird in our motel parking lot in Rio Grande City. I should mention before I get into a description of our Classic quest that many details of this quest have been omitted for the express reason that this information is classified Classic information proprietary to Tony Frank, our fearless Classic leader.

After leaving the motel, we went to a local road for Common Pauraque, Poorwill, and Lesser Nighthawk, and then to Salineño, where we got the expected, including Red-billed Pigeon, but not a Muscovy Duck (the bird I wanted most; is it going to be a nemesis bird all year?). After that, we heard White-collared Seedeaters at the Zapata library. Hopefully I'll see one this year, but hearing a bird counts, too.

In the early afternoon, we started getting into serious warbler territory at Frontera Audubon, with its expanse of newly budding brush and trees, and water, encouraging warblers to flit among the branches in search of insects as they rest on their northbound migration. There we found Blackburnian, Nashville, Tennessee, Chestnut-sided, Kentucky, Black-and-white, and Worm-eating Warblers, American Redstart, Common Yellowthroat, and Yellow-breasted Chat, plus Yellow-bellied, Least, Willow, and Acadian Flycatchers, Warbling and Philadelphia Vireos, Swainson's Thrush and Veery, a stunning Rose-breasted Grosbeak, and both Black-billed and Yellow-billed Cuckoos. A great place.

We raced over to Sabal Palm and then Port Isabel Road, where we found Grasshopper and Botteri's Sparrows. We ended in the Brownsville area by seeing both Green Parakeets and Red-crowned Parrots at dusk, but the day wasn't done. We drove back west to Bentsen State Park, arriving at 8:30 P.M. Shortly thereafter, David Sarkozi whistled in an Elf Owl, Eastern Screech-Owl, and Ferruginous Pygmy-Owl. There were Common Pauraques calling, too.

APRIL 30

On this second day of the Classic, we stayed in the Lower Valley and found Scarlet Tanager, Northern Beardless-Tyrannulet, Gray Hawk, Anhinga, and the usual other suspects at the various big refuges, such as Green Jay, Plain Chachalaca, and Buff-bellied Hummingbird. We then explored South Padre Island hotspots and added Magnolia, Hooded, and Cape May Warblers, Northern Waterthrush, Summer Tanager, and Surf Scoter (thanks to Scarlet Colley, who told us about the scoter).

It was time to leave the Valley and head north for sandpipers (e.g., Baird's and White-rumped) and for Masked Duck at the King Ranch (which we needed to get during the Classic, not just during scouting). We also learned of the location of a few lingering geese. In spite of the heavy winds, we were able to set up a scope and see them across a lake. We ended the day standing on a bridge in the pitch black, with David Sarkozi yodeling his Barred Owl call across the darkness, which resulted in an owl nearly landing on our heads.

M A Y

Warbler Waves and I Go North

NEW BIRD SPECIES SEEN THIS MONTH: 44
TOTAL BIRD SPECIES BY THE END OF THE MONTH: 580
PLACES BIRDED: Texas, Alaska, Washington, Michigan

MAY 1

We began the day in the dark on another lonely road, listening intently as the wind blew around us, eventually hearing five different nightjars: Chuck-will's-widow, Whip-poor-will, Common Pauraque, and both Common and Lesser Nighthawk in under an hour. This area is a relatively remote location known to our Classic leader that is sufficiently distant from the sounds of civilization and a sufficiently mixed habitat for these species. On a (rare) calm night, it is not difficult to hear them, but it was a challenge to pick out each voice from the sounds of the vegetation being blown in the breeze.

Our next stop, in the daylight, was for Field Sparrows at a site where we had found one the previous year. Our scouting had not found any Field Sparrows there this year, so we had little hope. Tony stopped the van, and we rolled open the back doors. Before I had a chance to get both feet on the ground so I could look around, we heard a Field Sparrow singing.

We were off to Corpus Christi, where we stopped at a lake for a few shore-birds and a Reddish Egret, and then at Rose Hill Cemetery where we found Canada and Cerulean Warblers, and at Blucher Park, where we added Bay-breasted Warbler. We drove the roads in Refugio, Calhoun, and Matagorda counties and eventually found a wet field with numerous Buff-breasted Sandpipers. Toward dusk we had very welcome flocks of Hudsonian Godwits flying over.

MAY 2

Today was our Classic team's Piney Woods day in Angelina and Jasper counties. Even before daylight, invisible Bachman's Sparrows were singing

A Reddish Egret hunts for food along the Texas coast (May 1).

around us. Around 6:30 the Red-cockaded Woodpeckers began to talk above us and then to fly from treetop to treetop. About 15 minutes later, Brown-headed Nuthatches excitedly appeared, squeaking and fussing as usual. Not far away we drove through an area where Swainson's Warblers were singing, followed by a single Red-eyed Vireo, a Wood Thrush, Yellow-throated Vireo, and a calling Red-headed Woodpecker. Further drive-by birding in Jasper County interspersed with a few brief stops revealed Yellow-throated, Pro-thonotary, Northern Parula, and Tennessee Warblers, a soaring White-tailed Kite, a fly-by Wood Duck, a sneaking Eastern Towhee, and a perched-up Prairie Warbler.

We checked several Beaumont locations but did not locate any Fish Crows. Sabine Woods and the nearby "willows" were good for more warblers, the highlight being a Golden-winged Warbler. While a Blue-winged Warbler was also reported, we were unable to find it, and in fact, we did not get one on the Classic.

We then drove to Winnie and down to Anahuac NWR and the High Island sanctuaries, popular locations during migration. At Anahuac were a Northern Harrier, many calling Sora, a calling Black Rail, a colorful Purple Gallinule, and Savannah and Seaside Sparrows. A long-necked American Bittern tried without success to escape our detection along one of the trails. We stopped briefly at Boy Scout Woods at High Island to check the blackboard to see if anyone had seen any goal birds, but not so. We did see a Gray-cheeked Thrush at the drip there before we headed to Texas City for our motel.

MAY 3

This morning we found a couple of Monk Parakeets at a "secret" spot of Tony's and then went to the Texas City Preserve for Attwater (Greater) Prairie-Chicken, which while not countable for my big year under the ABA rules because the population is not sufficiently established in the wild, is countable under the Classic rules. There was also a single Sedge Wren there.

We explored a couple of local water areas in Corpus Christi and found an Eared Grebe and a previously reported Pacific Loon among the larger Common Loons. Then we were off to the Galveston ferry and the Bolivar peninsula, where we were delighted to find a single Bonaparte's Gull sitting on the water, Whimbrels, a Long-billed Curlew, and a flock of Bobolinks. Back at Anahuac again, we found White-faced Ibises, and at least one Glossy Ibis (rare to uncommon in Texas). We drove to Beaumont to try once again for a Fish Crow and found one even before we reached our goal site. Then to Sabine Woods one more time. We saw that someone had posted a sighting of an Olive-sided Flycatcher at the willows. We raced over there, and without much delay we found it actively flycatching. That was our last bird of the Classic and number 548 for my big year.

I thought that would be my last bird for a while, but a Piratic Flycatcher had been reported at

The sky's cold and gray, the road rainy, wet
My bank account's empty and I'm deep in debt
My head's feeling fuzzy, packed tightly with fog
And sinking so slowly in dark soggy bog.
My eyes are so tired, my shoulders so sore
My thoughts stuffed with birds I don't need
 anymore
And with others that just refuse to be found,
That hid in the bushes not making a sound.
This portrait I've painted, unfortunate, but true,
Is *not* the full picture of what I'm going through.
This big year has actually almost always been fun,
In spite of the fact that I've stayed on the run.
But now I'm between and removed from the highs
Exclamations of joy now replaced by deep sighs.
I hope I'll have time, soon, for sleep and for rest.
I'll need them of course to finish this quest.
Together with willpower and drive and caffeine,
I hope they will take me through times yet unseen,
So when this year's over, this will be just a blip
On an otherwise magical, marvelous trip.

Pollywog Ponds in Corpus Christi. After the awards ceremony in Beaumont (we took second place with 306 species for five days), and after our team had gone back to Houston and I had my car, Sheridan and I drove rapidly to Corpus Christi, some 250 miles away, followed by Tony and his family in another car. Martin Reid had already arrived at Pollywog Ponds, had located the Piratic Flycatcher, and urged Sheridan and me to make fast tracks there. The flycatcher periodically would fly out of its mulberry tree and then disappear for long periods, causing Martin great anxiety that it would leave completely. Not to worry, however, because when we got there, Martin had his spotting scope trained on the Piratic Flycatcher sitting quietly, deep within the mulberry.

The Piratic Flycatcher that came to Corpus Christi was an unexpected rarity for the year (May 4).

MAY 10

I have terrors of missing my flight from DFW to Anchorage by being too engrossed in reading (it has happened to me in years past), so will wait until I'm on the plane, in my first-class seat. I am using frequent flyer miles, and first class was all that was available when I needed to go. Thanks to Birdtreks, a Pennsylvania-based bird-watching tour company, for taking care of getting me a reservation when none seemed available.

I have been racing around and doing client work since I got home after the Classic. I had stayed overnight in Schulenburg, Texas, because it wasn't wise to drive all night when I was so tired. Yesterday I did take a birding break. I went to Legacy Park in Arlington, east of Fort Worth, with visions of an Alder Flycatcher or rare warbler, but instead, there amid Indigo and Painted Buntings was a male Lazuli Bunting. They have always seemed like nemesis birds to me. I'll probably see a zillion of them later, but I don't have to worry about it now. I still need Alder Flycatcher though. Maybe I'll see one in Anchorage.

Bob Schutsky, the Birdtreks' leader (and owner) is sitting in the same plane row as I am, just across the aisle from my seat mate. He recognized me from

The mountains around Anchorage, Alaska, are stunning (May 11).

Red-necked Grebes were common on the Anchorage lakes (May 11).

my Web site photos and my current birdy outfit (pocketed vest, outdoor-type clothes). I had better restudy the birds that might show up in Alaska.

MAY 11

Because Alaska is so close to Asia, it is a prime place to find wandering Asian birds, particularly if the weather is stormy with westerly winds. I have arrived in Anchorage, at the beginning of the first of probably three to five trips to Alaska this year. The destination for this trip is Adak, an island on the Aleutian chain that once had an active U.S. military presence, evidence of which is everywhere in the buildings that remain. While it's not as far out the Aleutian chain as Attu, it is the farthest out the chain that birders can fly into now that Attu's airport has closed. The farther out, the more likely rare Asian vagrants will be found.

This morning I took a walk to Lake Hood, as I had briefly yesterday evening, and saw Barrow's and Common Goldeneyes, Buffleheads and Red-necked Grebes, and then today I walked farther down Spenard and Jewel Lake roads and found a long park. Highlights were singing Yellow-rumped Warblers, snipe (presumably Wilson's), a very close moose, many Black-billed Magpies, Black-capped Chickadees, Red-breasted Nuthatches, and a Bald Eagle near the airport.

I just want to get to Adak where I understand that it's 34 degrees and raining. Sounds like a typical Alaska island. The birds still count even though I will be wet and miserable (ought to count double). The plane to Adak is half cargo and half passengers, with the rows starting at row 15 behind the cargo area. I have three seats to myself.

MAY 12

We did get to Adak around 10:00 A.M. yesterday after a very bumpy plane ride and immediately drove out to see four Tundra Bean-Geese. There were two Parasitic Jaegers over the same lake, Lapland Longspurs on every road, and about two Rock Ptarmigans on every other road, cackling oddly as they flew. At Smew Lake was a lovely male Tufted Duck all by himself, although there were also Greater Scaup and Buffleheads on the lake. There were many Northern Pintails on Clam Lagoon, and then to my great delight we saw six winter-plumage Kittlitz's Murrelets. I got six new birds for the year in two hours. Not bad. We need shorebirds though.

MAY 13

Yesterday was a good day. We have a good group, one of whom is working on her 500th ABA area bird for her life list, and one of whom is up somewhere near 750 ABA area birds. I don't know what the leader's list is like.

Yesterday I got two new year birds—Red-faced Cormorant and Rock Sandpiper, both of which I will also get on the Pribilofs. Still, I'm glad I have them now. It snowed both nights we've been here, last night enough to whiten the rooftops but not the roads, and flurried during the day yesterday between sunshine interludes.

Although it's slow when there are no birds, I do enjoy wandering around an island with a chance of rarities any minute. Getting around on the Pribilofs is about half driving and half walking, or maybe a bit more walking,

Two of the four Tundra Bean-Geese fly over Adak Island (May 11).

and at Gambell it's all walking (unless you can commandeer an all-terrain vehicle [ATV]), but here we mostly drive, scanning narrow volcanic/pebbly beaches and long grassy pond edges and dumpsites, abandoned buildings, lawns of abandoned homes, and "forests." Forests are planted spruce sites where there are 1–50, but mostly 1–2, short, squat spruce "trees," usually scrawny unless they are tucked up next to a house. All of the forests are potentially resting/hiding sites for weary and hungry migrants. We have been putting out birdseed at many of the tree sites. I even brought along a couple of bags of seed to contribute to the cause. So far this year, it's only theoretical that birds will come to the seed.

Soon we will drive to breakfast, which is at a large, mostly unused school site that is quite well kept up from the military base days. One woman, Violet, almost single-handedly runs a restaurant there, cooking, serving, and being friendly. Her husband is there, too, mostly working behind the scenes. The dining room is huge, and the four of us huddle at a large table near the cafeteria-style counter. Some townsfolk also eat here, as do some of the other bird groups. I understand that the island has only 80–100 people. There were a few kids last night in the huge building that houses the cafeteria, which probably still serves as the school, plus being the community center with Wi-Fi and chairs for relaxing.

MAY 14

Yesterday it snowed and rained almost all day. Even the Adak locals were dismayed with the lateness of the snow. But it did not stop us hardy birders. We began with a brief tour of our in-town seed spots and then headed south through a more hilly area to Finger Creek Lake and Finger Creek. We were tremendously encouraged by the continuous sightings of birds. Nothing new, but we saw Snow Buntings, Lapland Longspurs, and Gray-crowned Rosy-Finches. We hiked up Finger Creek in stinging sleet and wind, but we saw nothing except a couple of very cute Winter Wrens. The hike back, with our backs to the wind, was much more pleasant but also birdless.

In the afternoon we drove toward Haven Lake where the Tundra Bean-Geese had been, but there were none. On the way there, though, a lovely Hoary Redpoll was on the road edge, oblivious to our presence. Later near Clam Lagoon I spotted an arriving Sandhill Crane, not a common bird here. On a bay we saw (in the rain) distant Laysan Albatrosses and Short-tailed Shearwaters, two closer Red-necked Grebes, a Horned Grebe, and a very close Red-faced Cormorant.

Our after-supper trip to Clam Lagoon at low tide was a rain-soaked walk on the mudflats, where shorebirds should have been, but there were none. The Sandhill Crane had come down to the flats, however, and a very obliging Lapland Longspur hopped close to us, so the trip wasn't a total loss. We got some exercise but no new birds for me.

Today was another rainy day with just a little snow. No new birds. We are just waiting for the migrants now, and I'm hoping they arrive before Sunday when I leave. I'm very glad for the Bean-Geese and the Tufted Duck, but more would be nice. I need Asian migrants.

> I wonder as I wander over Adak's brown hills,
> Will we ever find all our sought-after thrills?

MAY 15

Finally, a new bird. After a whole day of finding the same birds as yesterday plus our first Semipalmated Plover, tonight after supper we drove around and put out a new feeder made of a hubcaplike object I found that had blown off the roof of a building, and then four handsome Pacific Golden-Plovers flew in at the contractor's camp area. Number 559.

It's possible we'll go out on a pelagic trip tomorrow, but more likely we'll go on Saturday due to tomorrow's expected winds. I guess I should put on the patch tonight, take Dramamine, and eat dry toast for breakfast just in case. We probably won't know whether we are going out until after breakfast. It will be a short trip, so if I get seasick, it should not be for long.

MAY 16

We did not go on the pelagic today. It's set for tomorrow, my birthday. Today was a great day, and I got six new birds—Arctic Loon and Arctic and Aleutian Terns in the morning, Common Snipe and Tufted Puffin in the

Adak Island was beautiful in spite of the cloudy days (May 14).

afternoon, and Red-necked Phalarope tonight. It's as if the other three birding groups that arrived today brought the birds with them. We also had three Semipalmated Plovers tonight, so they are just arriving, too, after yesterday's sighting of just one. This is the first day that it did not rain on us at all. Good weather and newly arrived birds are hard to beat.

MAY 17

I'm 62 today, but so far I feel the same as 61. Birding began with the pelagic boat trip, where I got six new species for the year—Horned Puffin, Parakeet, Crested, Whiskered, and Least Auklets, and Wandering Tattler. The Whiskered Auklet was a lifer. The weather was brisk, but there was little wind as we headed out and no rain until the end of the trip. I wore the patch but did not take Dramamine this time. We did have some swells for a while, but they were quite mild. The tiny fishing boat was almost filled to capacity by the four of us. I was very glad that the waves and swells were not large. We went out past Adak and the next island to the southeast, and then out from the Bering Sea to the Gulf of Alaska. The Whiskered Auklets were in the passage by the thousands. Bob estimated 10,000–20,000. There were quite a few Tufted Puffins at nest sites on the high cliffs overlooking us and Ancient Murrelets among the auklets.

Ancient Murrelets stayed nearby as our boat left Adak Island for ocean waters (May 17).

Tufted Puffins nest on island cliffs near Adak Island (May 17).

The highlight of the Adak Island trip was the Whiskered Auklets (May 17).

When we got back to the dock, the walkie-talkie/radio message from the birding groups that had not gone out on the pelagic was that there were a Bar-tailed Godwit and a Bristle-thighed Curlew at Clam Lagoon. We skipped lunch and raced over there, but both had disappeared. Our group and two other groups each patrolled part of the lagoon. One group found the godwit, so the rest of us sped over there and saw it. As far as I know, the Bristle-thighed Curlew was never found again, although we certainly tried.

Tonight after supper we went out again, but no new birds. Hopefully we'll get more new ones tomorrow before we leave Adak. I'm at 572 species and holding.

MAY 19

I'm on a plane, feeling zonked. I spent some time on the flight to Anchorage from Adak reviewing my needed-bird list and trying to figure out how to get them all. I sure hope I see a lot of unexpected things in Alaska on my next trip, six days from now. Although I could have stayed in Alaska, I have client work that needs to be done before my long trip to Alaska at the end of May. It's hard to imagine I can keep it up for the next seven and a half months.

MAY 21

I left DFW and went to Michigan, essentially the only place in the ABA area to find a Kirtland's Warbler, and I accomplished my goal of seeing it. I took only one crummy photo, but that's okay. I saw two of them with the help of the biologist from the Mio ranger station and heard more, but none were close. It was too windy, so the birds were staying low. I went to the lower Upper Peninsula and saw a few warblers, Magnolia and American Redstart, but it was cold and windy.

Today after the Kirtland's Warbler trip, I went driving southeast of Mio and heard a distant Ruffed Grouse, so I got two year birds for Michigan. I'm now at 574. I looked and listened for a Connecticut Warbler, but no luck.

MAY 25

The beginning of a *big* trip to Alaska. I have a bundle of worries. Will my luggage get there intact (scope wrapped in sleeping bag)? Will the motel in

Anchorage store my duffel filled with tent, waders, and other gear? Will I and my luggage stay together? Will my clients and deadlines survive my being gone for a month? And way down the list, will I see good (i.e., new) birds? The adventure is beginning. I hope that there's not too much adventure on the plane trips to Seattle and then to Anchorage.

Flying, flying, somewhere out west. I finished an updated list of expected/ strongly hoped for birds. What I hope for, of course, is that wondrous west/ southwest winds have brought/are bringing birds, wonderful unexpected birds, and the usual Asian vagrants to the Alaska islands and the mainland. After I finished the list, I began restudying the bird book and the hoped-for birds. I'm in the middle of shorebirds right now and just had to take a break. One look at the page with Marsh Sandpiper and other possible vagrant shorebirds and my already-overloaded tired mind balked, so it's time to rest.

MAY 26

I went for a walk in Anchorage this morning. A couple of birds were singing, but it took me forever to find them due to the leafed-out trees and unbelievably loud calls of the Mew Gulls apparently nesting nearby and the Canada Geese flying around. One of the birds was an Orange-crowned Warbler. The other singer, after I made a lot of effort to try to see it, turned out to be a (Myrtle) Yellow-rumped Warbler singing his heart out. So cute, and so much not a bird I was looking for.

As I sat on the plane to St. Paul Island, I worried about my pack, computer, and camera, which were somewhere (I hoped) in the plane. Across the aisle from me was Dan Peake, and somewhere behind me were Martin Reid and Sheridan Coffey (all Texas birders extraordinaire). This plane, which went first to Dillingham and then to St. Paul, allowed me to feel every air current.

By the end of this one-month trip to Alaska, there's a possibility that I will be at or past 600 bird species for the year. I still need to do some serious California/western U.S. birding, plus mop-ups in places I have already been, as well as more pelagic trips.

During the flight I made the mistake of looking down. Our little plane was heading over open water. I don't know how I expected to get to St. Paul Island without it, but I would rather have looked at clouds blocking my view so I would not have to think about the water. To distract myself, I worked on a poem.

We did land safely, birded, and saw the St. Paul regulars—Gray-crowned Rosy-Finch, Lapland Longspur, Rock Sandpiper, and Red-necked Phalarope, plus Long-tailed Ducks, Northern Pintails, and Green-winged (Common) Teal. Then we headed over to Trident Seafood for supper after a wonderful detour for a Common Sandpiper. We had been about to fill our trays with the yummy food when someone called, and we raced outside to try to find the bird that had been called out. The sandpiper kept flitting away, landing at a distance, and flitting away again as we approached. All of us saw it and could count it if that was our interest. The Common Sandpiper became number 575 for the year and the only new one for the day. Wagtails and a Ruff had been on St. Paul, but we did not see either of these.

Why I Shouldn't Be Doing a Big Year

The most obvious thing is the money it takes
To fly hither and yon, to rent motels and cars,
To pay for the gas, the meals, the mistakes,
The sum of it all has just gone through the stars.
And then there's the worry that the plans will fall
   through,
Or the planes will fall down, or the luggage get lost,
Or the birds will not show, or I won't have a clue
Of what I am seeing. Did I mention the cost?
And of course there are phobias and gut-wrenching
   fears,
As we bump through the skies in a sardine-can
   plane.
I think about upcoming rafting with tears,
And I watch all that dough as it swirls down the
   drain.
Do you notice a theme here? I'm sure that's the case.
The horrendous expense is getting me down!
Yet my worrying leaves when I enter the chase,
And a smile of delight replaces the frown.

Lapland Longspurs abound on St. Paul Island (May 27).

Rock Sandpipers were on the rocks, in the snow, and in the weeds on St. Paul Island (May 27).

We had some excitement in our after-supper birding trek to look for wag-tails, when our van started smoking. At first we just thought it was blowing dust, but it was too black. Once we investigated, we found that the van was leaking some vital fluid and had been for miles. Our driver hailed a car, of which there are very few on St. Paul, and went to get another van. Six of us chose to walk back a couple of miles rather than wait around for rescue, in spite of the cold wind. It was a nice brisk walk, welcomed after all that bus and plane sitting, even though we did not add any birds. We did get great looks at Rock Sandpipers.

MAY 27

It began raining about suppertime, but it did not stop our birding around St. Paul Island. Before the rain, however, we had some brisk cliff viewing. I think I was the only participant in our van, except the leader, who had been here before and had seen the cliff birds. It is not possible to get sick of the puffins and kittiwakes and murres and auklets coming and going and sitting on their tiny rock ledges. I took many photos. I added the expected two year birds, Red-legged Kittiwake and Thick-billed Murre.

Parakeet Auklets cling to rocky cliffs on St. Paul Island (May 27).

We ended the day by tromping around a quarry, where there are lots of rock piles and potential sites for passerines (little "perching birds") to hide. Some of the group saw a Winter Wren, but I was off at another rock pile. During the day we also saw a King Eider, Harlequin Ducks, and Red-breasted Mergansers, as well as fur and harbor seals. The male fur seals are just starting to pull out of the water and onto the island, but the females will not be here for a while.

The food here is spectacular. We have breakfast at the "hotel," a barracks-type dorm that replaced the picturesque but apparently falling-down King Eider Hotel. My room has two single beds, two little closets, a shelf above each bed, a couple of chairs, a window, towels, and towel racks. There are bathrooms/showers down the hall. It is all more than adequate but nothing fancy. We eat lunch and dinner at the Trident fish-packing plant. It's cafeteria style, and while there's always at least one excellent seafood entrée, there are

Cliff-nesting Red-legged Kittiwakes are a St. Paul Island specialty (May 27).

Tiny Least Auklets pop up on the rocks on St. Paul Island (May 27).

also always other choices, such as last night's Cornish hen and lots of rice and potatoes, a salad bar, and desserts. Way too much, and all of it very tasty. It's good that we walk seven to eight miles per day. There is a television set in the dining room to keep us informed about the faraway world if we are interested.

MAY 28

In the morning it was too foggy to do much photography. I woke to pain in my tailbone and kidney areas, as a result I think of being in the back van seat yesterday bouncing over the bumpy roads. I vowed—no back seat for me.

The fog finally cleared off at midday, and the weather became very cold and windy, but not from the west unfortunately, which at least would allow a chance of bringing in Asian vagrants. I have the island blues—no new birds. Most of the times I've gone to Alaska islands, the potential has been so great, but the reality has been very few vagrants. Those are what I need this year. The most likely birds that I could add here are Slaty-backed Gull and Long-tailed Jaeger, but they have not arrived yet, and I only have a couple of days left.

MAY 30

I am on the St. Paul to Anchorage flight, with my pack beneath the seat ahead of me, my computer between my left kneecap and the side of the plane, and my camera, binoculars, and airplane lunchbox on my lap. A tight fit.

Yesterday we tromped over rocks and grass tussocks looking for a McKay's Bunting that had been reported. We found what's now decreed to be a *hybrid* McKay's Bunting. (A hybrid of two species is not countable as either species.) For a while, in my desperation to get this new bird, I was going to count it as a McKay's Bunting, whether or not anyone agreed with me. For now I have decided to go with the flow and call it "3/4 of a McKay's Bunting." With the far-out but pretty well-seen Long-tailed Jaeger today (the shape was that of a Long-tailed Jaeger, but details could not be seen), I'm at 578 ¾ birds for the year (the only person to do a big year with a fractional total). I've actually gotten quite enamored of calling it a fractional total. Of course, I can always hope that the experts change their minds eventually and call it a full-fledged McKay's.

MAY 31

Yesterday I was unable to find anyone who knew a particularly good spot for little owls (Boreal or Northern Saw-whet), so I went to the Eagle River Nature Center. I found no owls, even though I'm sure they were there somewhere. There was a calling Alder Flycatcher in a wet area along one of the trails, a calling Wilson's Snipe perched on top of a small conifer (sounding at first like a Goshawk), and a treetop Greater Yellowlegs. I also heard many Varied Thrushes singing their melodic monotones and saw a Brown Creeper and Downy and Hairy Woodpeckers. I think I need to go back to this area at night to look/listen for owls.

In the afternoon I drove up Arctic Valley Road in northeast Anchorage and walked the tundra. A couple of Golden-crowned Sparrows, a Savannah Sparrow, and Common Ravens were all I found. No ptarmigans. On the drive down the mountain though, I heard a Townsend's Solitaire in an area of pointy spruce trees.

J U N E

Alaskan Adventures

NEW BIRD SPECIES SEEN THIS MONTH: 24
TOTAL BIRD SPECIES BY THE END OF THE MONTH: 604
PLACES BIRDED: Alaska, Texas

JUNE 2

Yesterday I drove up toward Denali, getting as far as the road that goes
to Denali State Park before Sheridan called me on my cell phone to tell of a
reported Boreal Owl about 80 miles up the Glenn Highway near Sheep Mountain Lodge (about 160 miles from me). Since it was raining and I wasn't finding much, I turned around and drove toward them. A chance at a Boreal Owl
could not be passed up, but we found no owls. About 4:30 P.M. I gave up and
headed back to Anchorage to pack up for the next leg of my Alaska travels. I
am eagerly hoping for an influx of goodies at Gambell on St. Lawrence Island.

This morning I waited for the Wilderness Birding Adventures group to
gather at the Anchorage airport. We are supposed to have only 40 pounds
each of luggage, including binoculars, camera and lens, scope and tripod, and
carry-on. I know my belongings spread all around me are overweight.

I have briefly met the tour participants for the Gambell trip. Bert Frenz,
a Texas birder and caravaner, and some of his group are the other Texans on
the participant list. We are now coming down in Kotzebue. There is still ice
on huge areas of the water here. I assume there will be open water around St.
Lawrence Island since it is out in the ocean currents.

JUNE 3

I am sitting in the living room on Gambell, nearly every bone aching, eyes
bloodshot from the wind. After we arrived here, we almost immediately did
a sea watch, because an Ivory Gull had been seen. We watched icebergs and

A Little Bunting hiding in the boneyards at Gambell, Alaska, was a welcome treat (June 3).

Finally a nonhybrid McKay's Bunting was seen at Gambell (June 3).

alcids drift by, and I added White Wagtail, Black Guillemot, Steller's Eider, Little Bunting, Bluethroat, and a true well-seen McKay's Bunting on the first day. Finally, the McKay's Bunting is a full bird species on my year list, and no longer three-fourths of a bird. I got pictures of the bunting, so white.

The boneyards, where much birding is done, are essentially dumping areas for the leftover remains of slaughtered sea animals such as walruses. Old dried rib cages and other bones are piled and scattered about, with weedy vegetation protruding through, and dug-out holes where villagers have sought bones for their carving endeavors. Little birds straying to Gambell from Asia use these boneyards to hide from the wind (and from birders) in a landscape devoid of trees. Most of the rarities found at Gambell are found in one of the boneyards, named for their location or shape (e.g., "far boneyard," "circular boneyard").

Today was a marathon. After the sea watch and an Ivory Gull, we walked around the lake clockwise. When we got to the south end of the lake, we saw two Common Ringed Plovers, which I understand nest here, and a beautiful Yellow Wagtail. One of the other women and I slogged the whole way around the lake. That was when I nearly collapsed of tiredness, but when the call came in for a Red-throated Pipit, I went out to see it.

I'm so sore from walking—hips, head, all. I'm at 590 species.

Common Ringed Plovers nest on St. Lawrence Island, Alaska (June 3).

Gambell is a pebble-covered village on St. Lawrence Island (June 5).

JUNE 4

Again I'm recovering from being out at the sea watch earlier where the sleet was blowing at 20–30 miles per hour horizontally. I added one bird today, so far—Sabine's Gull, of which there were at least two in breeding plumage and one immature that flew by the sea watch. Plus, we had an Ivory Gull, or more than one, coasting by multiple times, and once actually briefly landing on and pecking at the water. All of this was just a couple of hundred feet or less off the beach.

JUNE 6

We are in a nine-seater plane from Gambell to Nome, and it's a beautiful sunny day. At the sea watch this morning, the wind was a bit brisk and cold.

What a good trip this has been, with the absolute highlight being the Jack Snipe that Jon Dunn of Wings found at the marsh north of the lake. All of us went by ATV to the location, but regrettably I was out there without my camera. The bird was approachable to within 20 feet, doing its comical body-up-and-down, as if its legs could telescope and become shorter and longer. Later two of us developed a Jack Snipe dance and performed it (and unfortunately were videotaped) to celebrate the occasion.

I'm at 595 species for the year. It will be hard to get five more, in Nome, Anchorage, and Barrow, but maybe it will happen. The last new birds were Yellow-billed Loon, four of them, one photographed, flying by at the sea watch; a nonadult Slaty-backed Gull; and a very trusting Gray-tailed Tattler out at the far reaches beyond the lake.

Five of us who participated in the Gambell trip are continuing on a Nome trip afterward. I hope Nome is a bit warmer than Gambell and there is no rain. It would be nice not to wear rain pants. Right now I'm sweltering in the sun pouring in the plane windows.

I have actually managed to get quite a bit of sleep on this trip, in spite of our not getting in from evening birding until 10:30 or midnight each night. Due to the lack of time spent back at our house and the fact that there was only one bathroom and shower, I didn't spend much time getting or staying clean. The food, however, cooked by the leaders, was spectacular. The group was congenial with not too much irritability or bad moods. Tiredness, yes, and aching bodies, yes, but spirits were usually high as we raced out for each reported bird. Every morning on Gambell, others would get up long before I did, and at the last minute I realized I had to face the cold and would struggle out of bed. Most of our rooms were upstairs, and we kept the door shut to the downstairs so it would not get too hot while we were sleeping, and it surely did not. I pull on more layers quickly as I get up, brush my hair (pointless), and lower myself carefully down the very steep stairs, open the door to the somewhat warmer living room/kitchen, and check out the bathroom line, and/or eat muffins or cooked cereal while I wait.

Sometimes I got a ride to the boneyards, but mostly it was slogging there or slogging to and along the seacoast. In the middle of the day, we usually trooped back for lunch. Often most of us birded together, except for the occasional few who weren't as eager to be outside all the time. Except for the coldest day, we pretty much birded/tromped or were ported by ATV all day long. Downtime was spent eating and waiting for a call on the radio from someone else who was out birding.

JUNE 9

On the afternoon of June 6, after we had arrived in Nome, we joined our leaders whom we met before going to Gambell, and headed off in two vehicles along the road toward Council/Safety Lagoon Sound. The birding was good, with "stonking" (one of the favorite words of a British birding friend) looks at Red-throated Loons, the usual shorebirds and gulls, plus a very close Aleutian Tern, a third-year Slaty-backed Gull, Hoary Redpoll (the usual species here), and Bar-tailed Godwit, as special goodies. There were no new birds. I left Gambell with 595 species on my year list. The leaders, who knew of my big year, were (painfully, I'm sure) aware of my desire to reach 600 as soon as possible, or at least in Nome. It did not happen on June 6.

On June 7, we left at 4:48 A.M. for Kougarok Road, the Bristle-thighed Curlew nesting location. The day was cold (34 degrees) and cloudy, with creeks partly frozen. My first new bird of the day and for Nome was Willow Ptarmigan, of which there were many. The first was a very attractive rusty-headed male with a white body. Along the roads on this and each subsequent day were Long-tailed Jaegers, Gray-cheeked Thrushes, Orange-crowned Warblers, Northern Pintails and Northern Shovelers, and "lappies" (Lapland Longspurs). Arctic Terns, Say's Phoebe, and five Short-eared Owls were there on June 7 but less common otherwise.

An Arctic Tern perches on a small bridge outside Nome, Alaska (June 7).

Long-tailed Jaegers are unmistakable in spring in western Alaska (June 7).

About 8:30, we arrived at the hill where the Bristle-thighed Curlews nest on top and climbed the three-quarter-mile tussocky gradual slope. It is not a difficult hike but must be done carefully, as the tussocks are not a stable foot support. Mostly you just walk between tussocks. Long before we reached the flatter area, we heard and saw Whimbrels, which are superficially much like the curlews but without the buffy rump and tail and with a less splotchy appearance. There were also many American Golden-Plovers. Then we heard the call of a displaying Bristle-thighed Curlew and saw it as it coasted to the ground farther up the hill. We slogged farther up, too, and soon had better views of the bird, which was close enough that the distinctive bill shape and back pattern were clear in the binoculars, and through our scopes were even clearer. The Bristle-thighed Curlew flew up, displayed again, and came down quite near a Whimbrel and started walking along chasing the Whimbrel. Of course, it was a year bird.

About 10:35 A.M. we began the drive slowly back to Nome. We added Rough-legged Hawk, Bluethroat, Yellow Wagtail, and Merlin to the trip list. At about 12:30 we took a brief detour up the road to Pilgrim Hot Springs for our lunch stop. Unfortunately, I did not see the Northern Wheatears that some others saw on the way in. I was irritated that we did not try for better looks before eating, but we settled down for a tailgate lunch instead. Birds should always come before food, if there is a choice.

Finally, all of the lunch things were packed up and we started up the slope to look for Wheatears. None. It was getting colder and windier, and snow was coming down. A quickly flying bird that we were told was a female Northern Wheatear disappeared, and my frustration mounted. We climbed back into the vans, turned around, and headed back toward Kougarok Road. Near where the Wheatears had originally been seen, we stopped again, and after quite a bit of telescope searching through the snowflakes, we found a pair of Northern Wheatears way up the slope. I was very relieved that we got excellent views. Number 598.

At a later stop back on Kougarok Road, we saw a distant grizzly bear wandering about on a snow patch, ignoring us except for a long look down the slope toward us. The snow was coming down fast and furious by the time we reached a known Gyrfalcon area. Almost immediately, our leader called out a "gyr," and I saw it, a large falcon silhouette blasting along the side of the snowy mountain. Number 599. It was actually seen a couple more times before the snow was just too heavy for us to see anything. Other birds of note on the trip back to Nome included Wilson's Warbler, American Pipit, American Tree Sparrow, and a Vega Herring Gull.

June 8 began with hearing a melodious Fox Sparrow behind the house where the group was staying. We again took the Safety Lagoon road to Council on which we had the now usual birds, with my favorites being the Snow Goose, Short-eared Owl, Red Knot, Sandhill Crane, Stilt Sandpiper (about which the leaders were particularly ecstatic because it is unusual here), Pomarine and Long-tailed Jaeger, and Brant.

About 500 yards past the Safety Sound bridge, at the far side of the water area on the land side of the road, our leader Aaron spotted an Emperor Goose across a large body of water. Number 600! Lots of rejoicing, especially by my pals who had been with me on the Gambell trip. A major milestone for me.

Birding went on with a pair of Canvasbacks, White-winged Scoters, another Slaty-backed Gull, Pectoral Sandpiper, and a Peregrine Falcon perched in a field. We decided to try for Arctic Warbler before supper instead of eating at our usual time, so we headed back to Kougarok Road. Although the iPod was played at a number of places and we listened intently, we did not hear a response at first (tour groups, while generally very good about using taped songs sparingly, are of course often under pressure to use them so their

Brilliant Red Phalaropes were common in the Barrow puddles (June 11).

paying customers—us—"get" their sought-after birds, and therefore they judiciously use them). We heard one quite a way up the hill of willows and got a distant view. We hiked/bushwhacked up the hill to try to get a better view, but the bird moved back down toward the road. It kept singing, so more and more of us got better views.

Today's (June 9) birding was on the Nome-Teller Road in the cold, often snowy (34 degrees) weather. We added American Dipper, Wandering Tattler, Snow Bunting, Rock Ptarmigan, Baird's Sandpiper, Black-bellied Plover,

My only year bird for Barrow in June was the Spectacled Eider (June 12).

Long-billed Dowitchers are paired up in Barrow in June (June 11).

and Ring-necked Duck to our Nome list. After that we packed, dined, and boarded the plane to Anchorage.

I am at 601 species.

JUNE 10

In my motel room in Anchorage, I have packed what I'll store here and what I'll be taking to Barrow. I am looking forward to this solo trip to a place

Steller's Eiders were common on the Barrow tundra (June 12).

A Pectoral Sandpiper puffs up and displays on the Barrow tundra (June 12).

that I have never been at the end of the world. I did not bird this morning—a combination of tiredness and lack of time to get anywhere and a lack of birds I could get in such a short time. It has been nice to withdraw, but tonight I'll be in Barrow with a rental car and bird again. The main goal there is Spectacled Eider, as well as a hoped-for miracle fly-by Ross's Gull and, of course, wondrous unpredicted vagrants.

JUNE 13

I am flying from Barrow to Fairbanks by way of Anchorage and a three-hour layover. My minimal goal of seeing a Spectacled Eider in Barrow was met, and that's it. It would probably have made sense to hire a guide, except I understand that the local Barrow guides mainly know the eiders and may not "do" shorebirds. None of the tour companies' schedules fit mine. In any case, I did not find any shorebirds that were new. Asian vagrants did not show up while I was there.

The tundra around Barrow was relatively easy to walk on, soft and squishy moss (like sphagnum) with puddles and rivulets that mostly could be walked across and were not too deep. There is a lot of melting going on, and I expect the depth of water will increase, and perhaps the breeding birds will, too.

If I don't get a Ross's Gull elsewhere, I will probably be back in October or November.

Besides Spectacled Eiders, I also saw a few King Eiders and about 10 Steller's Eiders, a couple of which were quite close to the road. Shorebirds included Red and Red-necked Phalaropes, the former particularly beautiful and abundant and present in nearly every puddle. There were many Pectoral Sandpipers and a few Baird's Sandpipers. The Pectoral Sandpipers were loud and brash in their displays holding forth across the tundra. Also there were Long-billed Dowitchers, many Semipalmated Sandpipers, a few Semipalmated Plovers, Black-bellied Plovers and Dunlin, also displaying, and one Stilt Sandpiper. The most evident birds on the tundra were numerous Pomarine Jaegers squawking, diving, zooming past, sitting on knolls, everywhere. They came very close as I walked about, acting as if I were near a nest but not dive-bombing me. I saw a lot of their apparent prey; it's clearly a lemming year. There also were some dark Parasitic Jaegers and at least one Long-tailed Jaeger. Ducks, besides eiders, were mainly Northern Pintails, everywhere, in groups and in pairs. I also saw a couple of Eurasian Green-winged Teal (not currently counted by the ABA as a separate species), many Long-tailed Ducks, and two Northern Shovelers. Gulls were limited to Glaucous Gulls, even though I tried hard for a Ross's Gull.

Owls were sporadic, mainly ghostly Snowy Owls that did not allow me to approach very close. Yesterday, two Short-eared Owls perched on grassy bumps about one-fourth mile apart and relatively near the road. There were also a couple of pairs of Tundra Swans elegantly floating on new melt ponds, and similar numbers of pairs of White-fronted Geese. Passerines were limited to the ubiquitous Snow Buntings, especially in town, Lapland Longspurs mainly on the tundra, and a couple of singing Savannah Sparrows on Freshwater Lake Road.

Just before I turned in my rental car yesterday, I found a winnowing Wilson's Snipe high over the south side of the residential area of Cake Eater Road (what a wonderful name—it made me hungry every time I saw it).

The Barrow experience was like many frontier/island towns of Alaska—lots of ATVs, gravel roads, junk lying all around with no place to dispose of it in the frozen tundra. Barrow is a "city" with a Wells Fargo bank, hotels, including mine, that had Wi-Fi, car rentals (mine a 2000 Ford sedan with broken parts and squeaks and rattles, but functional), restaurants (I only tried Arctic Pizza for a vegetarian burger), and at least two grocery/general stores.

Paired Tundra Swans float on the Alaska tundra near Barrow (June 11).

Most things appear to be owned and/or run by natives or the native corporation, Ukpeagvik Inupiat Corporation (UIC). I paid $50 for an annual permit that allowed me to walk on the tundra, and I'm glad that I did. I'll be able to wander around if and when I come back in the fall.

When I get to Fairbanks, I will join the people who are going on the "chickadee trip," though I will be late for the orientation, and Lena will be even later as she is coming in from a birding trip to Chevak. Tomorrow the big raft trip will start. I am a nervous wreck about the details and about whether I've brought the correct gear along. It was for the Gray-headed Chickadee that I risked taking this trip with its very horrifying prospect of rafting down the river. In the North American continent, this chickadee is found only in this area of Alaska and in a small area of the Yukon. If it weren't for Lena, however, I still would probably not be going on this trip, but she is an avid rafter and I can't back out.

JUNE 14

As I lie on my air mattress, head on my dry bag, mosquitoes are buzzing around, but so far no bites. My tent is set up next to me, and while rain seems unlikely, I expect it will be cool tonight. Right now the sun is hot, but the wind is heavenly cool. This is the first time I have been outside without long johns and gloves for a very long time. We are out here in the Arctic NWR, mountains all around us, through which we flew on an hour-long, breathtaking (in many ways) flight. There were only a few little bumps to remind us that we were in a four-seater (including the pilot). It was very cozy, with each of us having earphones both to muffle the very loud engine noise and to talk to each other and the pilot, which we did for the whole flight. He was very personable, inquired about our interests, and answered questions about the area. It helped quell my flight fears to learn that he had been flying into this remote area for many years.

Right now we are waiting for the rest of the tour participants to be ferried over and through the mountains from Arctic Village, where a tiny airport has been carved out next to the mountains. It's totally silent except for a few distant voices of our group.

Our tent site is spread out at the base of an unknown north slope mountain in Alaska (June 19).

Late yesterday while I was reading in the bedroom at the Fairbanks Bed & Breakfast, I had the windows open and was listening to American Robins and Yellow Warblers. Then something, perhaps a sound, caused me to look out and see an *Empidonax* flycatcher ("empids," which are drab little flycatchers, mostly indistinguishable except by their different vocalizations). What could it be? I checked the bird book and the Alaska guidebook and learned that there were only two empids here, Alder and Hammond's Flycatchers. I quickly dug out my iPod and briefly played the song of each out the window, and watched and listened. There did not seem to be a direct response, except the bird did eventually start "singing," and it was a Hammond's Flycatcher song. The bird called numerous times before quitting or moving on.

JUNE 15

Yesterday after she arrived here, Lena and I just walked around the camp plateau on the edge of the tributary of the Canning River and photographed flowers and mountains and ice. The "river" is mostly ice, and it looks to me, a nonexpert, that we'll need to begin with portaging a long way. Meanwhile, I'm bored and thirsty and tired. But of course, I'm also worried about the rafting. Did I mention that I do not swim at all and nearly drowned once? Now I have another worry. I understand that in spring, when the melting water creates fast-flowing streams, a channel can be gouged under the ice pack. It is possible that a hapless rafter could have her head removed as the speeding raft crashes into, and goes under, the carved-out low-hanging ice. Not a pretty thought.

Today was my first rafting, about half a day, and we probably went hardly any distance down the tributary. It was very shallow, and the trip involved lots of raft pushing and jumping off the raft and hauling myself back on the raft. I fell once when running alongside the raft, and water swept over me as I clung to the raft and was pulled along. In spite of it all, I did not drown, and was, considering how cold and totally wet I was, fairly cheerful. Of course my hip boots are sopping wet inside and undoubtedly will remain so for the rest of the trip.

JUNE 16

Today when we stopped at the confluence of "Tit Creek (River)" and the Marsh Fork of the Canning River, and left the rafts and crashed around

We were ecstatic to find the nest of a Gray-headed Chickadee in the Arctic NWR (June 16).

through the little willow stands, we found a pair of Gray-headed Chickadees, the single goal of this trip, dutifully and rapidly attending to their chicks and going in and out of a hole in a willow sapling while our group stood in a respectful semicircle about the nest tree. It was a tree in which Bob Dittrick (the leader) had previously, but not recently, found a nest, and it was our last hope for today (but not for the trip) to find the chickadee. I was, and am, elated, as was everyone else. The chickadee was number 604 for my big year, as big an expense, per bird, as I will have this year, because I can't imagine any other new bird that I will get on this rafting trip.

It rained a lot today as we bushwhacked through the chickadee habitat, and while it was sort of miserable walking in it, I'm glad we weren't rafting. Tomorrow we raft again, but the pressure is off, because we have found the chickadee. All we need to do is float/paddle to where we get picked up at the end of the trip and try for other birds as we have time. Of course, more chickadee views would be just fine.

This long-term camping (we have done only two nights so far) is great fun, with lovely scenery, birds, and so on, but also boring. There is much time when you stand around and try to be helpful and wait for time to pass until the next meal or the next walk. I could explore more here, but grizzlies are a real possibility, discouraging long solo walks. One can also sleep, and I'm catching up on that in spite of the hard ground.

JUNE 22

It has been a very intense six days since I wrote. It's hard to write when bent over in a tent, even though there is enough light any time of the day or night up on the Brooks Range. All the outdoor activity just took away my energy for anything but eating, sleeping, and, of course, birding.

Most days of the trip coffee was at 7:00, followed by breakfast about 8:00. Breakfast was later and later as the trip went on and the leaders got more tired. I usually slept until about 7:45. I could probably have slept until 10:00, but hunger, the need for the "growler" (more on this later), and peer pressure got me up. Once up, I was fine, not drowsy. Usually it was cold and/or raining, so it was even harder to get up.

On most days, we had to pack up all our gear, take down our tents, and truck it all down to the inflated rafts. These were loaded up with all the kitchen equipment, food, tents, personal dry bags, personal day packs, paddles, and fully rain-coated, hip-booted, life-jacketed us. About 11:00 (or later), we would be on the river, paddling forward, back, or right/left back, or mainly sitting, floating, or spinning down the river, and periodically getting out to drag the raft over rocks and rock bars. Many times when the raft got stuck, Bob and Ted (the leader and the only other male on our raft, respectively) would get out and push/pull/drag us to deeper water. When we all had to get out, I was very nervous, because at some point, when the water was deep enough to float the raft, but not so deep as to go over our waders, we would all have to get back on the raft. My big fear was that in the hurry to get going again, I would walk or be pushed or pulled into the water too deep for me to stay upright. There seemed to be too many ways for me to lose my balance or footing.

Each night (or afternoon) after we arrived at our new campsite, we hauled all our gear off the rafts. The kitchen equipment and food were piled at a designated spot relatively near the water, and we lugged our tents to a tenting area preferably at least 150 yards from the potentially bear-attracting food spot. Our leader(s) would get to work on setting up to cook and cooking while we put up our tents.

After we ate, which usually was finished at 8:30–10:30 P.M. (when it was still light out), we would disperse to our tents, and one of the leaders would make/set up the growler (I don't want to think about how it got its name). The growler was a neatly carved rectangular hole in the ground, some 6 by 18 inches by a foot or so deep. The upper layer of sod was carefully removed and placed a couple of feet away, and the dirt was removed and piled near the hole. A blue tarp was erected vertically and tied to nearby shrubs or upright raft paddles near the hole, between the hole and the camping area, and a life-jacket (PFD) was hung visibly nearby as a signal for whether someone was using the growler (PFD down on the ground) or not (PFD hung up). Next to the hole and behind the tarp was a plastic bag with a lighter and matches to burn used toilet paper, along with a roll of toilet paper and a dry match-striking stone for when the lighter did not work.

Before we broke camp each morning, one of the leaders would fill the hole with dirt and put the sod layer back on so the hole was covered and became invisibly blended with the surrounding terrain. The tarp and toilet supplies would be toted to the raft for use at the next campsite. Quite an ingenious system.

On June 17, we headed out about 11:00 A.M. in a bit of rain, seeing a few Wandering Tattlers, American Robins, and Arctic Terns on the float down the Marsh Fork of the Canning River, which is where we floated until near the end of the trip when we were on the river itself. It rained all night, and the next day we were thus provided with lots of water in the river. I did not know whether this was good or bad for the "big day" on June 18, the day we were to raft the "class 3" rapids. It seemed to me not to bode well because even before the rapids area, the water was booming and rushing along in deep, turning, swirling waves, tons of water wanting to go downward all together, heaving and roiling over itself in its attempt to get down the fastest. I wasn't quite sick about it, just very, very worried.

With the expert guidance of our leaders, however, we managed to avoid most of the rocks that were big enough to still present potential problems even in the deep water, and we just hurtled and/or spun over the others. I'm not sure I breathed for most of the afternoon that day. We were given rapid-fire directions, which we followed with as powerful a synchronized paddling

What a challenge birding can be, as I am helped across a raging torrent in the Arctic NWR (June 16). Photo by Lena Gallitano.

as we could (which was improved by a brief pep talk/team rally), and our raft just manhandled its way down the river.

We arrived at our campsite on June 18 a bit after 3:00 P.M., and I, with great relief that the day of serious rapids was over, set up my tent and wrote in my field notebook that "rafting's not so bad when you have a great captain, a willing team, and luck on the water." I was glad I hadn't bothered to bring my spotting scope and tripod on this trip—just another thing to worry about packing, being damaged, or getting wet.

Little did I know that new challenges were still to come that day. About 3:30 P.M., it was announced that we were going on a hike up a rushing stream that descended from the mountains near our campsite, forcefully blasting into the river. We were told that we should wear our hip waders, which should have given me the message that we'd be crossing the roiling water, but I climbed blithely along with the group through the willows along the creek until we got to an area where our only choices were to go back, ascend the bare rock face of a mountain, or cross the stream. I looked at the over-the-knee deep swirl with obviously deeper pockets between rocks and decided I would wait there while the others crossed, did whatever they were going to do, and returned. Everyone else was going across, the more timid ones being carefully kept upright by the leaders and a couple of the braver (nuttier?) trip participants who stood in the stream (I know not how). Knowing I would go down and need to be dragged to the opposite shore if I was lucky, or be carried out to sea otherwise, I also entrusted my clumsy, booted legs to the rapid torrents and the rest of me to those helpers.

We schlepped our way upward along the other edge of the rushing stream, up and down between the willows and over the mossy rocks, across scree slopes and tumbled rock slides. Someone behind me called out a sighting of a Gray-headed Chickadee, so we paused to check it out. There were at least two adults feeding at least two fledglings perched about 100 feet apart on the rocky cliff, some 20–40 feet above us.

But birding ended, and we trooped farther upstream to another must-cross-the-stream impasse. I let everyone pass, realizing that if I crossed again, I would have two more crossings to do when we came back down. This crossing was not as wide or noisy as the first, so I soldiered on across. We stopped at a rushing water-flooded cave too deep for my hip boots, even if I had felt like going through the narrow opening to where I understood there was a waterfall to be viewed.

Obviously I made it back across the two crossings, carefully tended by the guides (one of whom carried one of the trip participants across the stream because his boots were too short). We also saw an American Robin nest with at least one nestling, Say's Phoebes, Gray-crowned Rosy-Finches high on the cliffs, and a Golden Eagle nest (big pile of sticks but no bird).

It was a very cold night camped on a sandy rock spit, but again, I slept like drugged, only waking as I turned over and tucked extra clothing around the sleeping bag neck opening to keep the frigid air out.

The next morning (June 19), as I descended the very steep slope beneath the growler, I heard the unmistakable call of a chickadee, and with a small bit of poking about in the willows, found an adult Gray-headed Chickadee near our campsite. I think I was the only person who saw a chickadee on three days.

That day after lunch on a gravel bar across the river from the nest of an American Dipper under an overhanging rock ledge about 20 feet up, we stopped again to walk across an upland, mossy boggy area—this time for Smith's Longspurs. Bob spooked up the first one, which took off for parts unknown. Not too long after that, a male took off from very near my feet and landed some 75 feet away. I called out, and others also saw the bird, picturesquely sitting near a white flower. A couple more Smith's Longspurs were found as we left the area. We also saw Dall sheep that day, and I believe that was the day we spotted a group of more than six caribou with gigantic racks on their heads walking along on the gravel bars very near our raft.

On the morning of June 20, after taking my tent and gear down to the raft, I took a solo walk since the weather was quite nice. I saw another adult male Smith's Longspur as I walked over a mossy, hilly area, but I always kept an eye turned toward the lower campsite to be sure there were still tents up or still being taken down, and that I wouldn't be late for the put-in to the river.

Two times I got teary today as I realized somewhat to my surprise, that in spite of being fearful every time we got on or were in the rafts, and in spite of often feeling cold and miserable, I did not want the trip to end. I did not want to leave the beauty of the Arctic NWR, the absolutely stunning solitude of being on the river, and the companionship of the group and leaders. I knew I could never repeat the experience of my first rafting trip, my first view of the Arctic NWR, and my first intense camping trip, and I knew it would probably never be possible for me to come again. Being able to experience this wonderful place made me even more convinced of the importance of preserving this area from exploitation and damage, and I was glad our group did its utmost to leave it as we found it.

Not long after the realization that I did not want to end the trip, we heard the sound of a plane coming low through the passes upriver, and Kirk, the bush pilot, and his plane came into view, circled, and landed on the gravel and rocks near our tents. Again I was teary with the realization that I wanted to leave and was relieved that we were not totally isolated from the "real" world. It was (and is) time to get on with my big year by going places that might add birds and to get home to see Dave and do client work.

The last morning of the trip (June 21), some of us took a short walk up the hill from the camp before we left, but there was not much bird life. Although the schedule had been for us to all be transported to Arctic Village in shifts and then to wait together for a larger plane to go to Fairbanks, there was a

ANWR

Millions and millions of acres,
And miles of rivers that wind.
A refuge of breathless proportions,
A gem, and one of a kind.
With grizzlies and Dall sheep and eagles,
Rocky spires and green mossy rises,
And hidden in thick willow clusters
One of nature's tiniest surprises.
A chickadee, small and gray-headed,
Flitting constantly, feeding its young.
I sing of the need to preserve it—
A song that I know must be sung.

plane with space ready to go to Fairbanks immediately after some of us arrived in Arctic Village, so we disembarked from the four-seater, walked across the gravel to a nine-seater, and arrived in Fairbanks at noon, six hours early. That gave us time to shower and for me to repack for today, check, and delete e-mails, and make phone calls. I did some checking on a possible site in Fairbanks for Boreal Owls and rented a car so I could check out the Boreal Owls and get to the airport today. A couple of our group joined the downtown festivities for the summer solstice at midnight. About midnight, two of us drove to the yard where Boreal Owls had nested, but none were found, apparently having flown the coop. I got to bed about 12:30 this morning.

Chickadee Meditation

I could not see the forest for the trees,
Til I went north to seek chickadees.
Now the whole thing is clear, and sadly I fear,
That I'm killing myself by degrees.
There is something bizarre and absurd
About living one's life just to bird,
There's no rudder, no balance, no skills, and
   no talents,
Yet this mania cannot be deterred.
Don't ask if it makes any sense,
This big year, so driven, intense.
There's no reason, no rhyme, for such use of
   my time,
And no justice in such an expense.

Four of us from the chickadee trip birded in Fairbanks this morning at the Alaska Bird Observatory and Creamer's Field. We saw one of the many calling Alder Flycatchers, as well as Dark-eyed Juncos, Downy Woodpeckers, Lincoln's and Savannah Sparrows, Orange-crowned, Yellow, and Yellow-rumped Warblers, Northern Waterthrush, and Tree Swallows (going in and out of a nest box).

As I sit in the Seattle airport, it's dark outside. It's the first time I have seen darkness since I went to Barrow on June 10, some 12 full days of light, though of course some of that time was cloudy. Now back to "normality."

JUNE 30

Things are running late, so I will be arriving at the Portland, Maine, airport (via Washington, D.C.) at about 2:00 A.M. tomorrow, and then meeting and being picked up by my guide, Derek Lovitch, at 6:00 A.M. I originally met him years ago when he was one of the St. Paul Island, Alaska, guides, sporting bleached hair in imitation of the island's Tufted Puffins. He has since married and moved to Maine to run a wild bird store.

Since Alaska, I have been very busy, doing client work and bills, doing my annual three Breeding Bird Survey (BBS) routes, turning in the three BBS reports, attending church and singing in the choir, and making reservations for Arizona and for North Carolina later this summer.

Thoughts upon completing one-half of my ABA big year—some are expressed in the poems written earlier, but I am glad I'm doing this year. I wish I were doing a better job. I hate to think that there are regular birds that I have not gotten and may have missed. The Connecticut Warbler is the clearest example. By July, it's no longer singing, skulks, doesn't (hardly ever anyway) migrate through Texas or anywhere I'm scheduled to go. I have an e-mail inquiry on the Wisconsin listserv, but I have no real plans on how to get the bird. There's a fair number of other species that I'm close to clueless on how to get, such as Gray Partridge, various little owls, some western flycatchers.

It's interesting—I am 46 birds short of my minimal goal of 650 species for the year. I could theoretically get eight on this trip. Next is the Arizona–Nevada–New Mexico trip on which I might/should get quite a few, including hummingbirds, flycatchers, owls, sparrows, trogons. Maybe I'll be at 640 by the end of it, but I'm unsure whether that is optimistic, realistic, or totally unrelated to reality. After that, it's the North Carolina pelagic trips and St. Paul Island, plus sometime, West and South Texas, California, Florida, Barrow . . . who knows?

Maine Meandering and Nevada Nemesis

NEW BIRD SPECIES SEEN THIS MONTH: 45
TOTAL BIRD SPECIES BY THE END OF THE MONTH: 649
PLACES BIRDED: Maine, Texas, Arizona, Nevada, New Mexico

JULY 3

My trip to Maine was definitely a success. We heard (and briefly saw) the main goal bird, Bicknell's Thrush, on the evening of July 1, a long day.

After extended delays en route, in the very early morning the plane had arrived in Portland. By the time I found a cab, checked in, repacked for the camping trip, and got into bed, it was about 2:30 A.M. Derek Lovitch, my guide, arrived at 6:00 and off we went.

Our first stop was in the Scarborough Marsh area, where we quickly got our goal, Saltmarsh Sharp-tailed Sparrow, and Nelson's Sharp-tailed Sparrow. We had great views of both sparrows. The marsh was hopping with early-morning life. After the marsh, we went to Pine Point for Roseate Terns, about as common as the Common Terns, and they came very close to us. I had not seen these beautiful birds in the United States before.

We went to Rotary Park in Biddeford, where male Blue-winged Warblers had been reported, another bird on the want list that I had given Derek. We walked the mowed, wet, grassy trails listening for their distinctive songs but found only American Redstarts, Ovenbirds, Chestnut-sided Warblers, Common Yellowthroats, American Robins, an Indigo Bunting, Red-eyed Vireo, American Goldfinches, and Black-capped Chickadees. My feet got very wet, but I was embarrassed to complain about such a minor inconvenience in the face of my need for a Blue-winged Warbler. As we came through an open area dotted with clumps of trees, just before circling back to the car, we finally heard the very welcome song of a Blue-winged Warbler. When we found the singer, however, it was not a Blue-winged Warbler but a male Lawrence's Warbler (a hybrid of Blue-winged and Golden-winged Warblers). Derek was

The mother Spruce Grouse looks around at the intruders on Saddleback Mountain, Maine (July 1).

One of the Spruce Grouse chicks darts along after its mother (July 1).

ecstatic, and I was very depressed (but understood his enthusiasm for the rare hybrid). It did not count as a new bird for me. I was grateful, therefore, when Derek noticed that the Lawrence's Warbler's companion was a female Blue-winged Warbler.

At 8:30 we headed toward Rangely, the town nearest the Saddleback ski slope that we were scheduled to climb for the Bicknell's Thrush. Although I knew from Derek that it was possible to play a tape of a Bicknell's Thrush to lure it to a road, we had decided to backpack into a less public area to find the birds without disturbing them. We had sandwich wraps for lunch in Rangely after stopping unsuccessfully to look and listen for Mourning Warblers at habitats that seemed to have potential.

About 2:30, we began our hike up Saddleback Mountain with our full backpacks. Along the route Derek regaled me with tales of successful and unsuccessful trips with other birders who had hired him to climb the trail for the Bicknell's Thrush. I was worried that I would be the subject of his future tales of failures to reach the top, so I was greatly relieved that I managed to keep going past the "bunny slope" that had nearly felled an earlier similarly heavy-laden hiker. It wasn't too bad, so long as I took the time to rest every now and then, and to breathe.

I have just climbed Saddleback Mountain in Maine (July 1). Photo by Derek Kovitch.

The view from the top of Saddleback Mountain was spectacular (July 1).

What kept me going to the top was a female Spruce Grouse that was taking a gravel bath in the middle of the path up the mountain. When she decided that she should get off the trail as we approached with our cameras, three of her chicks appeared from nowhere and tumbled over the grasses to follow her off into the spruces. I didn't quite sprint the rest of the way up the slope, but I was ecstatic and my load definitely felt lighter.

The weather was potentially stormy that night (but currently lovely), so we chose a site for our tents close to an Appalachian Trail shelter. Before setting up our tents, we trekked up (without our packs) to the Appalachian Trail and took some pictures at the summit of Saddleback. We had wonderful views of the surrounding valleys from above timberline.

We went back to set up our tents and have macaroni salad for supper. At 6:16 P.M., we first heard a Bicknell's Thrush calling near our tents, and then one of them burst across the opening formed by the ski trail and dove into the short, thick spruces. We spent the hours until dark (about 8:45) wandering the nearby opening, hoping for more sightings but saw no more. We did hear about seven Bicknell's Thrushes and many Swainson's Thrushes, some of which we saw before we returned to the tents. We listened for Boreal and Northern Saw-whet Owls, but heard none, and we turned in.

I slept wonderfully. I'm learning to love camping and only woke up briefly a couple of times. It was a starry night and cool, but not cold. At 4:24 I awoke abruptly to the songs of a Bicknell's Thrush and a White-throated Sparrow and made myself get up. I knew Derek would be up soon, too, and I didn't want to hold up the bird-watching. Unfortunately, the Bicknell's Thrushes were silent and invisible the rest of the morning. After bagels and cream cheese, we packed up our dewy tents and headed down the mountain. Not too many birds were singing except a couple of tinkly Winter Wrens, some lispy Blackpolls, Swainson's Thrushes, American Redstarts, a Purple Finch, Black-throated Green Warblers, and a Least Flycatcher.

After we hiked down the mountain, we stopped in Rangely, and Derek called a friend who gave us insights on where to find Mourning Warblers, which we were still seeking. We found the recommended site, a hidden trail off a parking area along the road. Having heard that we would need to cross a river, I wore my wet tennis shoes without socks and waded across since I hadn't brought "wellies." It was not a rushing river and only about a foot deep, and it actually felt good once I got used to the cool water squishing between my toes. We were hardly across the river when we heard a singing Mourning Warbler, and then two more, none of which were interested in showing themselves. Although it was not always the case, ABA rules say that you can count heard-only birds. The reason the rules were changed was to prevent harassment by bird listers attempting to see every bird, for example, by coming too close to nests or crashing through fragile habitat or by playing tapes for long periods of time in an attempt to draw out a bird for a sighting. We turned around, recrossed the river, changed shoes, and headed for cattail marshes to look for Virginia Rails.

In spite of valiant efforts, we were unable to drum up any rails as we wandered coastward. Small wonder, as it was a hot July midafternoon, and we were looking for birds that are more active in the early morning or evening. We did see Black Terns, Bobolinks, Purple Martins, Northern Harriers, a Bald Eagle, an Osprey, and an Eastern Kingbird, among others.

We arrived at Pemaquid Point near Newport Harbor where we planned to go out for Atlantic Puffins, only to find that the coast was very foggy, definitely not good for sea watching and maybe a problem for seagoing. Not much we could do about it, however. Since we sorely needed sleep from our previous hurried schedules, Derek collapsed on a picnic bench for a nap, and I wandered off to sit on a rock and peer into the fog for birds over the water. It was pleasant, but I was worried about whether we would be able to

An Atlantic Puffin swims away in the fog off the Maine coast (July 2).

go out for the puffins (and our hoped-for storm-petrels). I had no other trips planned where Atlantic Puffins were a possibility.

When Derek woke up, the fog was still thick. We wandered over to the boat dock to see whether the boat was likely to go out to Eastern Egg Rock. The captain assured Derek that the tour boat was still going out and there was less fog at the island. We relaxed, but it did not look good for seeing storm-petrels on the water. At 5:30, the boat took off into the fog, and we listened to a naturalist tell us about what we would see soon, assuming we could see anything. As we neared the rock (they told us we were nearing it—nothing was visible), a couple of puffins darted by in the fog. When we got very close to the island, we began to see Atlantic Puffins, Black Guillemots, and Common Eiders on the water and flying terns (Arctic, Common, and Roseate). It was still too foggy to see much on the island itself. As expected, we saw no storm-petrels. It was a great trip though because of the puffins and because the fog gave the whole world an ethereal feel.

We headed toward Portland and discussed where to get supper. We decided (primarily because Derek convinced me that a proper visit to Maine not only included the ghastly Moxie drink and the yummy Whoopie Pies, which we had already tried, but also lobster rolls) to stop at Red's Eats, a classic roadside "fast" outdoor seafood place. I had a very good lobster roll—a toasted hotdog bun piled high with lobster meat, over which one could slather mayo or butter.

Today, I got up, medicated my zillion black fly bites (from Saddleback Mountain, and which were now inflamed and violently itchy), got a cab, and then hired a rental car for exploring on my own. I followed most of Derek's suggestions, beginning with some general birding at Capisic Pond Park in the Portland area, but I could not find any rails. I drove north to Bradbury State Park where Northern Goshawks had recently been seen. When I found the trailhead for Summit trail, I climbed the short (0.3 mile), steep trail that passed through a lovely tall mixed forest. As I stepped out onto the huge flat rock at the summit and glanced around, a large bulky accipiter flew low over the trees that I had just come through. I tried to put the camera into action, but it all happened too fast. Even though I stayed up there in the hot sun for about two hours, I never saw it (or any other raptor) again. The color, shape, and size were that of a Northern Goshawk, so I counted it (I saw a better view later in the year, which pleased me immensely).

That brought my list to 612 for the year.

I'm about to land in Chicago on my way back home. I'm next scheduled to fly out on Wednesday, July 9, on a multistate trip with friends to Arizona, Nevada, and New Mexico. I don't have plans to bird between now and then, but we'll see. I have client work and church activities and Dave's birthday all coming up, starting tomorrow.

JULY 9

Debra Corpora, Jean Ferguson, and I left DFW about an hour late. This is the first time the two of them have met, and I'm looking forward to our all birding together. Nothing (except a somewhat bumpy flight) has distracted me from planning our Arizona trip. I went through the Tucson Audubon Society's bird-finding guide to figure out which places to visit in three areas— Huachucas, Portal/Chiricahuas, and Santa Rita/Madera—by checking out where the birds that I want are found, or at least are possible.

At Miller Canyon at Beatty's Guest Ranch. I added Cassin's Kingbird, four hummingbirds (Broad-billed, Broad-tailed, Magnificent, and White-eared) and a Sulphur-bellied Flycatcher in the monsoon rains that came in and stayed. We shopped for groceries since our rooms have a refrigerator and microwave. We're set for the next couple of days.

JULY 11

July 10 was a very rainy day, so we had to fit in our birding during the least rainy periods. We went to Ash Canyon to look for hummers. Our first new year bird was a Black-headed Grosbeak. Then we saw many repeat hummingbirds, Arizona, Ladder-backed, Gila, and Acorn Woodpeckers, and finally a female Lucifer Hummingbird. After resting at Beatty's as the rain bucketed down, we finally noticed a letup and then a stop in the rain, so all of us went on a walk up the Miller Canyon trail with our rain gear and umbrellas. We added Western Wood-Pewee and Plumbeous Vireo (both heard but not counted earlier), Hepatic Tanager, Cordilleran Flycatcher, and then both Buff-breasted Flycatcher and Red-faced Warbler.

Today we awoke about 5:00 (with early-bird Jean's help) to a beautiful morning. Without too much grumbling, we ate a quick yogurt breakfast and then packed up and headed toward Carr Canyon. On the way over, we had a family of Gambel's Quail (parents and four young) along the road. On Lily Lane, we saw a male Montezuma Quail. After that success, we drove to Fort Huachuca to look for Elegant Trogons and Spotted Owls, neither of which we found. We had a very nice rain-free walk with more delightful Red-faced Warblers, after adding a Black-throated Gray Warbler at a picnic area.

About 1:00, we left Fort Huachuca and drove southeast through Bisbee and Douglas toward Rodeo, New Mexico. We periodically passed through quite heavy rain showers that were all around us. When we got to the dirt Stateline Road, the most highly recommended site for Bendire's Thrashers, it was not raining, so we decided to try for thrashers. We found none, and worse yet, the rain immediately moved in from the west in earnest, and the road started to accumulate water and the ditches immediately started to fill. We pulled over and stopped to wait since it was raining too hard to turn around without slipping into a deep ditch full of gushing water. For a while it looked like we might spend the night in our car, possibly floating. The road was flooding ahead of us, and it looked too treacherous with muddy shoulders and lakes behind us to attempt turning around. We had no visibility. About an hour later, the rain gradually slowed down, and we could see the mountains to the west. Finally, it stopped. Jean and Debra got out, checked the road surface, and decided that it looked hard enough to attempt to turn around. They stayed out to watch that I didn't go into the ditch; I made the turn, and we crept back a couple of miles to pavement through vast expanses of water.

We arrived in Portal 30 minutes later and immediately learned that a Violet-crowned Hummingbird was being seen at the lodge. While my burrito supper was being prepared, I saw and photographed the hummer.

JULY 12

We began the day walking up the road into the metropolis (a handful of homes) of Portal at 5:45 A.M. We saw some usual southeastern Arizona birds (Bullock's Oriole, Bridled Titmouse, Northern Cardinal, Curve-billed Thrasher) and then walked about half a mile up the paved road toward Paradise, seeing Blue Grosbeaks, Lesser Goldfinches, Bell's Vireos, one Rough-winged Swallow, Say's Phoebe, Gambel's Quail, Black-throated Sparrow, Canyon Towhee, Cactus Wren, Cassin's Sparrow, and Greater Roadrunner along the road. At David Jasper's place (a VENT tour guide), which was open to the

A Pyrrhuloxia sits on an empty feeder in Portal, Arizona (July 12).

Black-throated Sparrows were seen on our walk toward Paradise, Arizona (July 12).

public and has feeders, we saw nothing new for my year, but we added Pyr-rhuloxias and Lucy's Warbler to our trip list and saw more quail.

We tried going on to Stateline Road again for Bendire's Thrasher, but it was still too muddy. We saw a couple of Scaled Quail before getting back to Portal and breakfast, a great Spanish omelet. One nice thing about a small town with no fast-food place is that you must eat tasty "slow" food.

After that, we drove to Paradise, about 6 miles of a winding, narrow, rocky road. We were told that the road was passable in spite of the recent 4-inch rain, and it was. In Paradise, we found the George Walker House, where we peered into the yard and immediately saw our goal bird, Juniper Titmouse. It appeared to be a recently fledged one with a tinge of yellow still on its bill.

We were hearing increasingly noisy thunder by this time, and the sky was black. We bumped back over Paradise Road, but the rain soon caught up with us. We tried for Black-chinned Sparrows, but it was hard to keep the windows down and see out without getting wet, so we gave up and drove toward South Fork Cave Creek. We waited in the car for the rain to stop and eventually were able to drive slowly up the road, windows down.

When the rain seemed to be letting up, we decided to try to go to Rustler Park in the mountains primarily for Mexican Chickadees. A ranger we met assured us that the road, though a bit muddy, was passable even for our low-slung rental car. We found no chickadees or warblers, just singing Yellow-eyed Juncos, one Band-tailed Pigeon, and some Steller's Jays. We were just about to leave when I heard a Pygmy Nuthatch. After much peering about, we found it. I added two new birds today, the Pygmy Nuthatch (the last nut-hatch needed for my year) and the Juniper Titmouse (the last titmouse).

We headed out as rain with darkened sky and thunder was threatening again and stopped periodically when we heard chirps. The road to the west over Onion Pass was curvy, wet, sometimes muddy slushy, and often steep and narrow, but we got out, in spite of the downpour much of the way. We then headed to Madera Canyon's Santa Rita Lodge.

Tomorrow we go up the mountain again and then to Proctor Road and California Gulch, Melody Kehl (our guide) willing and the creeks don't rise.

Band-tailed Pigeons gazed down at us as we drove up to Rustler Park, Arizona (July 12).

JULY 13

About 6:00 A.M., we walked about one-third mile up the road from the
Santa Rita Lodge to Madera Kubo, a bed and breakfast, where both a Flame-
colored Tanager and a Berylline Hummingbird had been reported. Before we
got there, we could hear a burry-sounding tanager-like voice, and very soon
I spotted a singing, very yellow-orange bird with white wing bars, the Flame-
colored Tanager. Unfortunately, it dropped down from its treetop perch
before Debra and Jean saw it. Then it started singing again, and we all saw it.
Number 632. No Berylline Hummingbird was found.

We went back to our room, got gear for a longer walk, and drove to the top
of the Madera Canyon road to look for trogons. We had not hiked far up a trail

The Flame-colored Tanager was one of our most-wanted goals at Madera Canyon, Arizona (July 13).

when Debra saw a trogon-sized bird fly down the creek gulch. Soon we heard an Elegant Trogon barking just up the hill from us. It stopped calling and flew high through the trees, over the gulch, and away into the trees. We did not have time to try for a better view of this spectacular tropical canyon bird. It helped to think back to 2005 when an Elegant Trogon that had wandered to Weslaco, Texas, delighted birders for nearly a month. We walked back down the hill, also seeing a Hepatic Tanager, Plumbeous Vireo, and Painted Redstart.

Our next goal was a Black-capped Gnatcatcher on Proctor Road, where the bird had been seen recently, at the beginning of the Coronado area. However, all of our pishing and searching (in the infrequent nonrainy moments) did not turn up any kind of gnatcatcher. I did get a brief look at another new bird, a Varied Bunting.

We went over to Green Valley for lunch and then to meet Melody Kehl and other birders to go to California Gulch for the Five-striped Sparrow and Buff-collared Nightjar. This is one of the few places that both of these Mexican birds can sometimes be found. The group assembled into three cars. We headed south and then on increasingly bumpy, winding roads, often with rushing water crossing them or big puddles where the road went through the valleys.

When the cars stopped, we walked toward the edge of a flooded creek. As we stood on the edge of the turbulent waters after we reached the sparrow area, I realized that we were expected to wade across the rushing stream that was thigh high at its deepest where we had to cross. The brushy sparrow habitat was on the other side. We did not have waders or extra dry shoes or socks.

As usual, I was exceedingly reluctant to venture across the water, both due to my fear of falling (which in my phobic mind equaled drowning) and my distaste of having wet shoes, especially for another week of traveling. Once across, we walked along a creekside trail until we heard sparrowlike chip sounds, even above the noisy water, but could not find the calling birds. We wandered across more water, but now the wetness did not matter and the water level was lower.

Finally, Jean spotted a sparrow high up the slope, and we got to see our first Five-striped Sparrow. Later we saw another one somewhat closer, but it was hard to spot against the dark leaves.

About 6:30 p.m., we were ordered back across the rushing water. Time to go for the nightjar. We dumped water and pebbles out of our shoes and climbed the hill back to the cars, squishing as we walked. Once there, we drove a short distance to a plateau from which we could look at a gently rising slope covered with various mesquitelike shrubs and small trees and grass, across another little noisy brook. Melody got out chairs for all of us, a table, and a dinner of chicken, potato salad, and bean salad. Our chairs faced slope-ward as we ate and the sun set behind the clouds. As it got darker, we became quiet to listen for the nightjar.

We waited and waited. Spade-foot toads of various kinds started calling, a few bats came out, and the moon periodically peered through the clouds, illuminating the whole scene even after the sun was clearly gone. Unfortu-nately, we did not see or hear the nightjar. Since the bird did not sing and the early monsoon rains had nearly made the journey impossible to this site, it was sadly clear to me that the nightjar was going to be a "nemesis" for my big year, impossible to get to, and essentially impossible to find even if you could get there. One bird to take off my "might-see" list.

We bumped back to civilization in the dark. While I had a bit of a worry that we'd get lost, since it was only Melody's second time on part of the trail from Ruby Road to a different California Gulch access, I did not care because we were not on our way to any birds and I was depressed.

As we got back on the pavement, and the conversation up in the front of the car drifted to owls, I asked about Whiskered Screech-Owl locations and learned that Melody had found them calling recently at the top of Madera Canyon Road. I needed to be there in the dark; it was already nearly mid-night and would be dawn before 5:00 A.M. I decided (without consulting Jean and Debra) to head up to the top of the Madera Canyon Road as soon as we got back to Madera Canyon, stopping at our room to let them out to go to bed, assuming they would want to do that.

When we got back to our cabin, I was glad that they both wanted to go along for owls. Soon after we got to the parking lot at the top of Madera Can-yon Road, we heard a distant Whip-poor-will and then multiple Whiskered Screech-Owls, one of which we actually saw. Then to our delight a Northern Pygmy-Owl started up. First it was slow toots, and then a few more, normally paced notes.

JULY 14

We began to bird early, first unsuccessfully for Berylline Humming-bird and then unsuccessfully for Black-capped Gnatcatcher. Then we went to the Bog Springs trail where a Greater Pewee had a nest. Debra decided that because of tiredness and her bad ankle, she would not hike, but Jean and I headed up the trail toward the Bog Springs trail. At some point, we unknowingly passed the turnoff where Bog Springs trail went left and the Kent Springs trail continued straight. When we got to a later unexpected fork, we were not quite sure where we were and therefore did not know whether to go forward, left or right, or back, or to just sit down and panic. We took the left fork and eventually reached a different springs area. We then realized that to get to Bog Springs, we would have to either go back and find our missed turn or go forward and loop around to Bog Springs from the opposite side. We chose the latter, which worked just fine. The whole trip probably was a couple of miles longer than we had expected.

Once at the springs, Jean chose not to go down the final short trail because she was too tired, but I could not come this far without trying. The springs did not have any water, and at first no sign of the goal bird. I finally heard a couple of distant, distinctive Greater Pewee calls (a drawling *Jose Maria*), and eventually there was one high in the tree nearly above me, calling.

I climbed back up to Jean, and we hurried along the correct return trail, our steps quickened by the thunderclaps around us and by the realization that Debra was likely to be worried by our long absence. When we returned, we checked out of our room and tried once more unsuccessfully for the Berylline Hummingbird.

We went next to Tucson and the Desert Museum and Saguaro National Park West. Our goals were primarily Gilded Flicker and Costa's Hummingbird. We found very few hummingbirds at the museum, and they mostly seemed to be female and therefore tricky to identify. Luckily we ran into a docent, Barbara Bickel, a birder who told us that most of the hummingbirds were Costa's and that Gilded Flicker was unlikely at the museum. We all saw at least one Costa's Hummingbird and then drove off to the national park for flickers.

We drove up and down long gravel roads with saguaro cacti stretching for miles across the hills. We saw a couple of Gila Woodpeckers but no Gilded Flickers. Finally, we saw a flicker atop a saguaro, the only non-White-winged Dove on the saguaros. We looked it over carefully, and we concluded from its yellow underwings and red moustache that it was a Gilded Flicker.

It was time for one last trip back to Madera Kubo for the Berylline Hummingbird, but no luck. On the drive out of Madera Canyon, we looked for Rufous-winged Sparrows. Eventually, amid the Cassin's, Botteri's, and Black-throated Sparrows, we heard a couple of Rufous-winged Sparrows and saw them lurking in the brush. Lesser Nighthawks began to come out, and we headed to Tucson and our motel.

I'm at 641 species.

JULY 15

After I arrived in Reno (from Tucson) and rented a car, Linda Ford, a Dallas birding friend who had flown there to meet me, and I drove straight west to Elko. Our goal was a Himalayan Snowcock, a large grouselike bird introduced from Asia into the Ruby Mountains by hunters many years ago. I had never tried for them before because of their remote location. When I told my father (not a birder) years ago that people often found the snowcocks by hiring a helicopter to fly low through the mountains, my father looked at me in horror and made me promise not to try for snowcocks until after he was dead. He died 10 years before my ABA big year.

All around us in Nevada were mountains, sagelike plants, road, trucks, and nothing else. We decided to check out Lamoille Canyon, the site of the Himalayan Snowcock trail, that evening to be sure we could find it in the dark the next morning. Lamoille Canyon Road goes into Humboldt National Forest and ends at a parking lot and turnaround, from which various trails lead, including the trail to Island Lake. It was beautiful up there, filled with colorful wildflowers, mostly in yellows, purple-blues, and white. We hiked for about half an hour and then turned around so we could come down before dark.

JULY 16

We left our room about 4:30 this morning and went back to Lamoille Canyon. Early on in the hike we heard at least a couple of Dusky Flycatchers, confirmed by a quiet listening to the iPod. Violet-green Swallows zipped by, and we saw Mountain Bluebirds, a Townsend's Solitaire going back and forth between some pine trees and the rocks, and many American Robins along the trail. The hike to Island Lake was not too difficult, but we went pretty slowly anyway. It was spectacular, but we did not see or hear any snowcocks.

It was getting hot up on the rocks, and snowcocks are supposed to be primarily early-morning birds, so we hiked back down and drove to Ruby Lake National Wildlife Refuge. The refuge is a bigger, deeper lake version of Hornsby Bend (Austin), a vast expanse of shallow ponds and lakes. It had many more breeding birds and baby birds and a lot more hawks than in summertime Texas. The water was covered with American Coots, Mallards, Canvasbacks with youngsters, White-faced Ibis, Double-crested Cormorants, Ruddy Ducks with young, Canada Geese, Lesser Scaup, and Pied-billed Grebes, as well as a couple of Yellow-headed Blackbirds. As we drove out, we got a distant view of two Trumpeter Swans. We saw many black and pink Lewis's Woodpeckers, the most common bird of the trip along the roads.

JULY 17

Since we had not found any snowcocks, we tried again this morning, half an hour earlier. Unfortunately, the result was again negative, even though we hiked up way beyond the lake across a rocky, sparsely vegetated meadow to a verdant, boggy lake area. It was beautiful but very disappointing.

My sadness was relieved by the noisy chips and in-your-faceness of two MacGillivray's Warblers on one of the last switchbacks on our way down. Their actions made it evident that they had young ones very near, probably out of the nest and about to hop on the trail. A Clark's Nutcracker flew from a tree farther down, and a Yellow Warbler hopped in the aspens next to the parking lot.

The mountain view at Island Lake is beautiful, even if no snowcocks are seen (July 17). Photo by Linda Ford.

As I wondered whether they still made helicopter flights up to Lamoille Canyon to look for snowcocks, we drove back to Elko to pack up our gear. Trying to salvage something more from the trip, we headed north to Wild-horse Reservoir, which is supposed to, and probably does, have Chukars. All we saw was a nearby Clark's Grebe, as well as American White Pelicans and a Sage Thrasher.

Then we had the long drive back to Reno, 489 miles for the day. I'm still at 644 bird species.

JULY 18

The plane trip from Denver to Albuquerque was a bumpy ride, with convection galore. I've figured out some places in New Mexico to bird and have been thinking about what kinds of birds I still need to get this summer.

About 6:00, after Linda's birth-day lunch in Albuquerque, we drove to Sandia Crest with the goal of general mountain birding before dark and of finding owls after dark. We found mostly American Robins, Dark-eyed Juncos, and Chipping Sparrows, and a Grace's Warbler, new for the year. We did not find any owls, which was probably due to a combination of our being too tired to stay around until it got completely dark and the fact that it was mid-July, when owls are mostly silent.

Half Through

The year now is half done; the race is more
   than half run.
The birding's been great, so whatever my
   fate,
It's been cool; it's been neat; it's been fun.
But there's something that now must be
   said; it is swirling about in my head.
It is grim to miss birds, too depressing for
   words,
It's a certainty I'm facing with dread.
Already it's just as I feared, the list growing
   of birds disappeared,
They've stopped calling, or hid. Is it some-
   thing I did?
Second-guessing a bird can be weird.
It's much too late to quit now. It would be
   just like breaking a vow.
In spite of the cost, and the sleep that I've
   lost,
I'll keep on, though I can't fathom how.

JULY 19

We got up today at what we hoped would be early enough to let us get to Jemez (HAY-muss) Falls in time to see the early-rising Black Swifts. It took longer to get there than we had thought. We arrived at the falls parking lot about 7:50 A.M., long after first light. On the walk to the falls, we saw a very industriously tapping, bark-ripping American Three-toed Woodpecker. In spite of waiting around a couple of hours, we did not find swifts of any kind at the falls, just Violet-green Swallows.

We walked a short distance on a piney trail, continuously surrounded by the high-pitched peeps of Pygmy Nuthatches and hearing invisible empids and Western Wood-Pewees. We found Mountain Chickadees and White-breasted Nuthatches up in the pines. Back near the parking lot we saw a few Western Bluebirds, as well as a Hairy Woodpecker ferreting ants from a dead tree lying on the ground.

We drove east, stopping when we heard or saw or thought we might find birds of interest. What we found were a single male Red Crossbill perched high along the road, a stunning red and yellow male Western Tanager at a parking lot that was overrun with ground squirrels (goldish, striped backs), and a very pink-red-gorgeted Broad-tailed Hummingbird amid many sphinx moths hovering at the flowers. We also found a meadow where modest patches of ice and snow remained under the trees. Eventually we wound our way around Los Alamos and back to our motel.

JULY 20

We went back to Jemez Falls this morning, this time arriving about 5:30 A.M. after a drive of one and a half hours. An astounding regal elk appearing on the road right ahead of us was the highlight of the trip. Once again, we waited and waited for the swifts. It was very quiet, except for the continuous bubbling splashes of the falls. Finally, Linda pointed to two swifts up high, and then we saw two more large dark swifts, low, apparently dashing away from the falls.

We left the falls about 7:10 and headed east, only stopping briefly at a wide curve overlooking a burned/logged area with many dead snags widely spaced across a little valley. It was a woodpecker heaven with many flickers, mostly but not all red-shafted, and a briefly seen male Williamson's Sapsucker, plus a Black-headed Grosbeak, Steller's Jays, and two lovely perched-up Band-tailed Pigeons.

We headed north, our goal being Canjilon Lakes, which our New Mexico guidebook said was a good birding spot. However, I missed a right-angle turn, and we took an unplanned jaunt for an hour. After we discovered the error and retraced our steps, we continued north. Just as we came around a gentle curve, we were stunned to see a pickup truck sailing through the air and then landing upside down on the road, spinning around. It was not a sight that could be forgotten, and it was difficult to continue. I was shaking for some time. Other people who were much closer and had seen more of the accident got out to deal with the situation and waved us onward. We could do nothing anyway, so we kept on to Canjilon. The New Mexico guidebook did not tell us which direction to go out of Canjilon to get to the lakes themselves, and we missed the sign. We did another unplanned trip on a right fork, getting Linda her first Black-throated Gray Warblers and a nice swallow assortment, plus some beautiful Lazuli Buntings. The left fork, which actually went to the lakes, was nice, too, but yielded nothing new.

JULY 21

This morning, we allowed ourselves to sleep in, but by 8:00 we were at our last intended destination, Three Gun trail, a bit east of Albuquerque. Very quickly we heard and then saw a couple of Black-chinned Sparrows, my goal, and then it was time to go our separate ways, mine being back to Texas.

JULY 28

I'm driving west on I-20 in Texas—shades of my Texas big year in 2005. My goals, assuming the Guadalupe Mountains are not too flooded, are Spotted Owl, Virginia's Warbler, Gray Flycatcher, and, of course, rarities. I have not birded the past five days since I returned from New Mexico, except the Fort Worth Audubon Scavenger Hunt on Saturday. I now have some trips scheduled: Florida this week for a couple of days primarily for Antillean Nighthawk, and perhaps the Mangrove Cuckoo; Utah/Nevada in early August to try again for snowcock and hopefully other "chickens"; Arizona in mid-August for Berylline Hummingbird and flycatchers that I'm missing, Spotted Owl if I do not get it this week, and Mexican Chickadee.

I just realized that no matter which way I travel, I could possibly get a new year bird, but with the exception of California and North Carolina pelagic trips, most trips are unlikely to produce more than two to three species now. The number of dollars per new bird species is increasing rapidly with each new bird.

There are miles and miles to go, and it's hot (about 104 degrees) and birdless. As birds get more and more difficult to find this year, and the money needed to do so increases, so much will be required (effort/time/miles/dollars) for relatively so little. I knew that going in, but it would be nice not to have to return to some areas, besides the Metroplex (Dallas–Fort Worth area).

JULY 30

I am heading home. Viewed from the results of this two-day quest, this trip was a failure. I did not find a Spotted Owl even though I did the most thorough job of inspecting tree branches on the Devil's Hall trail (in the Guadalupe Mountains) that I have ever done. When I started planning this big year so many months ago, I chose to put one of my photos of a Spotted Owl on the business cards that I made up to hand out to birders to tell them about my big year. Now, Spotted Owls have become a nemesis bird, not seen after trying multiple times in Arizona and Texas. Did I jinx it by putting the picture on my cards? I should have chosen something more common, like Starling.

Yesterday, I headed out too early from Van Horn to the Guadalupe Mountains, so I waited in the dark at the Pine Springs campground, afraid to start

A Canyon Wren consoled me on my unsuccessful hike for Spotted Owls in the Guadalupe Mountains of Texas (July 29).

up the trail until I could see whether the thunder and lightning were going to be a problem. The storm appeared to be east of Pine Springs and not getting closer. About 6:00, I began the hike up the Devil's Hall trail. There were many singing Black-chinned Sparrows, one of which was gathering grasses, perhaps indicating that they were nesting now that it had rained. The other birds were all the usual ones—Canyon Towhee, Plumbeous Vireo, Canyon, Bewick's, and Rock Wrens, Cordilleran Flycatcher, White-throated Swifts, White-breasted Nuthatch, and Western Tanager, but no owls.

I went over to the Frijoles Ranch, where in 2005 it was easy to get Virginia's Warblers, but not so this year. Onward to Rattlesnake Springs in New Mexico, where a Ruddy Ground-Dove had been reported. I did not find any ground-doves but did see an unexpected Zone-tailed Hawk darting into a tree.

This morning I slept a little later. A couple of years ago, someone found a Spotted Owl at/near Pratt Cabin on the McKittrick trail in the Guadalupes, but the gate to that road does not open until 8:00 A.M. At the Frijoles Ranch, where I went instead, I found nothing noteworthy. I went back and found the gate to the McKittrick site open. I found no new birds for the trip except a Warbling Vireo, a much unexpected male Hooded Warbler, and a Gray Flycatcher, seen well in spite of its drabness.

I cut short my trip because of building cumulonimbus clouds all around and hustled down the mountain. I had one new bird for the three- to four-day trip.

JULY 31

My goal on this trip to Miami is Antillean Nighthawk, plus any rarities. I'm flying on last-minute frequent flyer miles on a very bumpy evening trip.

Spotted Owls and St. Paul Sandpipers

NEW BIRD SPECIES SEEN THIS MONTH: 17
TOTAL BIRD SPECIES BY THE END OF THE MONTH: 666
PLACES BIRDED: Florida, Texas, Utah, Nevada, Arizona, North Carolina, Alaska

AUGUST 2

Florida turned out better than expected. It started out well because I arrived in Miami a bit earlier than booked. Of course, some of that benefit was eaten up by a long wait at the car rental spot, compounded by a problem car (flat tire warning on instrument panel) requiring me to return the car immediately and get in a shorter line to get a different car.

I slept three and a half hours in Florida City and was in such a hurry to get going that I left my alarm clock at the motel. At about 4:30 I got up and drove south as fast as I legally could toward the Marathon airport, which seemed to be the first possible place for Antillean Nighthawk that I might reach by around dawn. The Florida bird books mostly noted that these nighthawks were active at dusk, but at least once I had seen the phrase "dawn and dusk" in the discussion of Antillean Nighthawks. I assumed I would need all three dawn-dusks of this trip to get the nighthawk. I didn't know if dawn would work or if Marathon airport still had any nighthawks.

I was delighted when with windows rolled down as I approached the airport at early daylight (6:30), I heard the unmistakable pit a pit pat of Antillean Nighthawks. It was still too dark to see their zooming bodies, but eventually I saw a dot in the light sky out over the trees across the airport. Soon I could hear more of them overhead and see three close by. I didn't hear any Common Nighthawks for about 20 minutes after I got there. By sound only it seemed like there were four to five Antillean Nighthawks and one to two Common Nighthawks.

With my goal accomplished, I continued south, uncertain of what to do. I had no lead on my other needed Florida birds (Smooth-billed Ani and Mangrove Cuckoo) and/or time to go for them (Budgerigar on the west coast of Florida), but who knew? Maybe I would find a rarity. It's a good thing that I stopped at Marathon. On my way south I stopped at five or more so-called Mangrove Cuckoo spots and then wandered aimlessly around Key West and the birdless airport after an early supper. There were no nighthawks at all at Key West.

This morning I slept in until 5:30 and then headed to the spot that had seemed to have the most potential of the Mangrove Cuckoo places I had checked yesterday. I arrived at a road into the mangroves on Sugarloaf Key and drove slowly to the bridge, beyond which was the best area as far as I could tell. Slowly I cruised down, periodically stopping, getting out, and listening.

As it got hot and the birds became silent, I reminded myself how grateful I had been for the nighthawks at Marathon and gave up to head toward Miami. Birding was done, and it was time to move onward. Finding a Mangrove Cuckoo would either have to wait for another trip, or this hard-to-find cuckoo would become one more of my growing number of misses for my big year.

About an hour later I found an NPR station with my favorite program, "Wait Wait Don't Tell Me," and settled in for a relatively happy hour of slow driving in heavy traffic, hoping the radio signal would last. Everyone in Florida who owned a boat or a mobile home was heading north, slowly, ahead of me. Birding was almost forgotten, and then the second astoundingly good thing happened on the trip—a Mangrove Cuckoo flew across the road immediately ahead of me with its unmistakable cuckoo shape and brown buffy underside. I was completely stunned by the unexpected bird out of nowhere!

I have now gone beyond my originally stated goal for this year of 650. And of course I am slowly working toward my real goal of 700. I was pretty sure that I would make it to 650, but 700 is not a certainty. It does require that all my pelagic trips go out. For now, I'm very happy with where I am in my big year. My next trip is back to Nevada.

AUGUST 8

On Monday evening (August 4) I flew uneventfully to Salt Lake City. The next morning I left my motel for Elko. The road continued forever along Salt Lake and miscellaneous ponds and puddles interspersed with salt areas that looked exactly like new-fallen snow, giving me a brief moment of homesickness for flat, central, snowy Wisconsin. I saw few birds in Utah—two White-fronted Geese flying over, Double-crested Cormorants, an American White Pelican sitting sadly on the railroad tracks, and Common Ravens. In Nevada I headed north to Wildhorse Reservoir to look once more, unsuccessfully, for Chukars. The only noteworthy thing about the trip was a couple of mini-plagues of Mormon crickets, with the road being dotted black with dead or slowly hopping, wounded crickets. The ravens along the road on the fence posts were sitting there looking rotund and stuffed.

At the reservoir I saw many Western and Clark's Grebes, American White Pelicans, White-faced Ibises, and miscellaneous unidentified ducks. A walk on the trail revealed quite a few Horned Larks and Vesper Sparrows, but no Chukar, which I was told can be found better at dusk. But I could not stay that late.

In the early afternoon, I headed south to Lamoille Canyon. My plan this time was to backpack up in the afternoon and camp at Island Lake, and therefore not have to drive in and hike up in the morning.

The climb was the closest I have ever come to giving up on a backpacking hike due to the combination of not enough sleep, too much driving, too little recent exposure to high elevations and thin mountain air, and 2 miles of continuous up with a very heavy pack. My legs got very shaky, my head so blacked-out feeling, and my lungs so sore. The trail to Island Lake has few boulder seats on which to rest a heavy pack or just sit. I knew that if I took off the pack, I'd have real difficulty in putting it back on, so when I was tired, I just stood and panted and trembled until I could put one foot ahead of the other again.

I got to the top about 5:30 (under two hours), which was not too bad. The looming clouds kept me going. I did not want to put up my tent in the rain, nor did I want my sleeping bag and air mattress (or me) to get drenched. I had extra plastic garbage bags along to stuff things in or to put over me, and my raincoat and umbrella. None of these were needed, because it did not rain on me or my campsite.

I snacked rather than ate a big supper and then moseyed about the lake area to see what was around. It was too light to go to bed. A Clark's Nutcracker, some Cassin's Finches, Mountain Chickadees, Northern Flickers, an American Robin, and a Rock Wren were it. About 7:45 I crawled into my tent. I was just dozing off when a loud, unfamiliar bird call woke me up, and I scrambled back out of the tent. I was almost convinced that it was a snowcock.

Lewis's Woodpeckers were noisy parts of the roadside wooded areas south of Elko, Nevada (August 6).

I didn't need to contemplate counting the uncertain sound, however. At 5:10 the next morning (August 6) I woke up and saw through my tent "windows" that it was just beginning to get light out, so I dragged myself out, many parts of me aching, not only from the climb the day before but also from sleeping on an angled slippery air mattress at one end of the tent.

I grabbed a few granola bars and a water bottle and headed out and up the "mountain meadow" (a slope of rocks and boulders with flowers and gravel between), toward the upper cinque, where Linda and I had wandered our second day in July. Much less water was flowing now, and I was able to head off to the left, behind the lake. I would have gone much farther left, but at 5:50 I thought I heard the whistled *bugle* call of a snowcock off to the right. I did not hear it again until 6:07, much closer, now that I had walked toward the first call. At 6:20, and at roughly two-minute intervals thereafter until about 6:45, I heard one to three Himalayan Snowcocks calling, from slightly different directions, but all generally to the right, an area that Linda and I had concentrated on. At 6:38, I saw a distant silhouetted lump off to the right where the sound was coming from, snapped a picture, looked up again, and the lump was gone. Later study of the blurry distant picture confirmed a brown body and light neck and head. I had heard and seen a Himalayan Snowcock.

After an easy walk down the mountain trail, I stopped at a picnic area on the Lamoille Canyon Road to plan my itinerary and eat amid five to eight Lewis's Woodpeckers, including fledged young and some still in the nest holes in the trees, all making lots of noise and flying about.

I decided to go next to Cedar Breaks National Monument in Utah to look for Dusky Grouse. I much enjoyed the trip but found no grouse. I did find many Pine Siskins, Mountain Chickadees, Orange-crowned Warblers, Brown Creepers like little bugs simultaneously working a little section of trees along the trail, Common Ravens, Pygmy and White-breasted Nuthatches, a Clark's Nutcracker, Ruby-crowned Kinglets, a Lincoln's Sparrow, and a single Three-toed Woodpecker.

This morning was beautiful, with a golden pink sky and a rainbow as I turned west, north of Salt Lake City. The fields were golden, too, and sudden tears came to my eyes for a friend who died after moving to Logan, Utah, last name of Golden. The scenery west of Logan was beautiful the whole way, about 112 miles toward the west and Snowville and then toward, but not to, Lynn. Along the road were a couple of Golden Eagles and an American Goldfinch. Definitely a golden day, but not a chickeny day. The other bird highlight was a little flock of Juniper Titmice, in junipers of course, on the way back to Salt Lake City. It was the first time I had ever seen them without doing a major targeted search for them. I also had a great view of an Olive-sided Flycatcher.

The flight home was uneventful, which is always good.

AUGUST 10

I played hooky from church today. I realized that if I were to have a chance at Yellow-green Vireos, I needed to go for them while they were being reported in the Valley (Texas). It was an uneventful trip, highlights being a fly-by Yellow-billed Cuckoo, a Mississippi Kite in La Grange, and Crested Caracaras south of Refugio. The latter made me feel homesick for nonstop Texas birding and the excitement of 2005. I miss seeing South Texas birds as I wander the rest of the country.

This morning I headed to the Brownsville airport neighborhood where Yellow-green Vireos had been recently reported and stayed about an hour. Many birds were singing, but I did not hear a vireo. I went over to Sabal Palm

Audubon Sanctuary and hastened to the boardwalk, where I knew they had been in previous years. At first all I could hear and see were Couch's Kingbirds, Golden-fronted and Ladder-backed Woodpeckers, White-tipped Doves, Long-billed Thrashers, and noisy Plain Chachalacas. Two Groove-billed Anis sneaked past to a scrubby area. Then I heard two vireo-sounding notes and then a Yellow-green Vireo singing nonstop for over a minute. After staring fixedly in the direction where the vireo sounds had been, I saw the tree leaves wiggle, and a bird hopped to an open branch very briefly, but long enough for me to see its yellow sides and lanky vireo appearance. Number 653.

Dickcissels serenaded me on my drive out of Sabal Palm. Hoping for something else, I checked out areas where Tamaulipas Crows have been in previous years, but all I found were Inca Doves telling me "no hope." And there wasn't.

I made the slow drive west to look for a Hook-billed Kite at Anzalduas County Park but wasn't as lucky as in 2005. I may miss that bird in 2008, but I'll try again. At 11:20 it was time to head home and get to work.

A Dickcissel "song" is more like an insect song (Texas, August 10).

AUGUST 18

I am due to fly to Dallas–Fort Worth from Tucson in about 15 minutes. This trip to Arizona has been unexpectedly good, even great, but of course, I will still need to come back for more Arizona birds.

I arrived at Tucson International Airport a little after noon on August 14, picked up a car, and headed to Madera Canyon. My initial goal for the trip was Berylline Hummingbird. I checked in at Santa Rita Lodge and drove up to monitor the Madera Kubo feeders for a while. After an hour or so, I went to plan B, which was to walk to Bog Springs (now that I know the right way to go), where more than one Berylline Hummingbird had been seen within the past week.

My late afternoon hike to Bog Springs was nice and uneventful, except for four Montezuma Quail—two along the drive into the Bog Springs campground and two near the beginning of the trail. But I saw no Berylline Hummingbird. That night as it got dark, I went over to Proctor Road, hopeful for a late Black-capped Gnatcatcher, but it was too dark by the time I got there. I did hear a very talkative Whiskered Screech-Owl but no new birds.

The next morning I was back on the Bog Springs trail at 6:15. I hung around the springs for a while after my fast 45-minute hike. Then, high above in the leaves was a dark hummingbird, small, hovering, and disappearing. Shortly after, I heard the unmistakable (I had listened earlier to my iPod) scratchy sound (to my ears, sort of like a combination of Anna's Hummingbird and Bewick's Wren) coming from a cedar. When I looked, I saw a hovering, dark green Berylline Hummingbird. On my way down at the top of the side trail to the springs, a quietly talking male Montezuma Quail slowly clucked his way across the trail about 15 feet from me. I also heard Dusky-capped Flycatchers and saw Black-throated Gray Warblers, Wilson's Warblers, and a couple of Black-tailed Gnatcatchers.

After I got back to my car, I visited Montosa Canyon for Black-capped Gnatcatcher. A couple of Varied Buntings were serenading me, a Pyrrhuloxia chirped, and Bell's Vireo was scolding, and then I heard the quiet but harsh-sounding call, twice, of a Black-capped Gnatcatcher. I saw movement, mostly hidden in the bushes, and was able to see two gnatcatchers, one a Black-tailed and one a Black-capped Gnatcatcher. A better view would have been nice.

I drove to Miller Canyon on the afternoon of August 15, planning to check in and walk up the canyon where one or two Spotted Owls had been seen every day since the first of August. Slam dunk, I thought, and about time. But I learned from the lodge owner that no one had seen any owls that

Black-throated Gray Warblers were commonly found in the Arizona mountain woods (August 15).

morning, despite much looking. I valiantly trooped up the trail to where I thought the owls had been (not far enough, I learned later), but of course, there were no owls.

That night I went up the trail in the dark, hoping at least to hear one. I had been told that they often could be heard, sometimes even hunting over the orchard at Beatty's lodge. I heard nothing, except a distant sound, which might have been an owl of some kind, but was hard to hear over the sound of the rushing creek.

The next morning (August 16), being ever hopeful, or perhaps quixotic, I trudged up the Miller Canyon trail again, visually stripping each branch—no large lumps that weren't wooden. I did see quite a few Red-faced Warblers and Painted Redstarts, but they didn't cheer me up. On my arrival back at Beatty's, I talked to Tom Sr. and to Helen Nelson (from Fort Worth, who stays at Beatty's with her family each summer). I told them of my big year and begged them to call my cell phone if an owl was sighted before I was due to leave Arizona in two days. I gave them my card, sadly, and perhaps ominously, bearing the Spotted Owl photograph. Was I never to see another one?

I picked myself up, said good-bye, and headed for my next goal, Sonoita/ Patagonia. I sailed through Sonoita to Patagonia and to the rest area made famous over the years for all its wonderful sightings. For many years Rose-throated Becards had been reported there, even nesting, but none had been reported this year, nor did I find any. My goal was Thick-billed Kingbirds (my worst nemesis in my 2005 Texas big year), which are regular in Patagonia. I strolled the trail along the river/creek across the road from the rest area, seeing noisy Yellow-breasted Chats and Yellow Warblers, but no flycatchers at all.

Across the road at the rest stop, I walked the length of the area, looking and listening. Near the south end, I heard the unmistakable whistled call of a Thick-billed Kingbird coming from a silhouette at the top of a dead tree. The bird sailed out and back, and I circled around below it to get a better angle that was not directly into the sun. It was definitely a Thick-billed. It left the perch for a while, went up the scraggly slope behind the rest stop, and then returned with a second kingbird—Mommy and Daddy apparently.

I went back to Sonoita, where I was staying this evening after a detour to nearby Las Cienegas to look for Bendire's Thrashers. A few Northern Mock-ingbirds gave me pause before I realized that they weren't Bendire's Thrash-ers. Sparrows were numerous (Cassin's, Botteri's, Grasshopper, Chipping, Black-throated, Lark). I also disturbed a Gambel's Quail covey dusting in the road. At Empire Ranch Road, I drove until the road mostly disappeared in a large puddle. I was already nervous about continuing, having fishtailed my way through some mini–sand dunes deposited previously by former floods. One good spot at Las Cienegas was the sycamore/big tree grove along the river behind the headquarters. The trees rang with the screams of Zone-tailed Hawks, but I saw only one. The bushes were alive with Lazuli Buntings and warblers—Common Yellowthroat, MacGillivray's, Yellow, Yellow-breasted Chat, and Nashville, and then finally, a Virginia's Warbler, which was shy, skulking about at the edge of the grove. Two new birds for the day. The Ben-dire's Thrasher would have to wait.

I stayed that night at the Sonoita Inn, big and spacious. I was barely in my room when the sound of rain beating on my windows drowned out any other sounds. I was very grateful that it had not rained when I had been at Las Cien-egas, or I would probably have been stuck in or between the flooded draws.

The next morning (August 17), I headed north, stopping and listening again for Bendire's Thrashers. None. My activities were apparently suspi-cious looking, and I was pulled over by the Border Patrol to "be sure I was okay." They looked dubious about my claim to being a bird-watcher looking for Bendire's Thrashers, but they did not haul me out of my car or investigate further.

My goal was Madera Canyon again. I had checked with people at Portal and been told that the road to Rustler Park was likely to be impassable due to recent rains, so I decided to just go birding up the Old Baldy trail at Madera. This trail held very good memories for me, even though I also remembered severe lung gasping there, too. Better though were the Aztec Thrush and the Crescent-chested Warbler I had seen there in January. Maybe I would find another rarity or one of the warblers that I was still missing, Olive and Hermit. I could not think of any other birds to chase in Arizona, or at least any birds for which I had any idea of where to search.

I headed west on Sahuarita Road and then down to Madera on the old Nogales Highway. On the way I saw a teetering Gambel's Quail on a power line. But I barreled on, eager to begin the climb as early as possible. I arrived at the trailhead at about 8:00 A.M., the weather still cool and pleasant, even cold, as I started the climb. I was determined to savor the climb, not charge up the trail as before.

I was surrounded by calling Sulphur-bellied Flycatchers, tail-flaring, singing Painted Redstarts, and screaming Mexican Jays. A couple of Bridled Titmouse flocks with embedded Black-throated Gray Warblers, a single Blue-headed Vireo, vocal White-breasted Nuthatches, a distant Elegant Trogon, a Dusky-capped Flycatcher in a tree over the trail, a Black-headed Grosbeak hopping on the ground amid Yellow-eyed Juncos, and a female Rufous Hummingbird were highlights of the walk up.

Then amazingly I was in the midst of a little family of at least three Buff-breasted Flycatchers. All were within 3–4 feet of the ground and 10–12 feet of the trail. While Jean and Debra and I had seen one in July, it had been a distant, dark woodland view. These were very vocal and well seen.

The flycatchers alone would have made the trip worthwhile, even if all the other birds had not, but shortly I was in the high pines area with many tiny birds high at the top of the pines. Some were Grace's Warblers, 20–25 feet from the tops of the trees, but I heard one tiny birdsong way up, sounding periodically and tantalizingly like part of an Olive Warbler song. Its chip sounds were good, too, but I couldn't see the bird. Finally, I saw that it had yellow under its chin and breast. It seemed to have white outer tail feathers, but I wasn't sure it was not another Grace's Warbler. It flew to another pine, and I had a better view. It did not have black on its breast, so it wasn't

One of the Spotted Owls begins to disgorge a pellet at Miller Canyon, Arizona (August 17).

a Townsend's Warbler, nor black stripes on its sides like a Grace's Warbler, but it did have a black eye patch, a field mark of Olive Warblers. A new year bird.

I walked farther up the trail, but then decided (about 11:40) to head back down. It was just warming, though not bad, and I couldn't imagine topping, or equaling, the Olive Warbler. After 20 minutes, I turned on my cell phone to see if I had enough signal to call my husband. I did, but it was weak. I put the phone back in my pocket but almost immediately heard the sound that indicates that I had voice-mail messages. Two messages (from Tom Beatty and Helen Nelson) told me that the Spotted Owls had been refound that morning!! My heart nearly stopped. Once I recovered, I started running, fast-walking, tripping down the trail. If I hurried, there was time to try for them, and presumably get them, since Spotted Owls roost by day.

I arrived back at Beatty's about 3:30, and Helen Nelson came out to meet me. She had seen the owls that morning and agreed to accompany me back up the trail. Just before 4:00 we arrived at the first creek crossing where the owls had previously been seen on a daily basis, and we crossed it. Helen peered up into the canopy, muttering that she sure hoped they were still there

My fledgling painting career was begun with painting the two most welcome Spotted Owls at Miller Canyon, Arizona (August 17).

and that they had already moved once that day. My heart sank—was this going to be yet another failed Spotted Owl quest?

But no. We could see two full-size, fully feathered Spotted Owls huddled together on a horizontal maple sapling branch just over the trail, maybe 15 feet up. Of course, I took many pictures. The birds stayed put, even when two other hikers walked under them. One of the birds turned around on the branch and scratched its head, and the other stretched its head upward, opened its beak wide, and coughed up a pellet. Then both settled back to sleep.

I was absolutely overjoyed. Not quite speechless, but words just could not express my elation. When we got back down the trail, I showed the pictures to one and all (Nelsons, Beattys). Tom Sr. said jokingly (I think), "You've seen one, you've seen them all." I noted later when looking more closely at the pictures that bits of down were still sticking out through the feathers, so probably these two birds were this year's young.

It was time to head to Tucson for my trip home. I am at 659. In two days I'll be off to North Carolina and then to Alaska. In North Carolina, I am going out on two pelagic trips. The originally scheduled trip to go to the ocean area off North Carolina that is best for White-faced Storm-Petrels did not fill, so I will not have a chance for them. I still need other Atlantic pelagic birds.

AUGUST 24

My trip to North Carolina got me five pelagic species, the five that I had deemed most likely on that trip, and nothing more. When I arrived on August 21, my friend Lena picked me up from the airport. We stopped to pick up food for supper and then went to her house. At that time, Hurricane Fay was pounding Florida, and I was concerned that we would be weathered out of the pelagic trips. I was also worried that if we did get to go out, we would live (or die) to regret it, getting sick as dogs from the predicted ocean swells of at least 5–7 feet. I needed to go out—this was my last chance for Atlantic Ocean birds.

A Pomarine Jaeger coasts by the boat on a North Carolina pelagic trip (August 23).

I am taking a picture of one of the North Carolina pelagic birds (August 23). Photo by Lena Gallitano.

I got unwelcome news as we drove east to the Outer Banks of North Carolina—a Jabiru, one of my most desired birds for the ABA area—is near Raymondville, Texas. I cannot go back to look for this huge stork until September, and it's unlikely to still be around. The reports say that it was in Texas for over a week before hitting the hotlines. I so want to see a Jabiru, which in my mind is "worth" a whole lot more than some regularly seen pelagic bird. It's certainly bigger. But in a big year, all the species count the same. [Note: The Jabiru did *not* stay around for long and was gone when I got back to Texas.]

Lena and I had a good drive, stopping at a few places to look for birds. Except for a couple of nonpelagic species (Virginia Rail and Henslow's Sparrow), it was unlikely I could find anything new for my big year. We stopped at the Voice of America site of a colony of Henslow's Sparrows (invisible this year), and Pea Island (no rails). We did not expect anything much in the middle of the day in late summer.

Both pelagic trips, August 22 and 23, did go out, and the weather was similar both days, partly sunny, medium winds, low 80s at most, and no rain. The waves were very bumpy both days, and the birds very similar both days—Cory's, Audubon's and Great Shearwaters, Wilson's and Band-rumped Storm-Petrels, and Black-capped Petrels (at a distance mostly, with their characteristic above-to-below the horizon arcings). Also we had Red Phalaropes, Pomarine Jaegers, a Masked Booby, and Sooty and Bridled Terns. We saw the usual inshore birds: Great Black-backed Gulls, Royal Terns, and Brown Pelicans.

My anti-seasickness regime of ginger capsules, preferably beginning a couple of days before the trip, Bonine before and on the trip, the Scopolamine patch, and Tums, kept me from getting sick. That and a careful diet before and during the trip, and my little sung calming mantra. But nothing kept me from being sleepy. Everyone seemed to be equally sleepy, a sort of narcolepsy or something in the air, or perhaps just due to a rocking boat lulling us all.

Unfortunately, day two added no new birds, but of course, I could not have known in advance.

Birding Musings after Pelagic Trips

Like a wobbly yellow ducky in a bathtub full of
 waves;
Our boat is bobbing wildly; I hope my gut behaves.
Yesterday the birds were great. I even added five.
Today is just a rerun. I guess that I'll survive.
Every bird that's added is a bird no longer sought.
Sort of like in fishing, when a fish that's caught is
 caught.
It's funny that the birds now are mostly one by one.
Nothing like last winter when the search had just
 begun.
Will they come out even, the time and birds
 remaining?
Whatever is the outcome, I'll do without
 complaining.
And so I'll keep on traveling, by boats and planes
 and cars.
All the time I'll say my prayers (and wish upon the
 stars).

AUGUST 25

I am on my way to St. Paul Island, my second trip there this year, without even stopping at home after my North Carolina trip. Up in Anchorage it's mostly cloudy, about 70 degrees. This flight stops in Dillingham on the way to St. Paul. Down below I don't see snow yet on the mountains, but the sky is wintry. Imagine what it will be like when I go to Barrow in October. I'll need to be sure that I don't have anywhere critical to go after that trip because the weather often delays flights in winter.

AUGUST 26

Yesterday was a great day—I got two new birds and now stand at the evil number of 666. I am the only nonleader birder here now on St. Paul Island, and the only person staying at the hotel. There are two leaders, Scott Schuette, who was here in May, and Dave Porter, one of the guides on my June trip to Nome.

When I arrived, the leaders, hearing that two of my goals were "anything with 'stint' in its name" and Sharp-tailed Sandpiper, took me out to a couple of "shores" here (edges of watery areas). Since it was such a wet spring and summer, the ponds have little shore and hardly any place for a shorebird to land.

Our first jaunt to Antone Slough produced some recently arrived shorebirds, six to seven Western Sandpipers and a newly-arrived Red-necked Stint, which cooperatively allowed us to take pictures. We then went to supper. It's halibut season here, so we will have that as a choice every night (and maybe at lunch, too).

After supper we headed west and checked out various bodies of water for gulls, ducks (unlikely now), and, of course, shorebirds. About halfway on an extended walk around Webster Lake, a Sharp-tailed Sandpiper flushed and landed not far away.

Any new bird now would be wonderful, but there aren't many realistic

A Red-necked Stint was a very welcome shorebird on St. Paul Island (August 27).

Sharp-tailed Sandpipers are best found in the ABA area on St. Paul Island in the fall (August 26).

possibilities. Of course, there are lots of unrealistic possibilities, and that's what I will look for. The two guides are here to help me, to some extent, but they are here mainly to record birds for the island survey. They are hoping to break the year record for number of species. Our goals are mostly compatible, although to them a lower-48 warbler is about as good as an Asian one. Whatever our goals, our sightings will depend on what birds arrive and whether we find them.

AUGUST 27

I have seen Sharp-tailed Sandpipers all three days, and Red-necked Stint the first two days. Yesterday was cloudy and windy and cold, while today is sunny, windy, and cold. We had our first (for the fall trip) Pectoral Sandpiper today, a Steller's Eider in female-type plumage, and an adult-plumaged Slaty-backed Gull.

Although I'm always, or almost always, hopeful of getting another bird here for the year, I probably should have scheduled a shorter trip. You never know. It's certainly a day-to-day thing, this doing a big year. No chance of predicting the birds—just like the weather.

AUGUST 28

It takes fortitude to sit on a rainy island without new birds and mostly without reading material or anything else to amuse myself. In an hour, one of the two leaders will pick me up for an afternoon of birding in the cold, windy drizzle. I can't say that I have no hope of a new bird, but it's very close to that. I'm just twiddling my thumbs until time to leave.

AUGUST 29

Unfortunately, St. Paul was and still is fogged in, and no planes are going in or out. I'm so disoriented. I had to cancel my motel for tonight in Anchorage and change my flight from Anchorage since I am unlikely to be able to get there in time. If I don't get out tomorrow, it impacts my California trip on Tuesday, and I need to do some client work before I leave to go on that trip.

AUGUST 30

It's still foggy out and little visibility. In seven-plus hours a plane is due in here. Early this morning about 4:00, I had a little adventure to break up the boredom. Getting up in the middle of the night, I put on my robe and picked up my room key from the chair beside my bed as usual before a trip down the hall to the bathroom. I shut and locked my room door and then realized that what I thought was my key in my hand were my eyeglasses. I was locked out of my room. The opposite of claustrophobia I suppose, but I was panicked. I was the only one in the hotel, and there was absolutely no one around to ask for assistance. It was nearly three hours until I was due to get up, and I had no bed.

I wandered down the hall, hoping to find someone. The office door had a list of phone numbers, including one to call after hours. After hesitating for about 15 minutes, not wanting to disturb someone in the middle of the night, I called from the hall phone. Someone answered but did not seem interested in helping me and hung up. I wasn't sure whether she would send someone or not, so I waited. About 5:00, I tried again, having found that the bedspread and blanket that I had pulled from the laundry room so I could curl up on the hall floor were not very comfortable, but no one answered. I left a message, but then decided as it was Saturday morning, probably no one would get the message for days. In my wanderings up and down the hall, I had noticed a small poster giving an alternate phone number to call, so I did.

I spoke to someone, who let me into my room 10 minutes later. So I got to sleep a bit more.

All's well that ends well, but there's still that misty fog.

My hope is fulfilled. Fourteen of us were loaded aboard a cargo plane about 12:30, two by two as into an ark, bound for Anchorage. So many people wanted to go on yesterday's canceled flight that they had to retrofit the cargo plane as a passenger plane.

Again today, I'm teary, thankful first for getting back in my room in the middle of the night, and second, for finally leaving St. Paul. If any new birds had appeared anytime after day one, I might have welcomed staying longer, but as it is . . . What I hope is that I can get back on tonight's flight to Texas. If not, I could try to get a car and look for White-tailed Ptarmigan around Anchorage. My heart's not in it though. I want to go home.

I need to explain what it's been like on St. Paul Island in the fall trip. The weather, of course, was wet. Birding there is a matter of driving the narrow, celery-lined gravel road to a chosen birding spot, climbing out of the van in rubber boots and raincoat, and if it's a narrow trail or heavy rain, adding rain pants. Then it's walking through thigh-high celery stalks and grass on a hidden, uneven-terrain "trail" over land thickly covered with wet vegetation, soaking legs and feet, and then staring out on a lake or the ocean, wind whipping you in your face, at very distant kittiwakes and Short-tailed Shearwaters, nearer Harlequin Ducks, shore-hugging Ruddy Turnstones and Rock Sandpipers, or tromping gravel roads between rock piles, and/or across higher elevations covered with grass squashed down by seals, or around a lake through celery without trails and no view of the ground beneath, with hidden caverns and rocks and ridges. Misty rain is still coming down. Or in another vain attempt to find a rarity, birding on St. Paul involves walking around

Fogbound

Staring out the window, foggy field of green.
Windmill's mostly hidden. Saddest thing I've seen.
Will it ever clear out? Will I ever fly?
All that I can think of—why's it happening? Why?
It's just an inconvenience. It's not a hurricane.
So I tell myself, but it's driving me insane!
My year is tightly scheduled—a blip becomes a
    mess.
The whole thing comes unraveled. My world
    descends in stress.
But wait, I can be cargo, replacing bags and things.
My hopes, from in the basement, ascend on silver
    wings.

and peering into crab pots that are piled in 20-foot-high stacks and extend in huge piles along the road, looking for little birds that have sought shelter there, or staring across a seal-strewn beach, or scanning the airport fence. More often than not, St. Paul birding is just watching an endless supply of Lapland Longspurs flying ahead as the van makes its way along the irregular road.

AUGUST 31

I birded Arctic Valley Road above Anchorage this morning but found no sign of any ptarmigan, in spite of two hikes way up to the rocky ridges. I was impressed with myself and how far I climbed. It was a beautiful upland mountainside, with willow brush in the narrow low depressions and stubby cold-tolerant plants nestled among and around the willows and extending as far as the eye could see. I will soon be flying to DFW, an all-night flight.

SEPTEMBER

Southwest Specialties

NEW BIRD SPECIES SEEN THIS MONTH: 25
TOTAL BIRD SPECIES BY THE END OF THE MONTH: 691
PLACES BIRDED: Texas, California, New Mexico, Arizona

SEPTEMBER 2

I'm hoping to get beyond 666 species today. My plane is scheduled to depart from DFW in 10 minutes for Los Angeles. It will be early afternoon there when I arrive. I plan to bird coastal Orange County today and am enthusiastic about the possibilities. It's high time that I do California birding before the breeding birds migrate south, out of the ABA area.

For years I have had a wintering Rufous Hummingbird, arriving generally in August. This year, after August came and went but no Rufie, I was quite sure that we were not going to have one visiting in our yard this year. Yesterday, as I blearily made my way through the house after having flown all night, she appeared, *tick-ticking* in the back of our yard, a female Rufous Hummingbird for the eighth winter. Having a wintering Rufous Hummingbird for multiple years has been, without any doubt, one of the most miraculous things of my entire life.

SEPTEMBER 3

Yesterday I left the airport in California to look for still-needed birds. At the Canyon parking lot (Back Bay Drive) were the typical expected birds, but not the hoped-for California Gnatcatcher. Across the bay, however, I spotted the first of many Elegant Terns.

I drove east along the coast toward Orange, where I was to stay last night. Just before dark I went to Crystal Cove State Park, which was supposed to have California Gnatcatchers. It does have singing California Thrashers. I got two new year birds in half a day of birding. Pretty good for so late in the year. A great start to a great trip.

My returning wintering Rufous Hummingbird female arrived at my yard on September 1.

Today I drove east, having plotted out a series of stops on my way to Ventura. The first place was a set-aside spot near a development (Ocean Trails) especially made for California Gnatcatchers. I did not hear or see one right away but ultimately heard a few and saw three of them. The first one scolded, popped up, and then darted across the trail. Clearly a gnatcatcher, by sound and locale. But I wanted a better view and ideally a picture. I got an out-of-focus picture of a pair of California Gnatcatchers climbing up a thin stalk. Their sounds seemed a bit more like cats than I had been led to believe by the tape, but they looked right—dark as they should be with a thin white tail edge and indistinct eye ring.

Shortly after I saw the first gnatcatcher, I took a trip down a side trail to the beach. As I came around a corner, I startled a small empid, which I realized (and confirmed by bird book and sound) was a Pacific-slope Flycatcher. I hadn't considered where I was going to get this bird, except they are on Santa Cruz Island where I was scheduled to go the next day.

After two new birds for the day, I am feeling pretty cheery but calmed down as I tried without success at the first so-called reliable spot (Sand Dune

Park in Manhattan Beach) for Spotted Doves, a countable introduced bird. I thought I might have one for a while, an oddly spotted Rock Pigeon near the park. I went to the other spot given in the most recent Southern California bird guide—Kenneth Hahn State Recreation Area. Eventually a couple of Spotted Doves sailed out of the woods across the mowed area above the park and landed in the trees. They were the right shape and color, but it was not a good view. It was good that on the last day of the trip I returned there and had a slightly closer view of two Spotted Doves.

When I got to Ventura Harbor, which took awhile because I got all turned around on my way, I checked in at my motel and then went to Foster Park, north of Ventura, to look for woodpeckers and flycatchers. Nothing new, but many Oak Titmice were calling and feeding young, and a Hairy Woodpecker zipped through.

A California Thrasher serenades me at sunset at Crystal Cove State Park, California (September 2).

An Elegant Tern cruises by our boat on the way to Santa Cruz Island, California (September 4).

SEPTEMBER 4

On the boat trip out to Santa Cruz Island this morning, the boat was filled to overflowing with kayaks, luggage, coolers, camping gear, and humans, including a birding group and a group celebrating some sort of annual event on the island. I saw Elegant Terns, Long-tailed and Pomarine Jaegers, murres, shearwaters, and many Red-necked Phalaropes.

The boat dropped off most of the gear and people at Scorpion Anchorage and then took the hardcore birders (mostly) to Prisoners' Harbor. Most of the other birders stayed near the docks at first. Hearing distant jays, I headed out on the road toward the sound. I did not see any jays, although I did see Bushtits, House Finches, Orange-crowned Warblers, a Black Phoebe, and a Pacific-slope Flycatcher. I went back toward the other birders, who had not seen jays either. We then heard jays where I had just been, so we all wandered back, with me tagging along a bit behind the group. I was worried about appearing to take advantage of their leaders' guidance when I had not paid for it. Unfortunately, as they wandered ahead of me, they saw a jay that I missed. Then, someone yelled out from the area near the dock, and I ran over. Two Island Scrub-Jays had decided to be friendly and visible, and everyone was able to see both of them, perched sometimes only 5 feet above us in the tree. It was a lifer, one of the main reasons for the trip to California—they are only possible on Santa Cruz Island.

SEPTEMBER 5

Today was much more of an adventure with more good news and more bad news than I had anticipated. At 4:30 A.M. I left Ventura, bound eastward to look for Le Conte's Thrashers and Mountain Quail. I'm sure the mountains were lovely, but it was dark as I carefully wound my way toward Maricopa up, over, and down the coastal mountains. The road leveled off on the interior plains, and I was able to start going a decent speed.

It was just beginning to get light when I suddenly saw a single stone, maybe 3 inches square just ahead of me. I was on top of the stone immediately after I saw it, unable to miss it. Blam! Whooosh! All of the air immediately left my right front tire, as I confirmed when I screeched to a halt and got out to check. Across the road was a darkened house, and next to it was a closed country store and gas station. Nothing else was around but fields and my injured metal-clicking rental car. I crossed to the store to check on its hours, but no sign was visible. A large dog began to bark in the yard next door and then loped over to check me out. I said friendly things, and the dog began to wag its tail just as the door of the house opened and a young man stepped out. I explained my problem, and he called the dog; together we all

To see an Island Scrub-Jay, one must go to Santa Cruz Island, California (September 4).

A Le Conte's Thrasher was one of the most welcome birds of the year (September 5).

walked over to check out my car. I had not even noticed that the tire rim was bent. He competently removed the mangled tire and replaced it with my rental car's puny spare. He advised me not to go over 50 miles per hour and also told me that the nearest garage was in Taft, some 30-plus miles away, just beyond the site where I had been headed to look for thrashers.

Carefully I drove onward, hoping my plastic tire would make it to Taft. There was no need to hurry. It wasn't even 7:00, and the garage would not open for a while. I plodded on and decided, without feeling much hope, to try for a Le Conte's Thrasher, which had been one of the hardest birds to get on my ABA life list, nearly impossible to find even with a leader's help, as it darted mouselike under and between desert plants in Arizona. I was pretty sure I would not find it in California and would probably be trying for it in Arizona as my ABA big year ended. But I wasn't likely to get it at all if I did not try, and I had nothing better to do until I got to Taft.

Just beyond Maricopa, I followed the guidebook's directions to take Petroleum Club Road and look and listen for thrashers, which I did. Nada. No surprise. I kept looking as I moved along the road and then pulled over and decided to walk across the patchily vegetated desert. The first sign of animal life besides the various tracks left in the dust was a perched-up Sage Sparrow, which immediately hopped down and tore off across the dirt, tail cocked upward.

Soon I noticed a distant bird scratching in the dust. I was excited to see that it had a thrasher size and shape. I quickly but unobtrusively sidled toward what turned out to a Le Conte's Thrasher, oblivious to me until I got just a little too close and it skittered off into the bushes.

Reality beckoned, so I proceeded to Taft and found the tire shop, where a very skilled mechanic bent the wheel rim back into workable shape and replaced the tire with a passable used one, all for a total cost of $23. I was on my way again, almost as good as new. It was only 8:45 A.M. I still had time to look for something else, although I was worried that the goal Mountain Quail would be silent and away from the roads by the time I got close to Mt. Pinos.

An hour later as I rounded a bend, a very upright quail with a skinny straight-up topknot sped across the road immediately in front of me. I stopped but realized right away that I needed to move off the road to avoid being rear-ended. I could hear more Mountain Quail talking gently just off the road, and I could see another quail's head over a dirt clump. I hurriedly

White-headed Woodpeckers were unmistakable among the other woodpeckers at Mil Potero Park in California (September 5).

parked 100 feet ahead, grabbed my camera, and rushed back. As I rounded a bend and got to the spot, two more Mountain Quail darted across. I tried for a picture but did not catch the birds in my photos. On the road again, I saw one more Mountain Quail about five minutes later—the second lifer in as many days.

What should I do? It was only 10:00. I decided to check out Mil Potero Park, which was supposed to be good for woodpeckers. And it surely was. At and near a dead pine, which I later termed the "mecca tree," I saw, in addition to Pygmy and White-breasted Nuthatches, a Northern Flicker, Acorn Woodpeckers, a Hairy Woodpecker, Oak Titmice, and my goal, two White-headed Woodpeckers. I never figured out whether it was sap or insects from the recently dead tree, but something in a couple of the ridges of the bark was absolutely magnetic for these birds. I explored Mt. Pinos after that and then put myself on autopilot for Indio, my scheduled resting spot for the night. What a day—three new year birds, one of which was a lifer. I was at 675.

SEPTEMBER 7

Early yesterday morning I headed to the Salton Sea after getting a bit confused about the route. I checked out places where the Yellow-footed Gull was likely, including the Salton Sea State Recreation Area, the Wister Unit of Imperial Wildlife area, Red Hill Marina (absolutely full of flying flies, maybe 1,500-plus immediately in the car and most probably still in the car), and Garst Street. Between Obsidian Butte and the water of the Salton Sea was a sizable gathering of pelicans as well as avocets, a few gulls, and some smaller shorebirds. Then I saw one large dark gull with yellow legs (and presumably yellow feet)—my goal Yellow-footed Gull.

Since my Southern California goals were mostly reached, I had been vacillating over whether I should gamble and take the time and effort to try for the Sinaloa Wren that amazingly had been in Patagonia, Arizona, almost two weeks. Now that I was so far east in California, and had seen the gull so early, I decided to go for the wren and began the long trip to southeastern Arizona. I took a quick detour to Riviera near the California/Arizona border for Ruddy Ground-Doves (not found) and then kept going to Sonoita, Arizona, a total of 585 miles for the day. This may seem crazy, but well worth it for a chance at a bird that was a first ABA area record. Now that I have lived in Texas for a while, I am used to driving such long distances to chase birds.

This morning I followed the car of another birder, and we joined the 30 or so birders at the road near the Patagonia Sonoita Creek Nature Conservancy area. About an hour later, we first heard the loud song of the wren, bursting out sporadically at different places along the creek. The bird itself was rarely seen either while singing or while silently darting between singing spots. While I heard it many times mostly before 8:00, I only saw a brief view of the wren. The Sinaloa Wren is certainly not a bird that I had expected to find in the ABA area.

At about noon, I began the boring, lengthy drive back toward Los Angeles, to turn in my rental car, and catch the flight home today. But the trip was not yet over. This morning I decided to try again for Nuttall's Woodpecker, a bird listed as "common" at many of the places that I had birded in the early part of the trip. I had stayed overnight in San Bernardino National Forest where the Nuttall's Woodpecker was supposed to be. I drove up and down some of the neighborhood streets of San Bernardino itself in the foothills and was delighted to see a small calling Nuttall's Woodpecker fly over me.

I drove toward Los Angeles, but still having a bit of extra time, I stopped again at the Kenneth Hahn State Recreation Area and saw two more Spotted Doves. I ended this trip at 678 species. In less than a week I'll be back in California, near Monterey for a couple of pelagic trips and some land birding.

SEPTEMBER 12

I am now on my way from DFW to San Jose via Denver, on one of my two scheduled flights today on Frontier Airlines. I love Frontier planes. Each one has an animal painted on it. This morning's flight was on a plane with a moose on the wingtips and on the tail. This one has a Rufous

Big Year Thoughts

I waited to see whether poetry would fill up my brain,
Now that I'd found myself stuck once again on a plane.
I thought of the birds that I'd seen in the months gone
    before,
And the as-of-yet-hidden birds, which were lying in store.
My mind traveled back to my innocence in late December.
What had I been thinking? I really just couldn't remember.
Did I think that I'd sail through this year and not be
    demented?
Did I think that this unceasing mania could be prevented?
I think I just launched out and trusted the fates to protect
    me,
And gave not a thought to the things that might rile or
    upset me.
Perhaps when it's done and my life is less of a blur,
I will find that what's happened is what was "supposed"
    to occur.

Hummingbird on the wing, and presumably also on the tail, and reminded me of Rufie, "my" female Rufous Hummingbird.

This is my last scheduled trip of September. I expect that I will go somewhere else as soon as I can figure out where and when, probably South Texas and Colorado.

SEPTEMBER 14

Yesterday morning at 5:30 I joined a full boat of birders at Fisherman's Wharf in Monterey. Before we even left the dock, we saw a Black-crowned Night-Heron in the dock lights, balanced on a line from the boat, carefully leaning out and stabbing a fish out of the water. Almost as soon as it was light, we started seeing the very smooth sea and Sooty Shearwaters, which this year were much reduced in numbers (we were told later).

After seeing many Pink-footed Shearwaters, I was elated when the first of a couple of Flesh-footed Shearwaters appeared. By then we had also seen Ashy Storm-Petrels, Buller's Shearwaters, and South Polar Skuas. Other birds that we had already seen early during the trip included all three jaegers (mostly Pomarine and Parasitic), both Red-necked and Red Phalaropes, Sabine's Gulls, and Rhinoceros and Cassin's Auklets. Storm-petrels began to

A South Polar Skua is a regular off the California coast (September 13).

A Red Phalarope flies across calm waters off Monterey (September 13).

appear in huge rafts on the horizon just after a single Leach's Storm-Petrel zoomed by the boat. Among the storm-petrels, with a lot of effort and patience I was able to see the single Wilson's Storm-Petrel (not new), a few Black Storm-Petrels (larger, slower flight), and a Fork-tailed Storm-Petrel (much paler, and difficult to see against the silvery water).

It was a great trip, with seven new birds (most of which were seen again on today's storm-petrel trip). It was another lovely cool day and mostly cloudy, so we were not cooked by the sun.

SEPTEMBER 15

My first stop today was at the Moonglow Dairy, where a Little Stint had been seen the day before. Although I was the first birder there, I was soon joined by about 30 others. Unfortunately, while many eyes increase the chances of finding a bird, they do not help one find a bird that has departed.

About noon I gave up and decided to go birding at Molera State Park for possible Vaux's Swift (maybe too early for them to be migrating through), Hermit Warbler, and/or Cassin's Vireo. I had an enjoyable, quite birdy walk for about three hours. The highlight, a single Cassin's Vireo, was seen early, slowly hunting the branches overhanging the water, yellowish sides with dull greenish side streaking, gray-green back, white belly, white eye ring. I also saw many Townsend's Warblers, Steller's Jays, Bushtits, and Chestnut-backed Chickadees, as well as a fly-by Belted Kingfisher, a little family of calling Nuttall's Woodpeckers, a couple of Bewick's Wrens, an American Redstart, a Spotted Towhee, and a Wrentit. As I drove out of the park, a covey of about 25 California Quail was busily scratching in the dirt along the road.

SEPTEMBER 16

This morning I went to Muir Woods, which I had never visited before. I had a great morning, peering up into the tops of the sequoias just in case a Spotted Owl was visible. You just can't see too many Spotted Owls. I did not find my real goal, Hermit Warbler, although I saw many flocks of Chestnut-backed Chickadees and Townsend's Warblers, and many Hairy Woodpeckers, a couple of American Robins, a Hermit Thrush, Brown Creepers, and a Winter Wren.

In the afternoon, I drove to Pinnacles National Monument with Lawrence's Goldfinches on my mind. My mind is the only place they were, sadly. In the real world I found House Finches, Lesser Goldfinches, Western Scrub-Jays, Black Phoebes, Phainopeplas, California Towhees, and California Quail. That was it for this California trip. Eight birds was very good, but of course they were "needed." My year total was 686.

SEPTEMBER 17

This morning my theme song was "Do You Know the Way to San Jose?" I didn't. I drove 101 north, and then I turned around because it had been over 10 miles since the San Jose sign. But I could not find any sign of the road I needed, so I drove south, did not find the road, drove north, and after an agonizingly long time, found the road to the San Jose airport. It was a good thing that I gave myself plenty of time. Now I'm off to Denver and then home.

SEPTEMBER 22

I have been on the road from home since about 3:00 A.M., driving west to Arizona. I hope that the reported Plain-capped Starthroat is still in Patagonia.

My reward for a very long day of travel was the Plain-capped Starthroat in Patagonia, Arizona (September 22).

My goal is to get as close to Patagonia as I can today and to be at Paton's early tomorrow. Paton's is a privately owned residence along Sonoita Creek adjacent to the Nature Conservancy preserve. The owners have graciously opened their backyard to all bird lovers, providing feeders and even a tent and chairs for the comfort of their visitors. Maybe I'll take a quick look/listen for the Sinaloa Wren, too; I would like a picture.

I will also try for Baird's Sparrow, Mexican Chickadee, and Bendire's Thrasher in Arizona, and possibly in New Mexico.

SEPTEMBER 23

I drove yesterday for about 15 hours, with the minimum number of stops and arrived in Patagonia before dark, jumped out of the car, walked around the Paton house, stared at the hummingbird feeders, and within 10 minutes had seen the Plain-capped Starthroat. I had not thought I would get it at all, but I gambled and won.

Today I went back to Paton's first thing, saw the Plain-capped Starthroat again, and then did an unsuccessful vigil at the Sinaloa Wren spot. Then I went to the San Rafael Grasslands for Baird's Sparrow. A little flock of Horned Larks was all I found. On the way back a couple of birds flew across the

The San Rafael Grasslands, Arizona, are where Baird's Sparrows winter (September 23).

wooded road near Patagonia, and one of them was a well-seen Red-naped Sapsucker. I'm at 688 species. I am in Portal now, planning to go to Rustler Park tomorrow for the Mexican Chickadee and possibly try for Bendire's Thrasher near here.

SEPTEMBER 25

I stayed in El Paso last night. I am going to go directly down to the Valley for the birds I still need (Muscovy Duck and Hook-billed Kite) rather than go home first.

Yesterday, although I missed Bendire's Thrasher both in New Mexico and Arizona, was a good day. I began very early, jumping in my car 10 minutes after I got up and heading without ado to Rustler Park, *the* place to get Mexican Chickadee in the United States. Unlike on my summer trip, the road was dry, the sun was shining, and I found wonderful birdy flocks. Bridled Titmice were the core of most flocks. Warblers abounded—Townsend's, Black-throated Gray, Orange-crowned, and a couple of Hermit Warblers. I saw Hepatic Tanagers, Bushtits, a Spotted Towhee, a singing Cassin's Vireo, and Mexican Jays. Near Rustler's Park, the tall pines were brimming with

Mexican Chickadees, mixed in with Olive Warblers, Townsend's Warblers, Ruby-crowned Kinglets, Steller's Jays, and at least one more Hermit Warbler. The gentle sun on the pine needles scented the whole area, both invigorating me in the cool air and making me want to curl up to sleep in the warm sun.

I had to leave to look for Bendire's Thrashers though. I drove up and down Stateline Road east of Portal, the back roads of Rodeo, New Mexico, and Gin Road between the two. I saw no thrashers, except one Curve-billed Thrasher. I gave up and headed to Texas. I'll need to go back to Arizona for Bendire's Thrasher and Baird's Sparrow sometime in the next three months, probably more than once, and also try to find Ruddy Ground-Doves.

Ninety-six days are left in 2008. That is not much time. Can I get 10 more, to 700, by then? It sounds simple, but some toughies remain. It's just one by one.

More Big Year Thoughts

Mindless mind, brainless brain.
Some things are just too hard to explain.
Roads keep winding, never-ending,
What's with all this time I'm spending?
But no matter. I keep going,
All the while, not really knowing,
When I get there, will I find it?
If I do not, will I mind it?
Three more months—I've got to do it.
Otherwise I'll know I blew it.
I tell myself; I must remember:
No more chances past December.

I saw a series of birds fly by at sunset at Salineño, Texas (September 25).

One of the fly-by birds at Salineño was a Black-crowned Night-Heron.

SEPTEMBER 26

I got to the Valley and Salineño last night about 5:50, which was almost two hours before sunset, two hours of not seeing Muscovy Ducks. Nobody else appeared except the Border Patrol (for a brief friendly chat). It was a gentle sunset, gradual, and accompanied by a succession of evening and night birds. About 35 Wood Storks came in to roost on the island up the river, followed by a couple of fly-by Common Ground-Doves, a Red-billed Pigeon, a couple of Mottled Ducks, an invasion of fluttery nighthawks (those I studied seemed to be Lesser Nighthawks), a single Black-bellied Whistling-Duck, a high-flying Roseate Spoonbill, an adult Black-crowned Night-Heron, and at 7:48, calling Common Pauraques, when it was nearly impossible to see anymore. I gave up and found a room in Rio Grande City.

This morning, determined to be there before dawn, I left early, arriving at Salineño at 6:11. It was very dark, with a crescent moon and stars. Mexican ambient light let me see the silhouettes of the far shore and the shine of the water through the patchy fog. At 6:25, three or four Great Horned Owls started hooting, mostly across the river, but one was on the island and not a Mexican owl. I also heard Lesser Nighthawk trills and a short burst of Eastern

Screech-Owls. A Great Blue Heron croaked at 6:32 as the stars were becoming slightly fainter in the sky, and ospreys started checking the river. The Great Horned Owls were still calling at 6:57 when two Wood Storks landed in silhouette across the river. The sound of birds increased—Olive Sparrow, Northern Cardinal, Ringed Kingfisher, and Blue-gray Gnatcatchers.

Then at 7:12 as I was peering up and down the river, I caught a peripheral glimpse of a big bird behind me—a long-necked, gooselike, slow-flapping silent bird flying up the river but over the northern shore where I stood. Having spun around, I saw that it had white in the wings. And it was gone—one Muscovy Duck. I waited for more Muscovies or for a Hook-billed Kite to join the many vultures at their liftoff between 9:48 and 10:13, but there were none. I headed home for some much-needed client time.

OCTOBER

The 700-Club

OCTOBER 1

My plane is due to take off in 20 minutes. I did not expect to be here in Washington. When I inquired on Birdchat about finding the various "chickens" that I still need for the year, experts e-mailed me to say "better now than later." Sooty Grouse and Dusky Grouse, which are mostly separated geographically, get harder and harder to find after snowfall, because they go upslope. Most everyone told me that Washington state was the place to go for both of them. In theory, I could get four chickens in Washington (five if I went to eastern Washington, which I probably will not do), plus two owls and Vaux's Swifts if I were lucky.

After church three days ago I went online, bought cheap round-trip tickets to Seattle, and reserved a car and a room for tonight only, since I don't know exactly what I'll do when I get to Seattle. I could go down to Eugene, Oregon, where a Wood Sandpiper was found yesterday, which might stay around, but . . . I'm excited at the possibilities for this sort of out-of-the-blue trip. Maybe I won't be so desperate when I take the inevitable Colorado/New Mexico trip in a couple of weeks (not yet scheduled).

I've gone through the Washington

Big Year

B is for "boy"; this has been hard to do!
I is for "ignorance"; that's part of it too.
G is for "great" when a new bird's been found.
Y is for "yelp" when the bird's not around.
E is for "each" of the birds of this year
A is for "all" that it's taken; I fear that
R is for "rest" that I'll need when I'm done,
In spite of the truth: it's really been fun!

state bird guide numerous times. If I get Sooty Grouse today (or tomorrow, which is more likely), I can go for White-tailed Ptarmigan (which in theory I could see later in Colorado) or I could go straight for Gray Partridge (not in Colorado) and Chukar (which I did not find in Colorado in April), or for owls (Boreal and Northern Saw-whet), which are also possible in Colorado, Vaux's Swift (leaving the country soon), Virginia Rail (should be findable in Texas), and Dusky Grouse (also in New Mexico and Colorado).

OCTOBER 2

Yesterday, after I picked up my rental car, I drove north into Seattle and then west toward water. I got lost a few times but eventually found the Bainbridge Island ferry dock and parked. The ferry was huge with multiple car decks and multiple passenger decks above that. It seemed to stretch across the entire waterway between Seattle and the island. It was a silent, smooth ride, and the Seattle skyline was beautiful.

On Bainbridge Island, I drove north and west toward Port Angeles. About five miles before Port Angeles, I found Deer Park Road, a winding, very narrow scenic road that climbs steadily, first paved and then packed gravel for about 16 miles, with sheer drops off the road edge with no wall to break a fall. It was nerve-wracking as I very carefully negotiated the curves, praying that no one was barreling down the road toward me or careening around corners. I met only a couple of cars, however, and all went fine. I saw few birds, mainly a few juncos and an American Kestrel, but no grouse, even though I went almost all the way to the top. I turned around as it got dark and even more carefully wound my way back down. At least in the dark I could have seen headlights of any approaching cars, but there were none.

Today I planned to go up to the Hurricane Ridge visitor center west of Deer Park, where Sooty Grouse had been reported very recently. It was still dark when I reached the lit-up sign along the deserted road informing me that the road ahead was now closed on Mondays through Thursdays. It was Thursday. What should I do? I turned around and went up Deer Park Road again. At least I was familiar with it. The early morning had fewer cars and more birds, many American Robins and Varied Thrushes on the road, the sound of Golden-crowned Kinglets, Dark-eyed Juncos, Common Ravens, and Red-shouldered Hawks. Again, I found no grouse, even though I drove all the way to the top. By this time it was raining gently, and the clouds were closing in. I was worried that the dirt roads would be slick when wet, so I reluctantly started back down the mountain. Shortly after I got back on the pavement, I called Dave. Just as I started to tell him that I had not found any grouse, out from the thick greenery at the edge of the road stepped a brown grouse, with a red-orange comb, a Sooty Grouse. I burst out with "Oh, my God" and tried to stop and get a picture, but the grouse was gone.

I headed toward Tacoma, glancing up continuously for swifts. None. Although it had rained earlier, it began to lighten up a little. I went toward Ellensburg, hoping to get out of the rain and find a Gray Partridge. In Ellensburg, I checked every single road and yard that was supposed to possibly harbor Gray Partridges, and then I checked all the sites again and drove a couple of additional roads that looked promising.

OCTOBER 4

Yesterday morning I retraveled the alleged partridge roads around Ellensburg and then went farther east to a Vantage area campground on Huntsinger Road, where Chukars are supposed to hang out. There were a couple of flocks of California Quail, with more in the surrounding sage. I saw no Chukars and heard only one brief call of a Chukar. As I drove south of the campground, I heard more and saw a head very briefly. After obsessing over whether to count an essentially heard-only bird, I did count Chukar.

By this time it was about 4:00, and I decided to give up, at least for a while, on anything gallinaceous. I sped west, intending to get to Monroe's Frank Wagoner Elementary School where I had been told that Vaux's Swifts were overnighting in a tall chimney during migration. I nearly did not get to the school before dark. I heard from the young woman who was doing the official swift count that about 300 swifts had already swirled their way into the chimney. I saw just one, a very unsatisfactory view, and darkness fell.

During the day, I had talked by phone to John Puschock, a Seattle bird guide with Birdtreks and owner of Zugunruhe Birding Tours, whom I had not yet met, who was keeping track of whether a Wood Sandpiper that had hung around west of Eugene, Oregon, was still there. He wanted the sandpiper for his lower-48 list, and I wanted it for my big year. About 3:00, he had gotten notice that the Wood Sandpiper was still around. We arranged for me to go to his house after my swift visit and to leave in the middle of the night for Oregon. There was no point in leaving earlier than that. We just wanted to arrive soon after dawn.

John and his wife had made up a bed for me to get a few hours sleep, after which he and I groggily, but with anticipation, climbed into my car at about 1:30 this morning and drove south about 300 miles in the pouring, wind-blown rain. The nasty weather required great concentration, which was not easily found as we became more and more sleep deprived. We reached Fern Ridge Reservoir west of Eugene at about 7:15 just as the rain stopped. We walked between flooded areas toward three people who were looking at the Wood Sandpiper through their spotting scopes. The Wood Sandpiper was waggling its rear end as it fed at the far edge of the water. Periodically it flew up and returned to the same general area. After about 10 minutes, all shore-birds took to the air, spooked by a Peregrine Falcon. The Wood Sandpiper and a Greater Yellowlegs, staying close together, flew toward and directly over us, giving me a chance for photos.

John and I looked around a bit to see what else was around and then walked back to the car, reaching it just as the rain resumed. Good timing. We loaded up our scopes and, after evaluating several possibilities, headed east to Redmond and then north to Yakima, Washington, to Vantage to look for Gray Partridges and Chukars, and then to Seattle. It was a nice drive, but we saw no "chickens" at all.

OCTOBER 5

This morning I did not get up very early, although if I had, I might have seen the ptarmigan(s) that had tracked up the new snow at Mount Baker by the time I arrived at 9:30. The tracks were nice, but a real live ptarmigan would have been much better than ptarmigan "ptracks" (my term when I posted a picture on my Web site). Mount Baker was lightly snow covered near the top, but the pavement was covered with slush and did not appear dangerous. I am glad that I went up, but I did not do more than walk the rec-ommended trail (Table Mountain) before snow started falling quite heavily. I was worried about the road up the mountain and left by noon.

I had extra time before going back to Monroe for the swifts (assuming that they had not all migrated south). I slowly drove south and still got to the school about two hours too early. I spent the time reading and repacking my luggage for the flight home.

About 5:50 P.M., I locked the car and strolled closer to the school, thinking I had seen a swift. Soon Vaux's Swifts were gathering over my head, gently twittering in their tiny voices. I saw 30, 100, maybe 350, beginning about 6:10.

Ptarmigan "ptracks" just are not quite what I was looking for at Mount Baker, Washington (October 5).

Vaux's Swifts swirl into a chimney in Monroe, Washington (October 5).

A few went in earlier, but about 6:20, they started in earnest. I got pictures of the chimney top plus multiple swifts as they swirled and plunged in. By 6:30 about half of the swifts were down, and it was too dark to get any more photos. I called John Puschock to tell him I'd seen the swifts, called home, and then headed for the airport for my midnight flight home.

I will have a day to recuperate before I go back west to California and Alaska.

OCTOBER 7

I am on my way to San Francisco for my Bodega Bay pelagic trip on Thursday (October 9). I have today and tomorrow in California to do land birding. I plan to try for Virginia Rail and Lawrence's Goldfinch in areas around San Francisco Bay. I probably will not get both, and may not get either, and I have little hope (but some) of getting a year bird on the pelagic trip, but I must try. We could see a Xantus's or Craveri's Murrelet or some wondrous vagrant. The most likely new bird is Ross's Gull in Barrow, where I go after California.

OCTOBER 8

After I arrived in San Francisco, I picked up my rental car and headed north to check out some of the marshes near Point Reyes for Virginia Rails. For months now, I have bemoaned the fact that I just have not gotten around to getting Virginia Rail for the year. It's true that when Debra Corpora and I were in Oregon in late February, we had undoubtedly heard a Virginia Rail in a marsh, but I had decided to wait for an actual sighting, or at least a clearer audio.

At Limantour Beach in California at a scenic marsh with dense, long cattail-like leaves, I got lots of audio and an oh-so-brief skulky glimmer of a Virginia Rail. I waited for a better view, but even though the bird was within 2–3 feet of me, it blended too well with the vegetation.

I wound around the coastal hills to Bodega Bay as dusk approached to check out the place where I was to meet the Shearwater Journeys boat in a couple of days and saw a silhouetted Great Horned Owl on a nearby power line, and then went to Rohnert Park.

Today I headed south to Lawrence's Goldfinch country (Mines Road in

A Yellow-billed Magpie in Santa Clara County, California (October 8).

Alameda and Santa Clara counties and into Stanislaus County). On the trip I had the quintessential stereotypic California experience, sitting stuck or barely moving in traffic. After three and a quarter hours, I got to Livermore and headed south on Mines Road, a beautiful, golden-hill area, with a winding, sometimes precarious road. Along the way, I stopped at places identified in the Northern California bird guides as being good for the little wandering goldfinches, typically areas with water. Everywhere was green, and birds were evident in the pleasant cool morning. Highlights included Spotted and California Towhees, California Quail, Wild Turkeys, Oak Titmice, Western Bluebirds, two Red-breasted Sapsuckers, and a Fox Sparrow.

At the Junction Café/Restaurant in Santa Clara County, I stopped to have lunch and watch birds under the trees. The noisiest birds were two Yellow-billed Magpies cruising between the trees and periodically flying down to the ground. Many Lark Sparrows, as well as Golden-crowned Sparrows, White-breasted Nuthatches, Oak Titmice, House Finches, and Yellow-rumped Warblers busily worked the area. A juvenile yellowish finch came down to the ground to drink from the rivulet of water coming from the restaurant drain pipe. After studying the bird book, I decided that it might be a Lawrence's Goldfinch, and I might be hearing them singing in the trees. But I was not sure.

Deciding that no more goldfinches were going to come down to the water for a while, I continued south and then east to Frank Raines Park, where I had my best year view of a Nuttall's Woodpecker, but little else. I reversed course about 4:30, stopping again for half an hour at the Junction stop where invisible California Quail had started up their *shi-poop-ee* calls all around and Mountain Bluebirds and a Nuttall's Woodpecker had arrived.

I stopped again at the pond across from the Digger Pine Ranch, where I thought I'd heard Lawrence's Goldfinches earlier, but had decided that it was just wishful thinking. After I hung out a few minutes on the roadside, a little finch flock appeared, three of them landing in a leafless sapling near the road, where a Western Bluebird already was perched. When I lifted my binoculars to check them out, I was stunned to see that two of them were honest-to-goodness adult Lawrence's Goldfinches with their dapper black goatees and forehead patches. Then another bird arrived and spooked them all, but it was okay.

Two Lawrence's Goldfinches were finally found after searching all day (October 8).

Oddly enough, I was a bit taken aback. What was I going to look for the next day? I had learned by checking my e-mails that my pelagic trip tomorrow had been canceled because of a gale warning. While that was disappointing, I was of course a bit relieved that I would not have to face seasickness possibilities.

OCTOBER 9

I made no attempt to get up at or before the crack of dawn today but leisurely headed out toward Point Reyes, cutting cross country at Novato. It was another beautiful morning, but I felt a bit aimless. How could I just bird, when somewhere (not in California as far as I could figure out) were birds I still needed and might be able to find? I birded at Five Brooks, with the expected birds plus Pine Siskins, a pair of Belted Kingfishers, and both kinglets.

OCTOBER 10

I am in Seattle on my way to Alaska, and now I learn about a Yellow-legged Gull in Newfoundland, apparently one that was there last fall, a La Sagra's Flycatcher in Florida, and a Dusky Warbler in California, and I'm going to Alaska. There's something wrong with this picture.

Ann and I boarded the plane for Anchorage, just a bit late. She's the one whose gift of *The Big Year* got me into all this, who has encouraged my big year and is an indefatigable, enthusiastic birder. Her goals for this trip are Ivory Gull, Ross's Gull, and polar bear. We hear an announcement concerning uncertainty about this flight due to the windy Anchorage weather. Two flights have already been canceled, but in spite of the wind, we're now leaving for Anchorage.

Obsession's my name, and birding's my game.
It won't be the same, when this year is over.
I've had "hunting" to do, but soon I'll be through,
I expect I'll be blue, no longer a rover.
The effort's been fun, though I've been on the run,
And I've hardly begun to know what I'm doing.
The hopes and the fears, the laughter and tears,
My life in arrears, the fabric ungluing.
No sorrow or grieving, no doubt—just believing:
This "thing" needs achieving, and so I'll keep at it.
The end now in sight, not wrong and not right,
It's been a good fight, but still I say "drat it"!

OCTOBER 13

I'm sitting at the Barrow terminal in the plane, expecting to depart about 11:00. It's quite light outside, with a bit of a breeze.

It's been a great few days. We arrived in Barrow on October 10. The next day after a late breakfast, since it does not get light before 9:00 A.M. in Barrow, we drove out to explore. Roads were snowy, some snowpacked, but mostly the roads were easily driven. Every now and then we found sheltered areas where the strong wind had not cleared off unpacked snow and there were deep, wide tire tracks through the drifts. Our rental car was an all-wheel drive and did very well, sometimes even plowing a new track.

At first we found very few gulls, until we approached the first of three relatively recent whale-kill harvest areas. These areas had been emptied of the majority of the bones and meat but were a bit bloody yet with remnant hunks of whale and a few large bones. The attending gulls were mostly adult Glaucous-winged Gulls, some nonadults, and just a couple of Glaucous Gulls, but no rarities. We saw a few Black-legged Kittiwakes, but we were still looking nervously for our goal birds, hoping we hadn't wasted our money and time to get to this remote area. All I "needed" for this trip were Ross's Gulls. I was hoping for Ivory Gulls, too, because they are beautiful and because I had gotten my lifer this year. Like Ann, I also hoped for a polar bear.

Just before we got to the last accessible area before the off-limits point (polar bears are too likely and dangerous there), we noticed a few smaller gulls coming overland toward the point—Ross's Gulls! In the low light, due to the low cloud cover and low sun, it took awhile to see the pinkness very well, but they were pink. Unlike other gulls, Ross's Gulls are a distinctly blushing pink, leaving me awestruck at their beauty. We saw many Ross's Gulls over the two full days

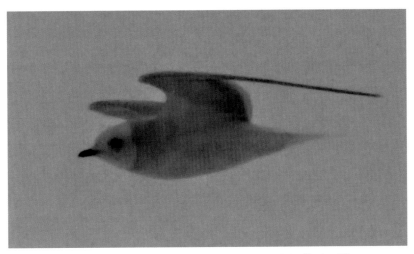

My first Ross's Gull was one of over a thousand Ross's Gulls at Barrow, Alaska (October 11).

An immature Ivory Gull has black feather tips on its wings and tail (Barrow, Alaska, October 11).

A ghostly adult Ivory Gull glides by land in Barrow, Alaska (October 12).

that we birded in Barrow. I estimated about 300 on day one, but when we made an attempt to count them yesterday when we were driving along the water's edge, we reached over 1,100. Almost all of them were flying west to east, and nearly all were adult "pinkies." On both days, two adult Ivory Gulls came by. We also saw a black-faced, back, and wing-tip-spotted first winter Ivory Gull.

We drove back and forth along the ocean, periodically stopping, rarely getting out of the car because of the icy cold wind—probably 20–25 degrees and 20–25 mile-per-hour wind. We noticed a couple of cars with people staring fixedly toward an off-white mass out toward the ice on the south side of the point. The lump was three sleeping polar bears, one adult and two half-size "cubs." The presumed mother pulled herself to her feet as did the cubs, but they did not go anywhere. Very photogenic.

Yesterday we also saw a single big polar bear out on the thin inland bay ice. He carried a piece of something dark, which looked at first like a person's jacket but was probably a piece of animal hide. He would toss the thing up in the air and go galloping toward it, shake it, worry it, and then repeat. Every now and then he would pound his front feet on the relatively thin ice and make a hole, through which he would disappear, reemerging again, still carrying the dark thing, which gradually decreased in size. Eventually he turned toward us and trotted our way. Oops! But when he reached land, he found what appeared to be a large slab of whale, grabbed it, and started dragging it across the ice away from us. Because of the size of the slab, he kept stepping

Birders don't mind seeing mammals, too—three photogenic polar bears in Barrow, Alaska (October 11).

on it, causing him to stumble a bit, after which he would grab the slab again and try to make further progress across the ice. After he was out on the ice quite a way, he set to work munching on the slab, and we went back to the mesmerizing task of pinky watching. It was almost impossible to leave them, but we did to wander a few inland roads and ate and slept.

Yesterday on one of our coast-edge drives, I saw a white lump along the road ahead and then saw it move, a totally white arctic fox. We saw five or six yesterday, a couple of which were not quite into their full white winter dress.

In addition to gulls and mammals, we saw many Long-tailed Ducks, White-winged and Black Scoters, a flock of Spectacled Eiders (identified from my pictures that night) and a single Common Raven. We did not see any owls. Some of the roads that would have been good to explore were just too snowy to risk driving on, especially for birds already seen on other trips.

We are in the air now (11:22), departing for home exactly on time. Down below it's all snow covered and white clouds. Winter is here. The sun through the window makes me purr like a soft, fuzzy cat.

OCTOBER 19

Yesterday I drove 738 miles from home to St. Louis. The first place I tried for Eurasian Tree Sparrow (ET) (a countable introduced bird with a limited range) was the yard of Bill Groth who was reported to have ETs in his yard. Yesterday, we could not find any, nor could we find any at the neighbor's. Having nested, the ETs have dispersed widely. What to do? St. Louis to Fort Worth is a long drive. He told me about Riverland Park, another site for ETs, and I went online and found some more places to go, which was a good thing.

This morning after a night in the motel with Shar, our dog that I had taken along for companionship, I went to the closest place along the river, North Riverfront Park. While the park had no ETs, I heard a few hiding in a dense bush across the road from the park, but I did not dare wander into the yard. It's often difficult, but important, for birders to respect property rights of others (even though birds do not) and refrain from trespassing while birding (and otherwise).

The next stop was Riverland Park. At first no ETs were visible. When I drove farther down the road and turned around, I saw three of them perched in a nearly leafless bush out in the marshy field. It was a great view, but when I reached for my camera, they flew away.

I'm at 699, with no immediate chase plans. What's next? How will I get to 700?

OCTOBER 21

I'm home, between birding. As I came out of the post office, a Northern Mockingbird was singing in the brisk, springlike air. Suddenly I felt as if I were surfacing from the obsessed big year push, that life and birding were beautiful, and that I was happy to be hearing a mockingbird singing and not be chasing or hardly even thinking about chasing birds.

OCTOBER 22

Of course, I'm back to chasing, or will be, as soon as my car is through its routine maintenance appointment. I'm excited that I am going to Florida tomorrow. I e-mailed Larry Manfredi to see whether Smooth-billed Anis were being seen in Florida. Although I have checked for them unsuccessfully each of the three times that I have been in Florida this year, rumor has it that they still might exist there. To my delighted surprise, Larry e-mailed yesterday saying that he had just seen some Smooth-billed Anis feeding young and that it was a good time to come. When I checked airfare last night, I just could not commit to spending so much money for the last-minute flight. But early this morning I could not sleep with the excitement and the certainty that I needed to go. I learned that Larry is available on Friday. I bit the bullet and reserved to go tomorrow (Thursday afternoon) and return home on Monday. I reserved a room only for Thursday night. I don't know which day I'll go up to look for budgies (my other main goal). "Budgies" are Budgerigars, the common parakeet cage bird from Australia. Although not native to North America, like a number of escaped birds of the parrot family, breeding colonies can become established in the wild in the United States and eventually be ruled "countable." Newly escaped birds, however, are no more countable as wild birds than chickens or domestic ducks.

If I finish birding early in Florida, I can try for a standby flight, or I can look for a rarity. I'll look through the Florida guide on the plane. With any luck, the Smooth-billed Ani will be number 700.

OCTOBER 23

I am on my way to Florida. Oddly enough, the people around me who noticed me perusing the Florida birding book were interested in my big year. One asked me whether I was going to be on Larry King—I don't think so.

OCTOBER 27

To cut to the chase (or after it, actually), I got the bird and then some. I arrived in Miami just after midnight on October 24, got to the car rental place, found my way out of Miami, and drove south to Florida City, about 36 miles.

After about four hours of sleep, I got up, showered, and went down to the motel breakfast, where I met Larry Manfredi and his son Phillip (no school that day). I drove the three of us to Old Griffin Road, Fort Lauderdale, to the spot where I had looked at least three times earlier this year. Within two minutes we saw two Smooth-billed Anis on an electric line, and more kept appearing. We saw seven of them (at least), some of which were going in and out of a thick tree (feeding young apparently). Hopefully soon more little anis will grow up there. Number 700! From now until December 31, anything else is gravy, or frosting (but not both). Seeing 700 bird species in the ABA area is a goal that many birders aim for in their lifetime; I'm astounded that I was able to do it this year—and the year is not over.

What should I do next? I had learned from Larry that Common Mynas are now officially countable since the Florida bird record committee and the ABA committee had both voted to accept them to be countable in Florida. We checked around Florida City and found some near a Burger King. While I had seen Common Mynas earlier in the year, those sightings were before the vote and did not count because these mynas were originally introduced into the ABA area. Number 701.

Smooth-billed Anis in Fort Lauderdale, Florida, was number 700 for my big year (October 24).

Common Mynas are definitely common in Florida City, Florida (October 24).

Also, unbeknown to me, apparently wild, countable Greater Flamingos had returned to the Everglades since I had last discussed them with Larry. Hurricanes had scattered the ones there in previous years. We headed south to Flamingo, Florida, trailering Larry's well-used motorboat to find us a flamingo. We had sandwiches, loaded our rain gear and binoculars into the little boat, and putt-putted away, saving time by taking a shortcut across what is usually an island but which we could cross because of very high water. Staying fairly distant from the shore because of shallow water where normally mud was found, we made a wide loop and started scanning the shore. I had assumed that we would see just a couple of flamingos at best. When I saw seven or eight pink birds up against the shore in the distance, I assumed that they were Roseate Spoonbills. But those were the flamingos—*eight* Greater Flamingos (seven light immatures and one darker adult). Number 702.

After staring long and hard at the flamingos, we headed back, faster this time, since Phillip wanted his dad to go really fast. We zipped along and soon were back in Flamingo. It was too late to head out anywhere else where I might find another year bird. I went back to Florida City, having decided to try for the reported La Sagra's Flycatcher the next day.

On October 25 I left the motel long before dawn and drove south to Big Pine Key/No Name Key where the La Sagra's Flycatcher had been reported once on October 9. It was unlikely to still be around but was worth a try. I stayed two and a half hours until 10:00, getting eaten alive by tiny flying insects that crept through my socks and into my hair and up my sleeves, and bit everywhere. I'm still itching. Otherwise it was a pleasant cool morning with White-eyed Vireos, Blue-gray Gnatcatchers, a Palm Warbler, Northern Parula, Orange-crowned Warbler, and Northern Waterthrush, and only one flycatcher heard, a Great Crested Flycatcher. Close, but not La Sagra's.

It was time to head north for the only other new bird I could think of that Florida might provide, the budgie in Hernando Beach. This was a much longer drive than I had anticipated. By the time I arrived, I had driven over 530 miles for the day, the last 15 of which were up and down the streets of Hernando Beach where the last remaining Budgerigars had been seen. Although for years huge populations had survived in Florida, they had dwindled precipitously and had become increasingly hard to find. I listened and looked, but I did not find any that night, and it got dark very fast. I found a nearby motel.

By 6:50 A.M. on October 26 I was again in Hernando Beach with the sky just beginning to get light. Again I drove up and down each street mentioned in the Florida birding guide, and all the in-between streets, peering down the streets and canals, listening intently for parakeet sounds. Although many birds were waking up, some of them noisy Boat-tailed Grackles, I could not hear or see any parakeets. Where were they? Had they all been extirpated?

After doing the complete route from north to south, and then south to north, I decided to do the whole thing one more time and then give up. I was on the second-to-last street of my route, where the Gulf was visible between the houses on Gulf Winds Circle, when I saw a little group of perched long-tailed small birds. Not grackles. Parakeets. Eight of them. This is the number that Larry had heard were still left in Florida. Number 703. It's a good thing that they were very visible—I did not hear them. Only when I was very near could I hear their little parakeet-talking sounds as they groomed and chatted to each other.

What to do? Maybe Henslow's Sparrows had already migrated south to Florida. The guidebook said that Kissimmee Prairie

With all the great composers, music through them
   streams.
Instead of counting sheep, they're singing in their
   dreams.
What is it with me? Birding is my song.
Birding makes my life; birding all year long.
Chuckling in my sleep, what a glorious day!
My eyes keep popping open; there's stuff I've got
   to say.
So what was so exciting, under the cloudy sky?
Why am I so happy? Let me tell you why:
Eight stilt-legged flamingos, lined up on the shore.
Could you really ask, do I still want more?
Seven Smooth-billed Anis, peeking from the weeds.
Number 700! Yet I have more needs.
Multitudes of mynas, near the Burger King.
Finally I can count them. Makes me want to sing.

Preserve State Park, on my way back to Miami, had Henslow's Sparrow in winter. The trip to the state park was through interesting Pileated Woodpecker habitat and places where I had not been before. At about 2:00 I got to the state park and found out from a ranger that Henslow's Sparrow might be found near a wetlands area in the middle of a prairie. Off I trudged, through the nearly continuous palmetto toward a distant area without palmetto. I found very few birds, just a Palm Warbler, appropriately, a probable Savannah Sparrow, and Turkey Vultures. And one big fat wood tick that hitched a ride in my car for a couple of miles as I drove to Miami.

OCTOBER 30

As I sit in my rental car in the Laguna Mountains, Cleveland National Forest east of San Diego, I am waiting for dark or at least for it to get darker. The goal is Northern Saw-whet Owl, probably not likely, but it's all that I can think of trying for before my two-day San Diego pelagic trip.

Having arrived in San Diego after midnight California time (later than 2:00 A.M. home time), I made myself sleep in today and did not get going until about 9:00 A.M. Then I dilly-dallied around, stopping for a sit-down breakfast and to read, eventually getting up to Cleveland National Forest to check out the areas that might be good for Northern Saw-whet Owls and look at the Mountain Chickadees. Now I know where the owls might be, having gone up and down each of the roads. I've chosen Morris Ranch Road to start actually looking and listening for owls.

OCTOBER 31

After traversing all the good owl spots in the dark in the Laguna Mountains yesterday, and then going back to all but one again, all unsuccessfully, I finally had success. I had just called Dave since it was near bedtime in the Central Time Zone and had told him that I had not had any owl luck. I then drove into the entry area for Wooded Hills Campground and turned around. I was so sure that no owls were around, and it was so dark, that I did not even bother to get out of the car but just rolled down the window to listen. Astoundingly, I heard a very close Northern Saw-whet Owl. When I got out of the car, I could hear a far-off owl responding to it. What if I could see one of them? I had never seen one at all and had only once heard one before, in New Mexico.

These birds, especially the nearby one, sounded very irritated, but they

A Mountain Chickadee talks to me in Cleveland National Forest, California (October 30).

did not call for long and I could not pick up any eye shine with my flashlight or anything like a little dark lump in the branches of the low bushy trees at the edge of the road. Then, a gentle noise started up low in the deciduous brush surrounding the base of the tree from which the calls had come. The new sound either had to be an owl, or some kind of mammal, perhaps a cat or skunk or mountain lion. With some trepidation I climbed up the dirt embankment beside the road and pointed my flashlight at the sound. About 3–4 feet from the ground, about 8 feet from me, sat an adult Northern Saw-whet Owl staring gravely at me. In my hurry to try to get my camera in place and somehow keep the flashlight aimed at the owl, I glanced down at the camera, and when I looked back, the owl had disappeared and all was silent except for the wind blowing through the branches above. I was weak with relief and joy. In spite of it being past Dave's bedtime, I called him again—I had to tell someone.

I went back to San Diego, some 50 miles west, to sleep. Of course, before I did sleep, I updated my Web site and e-mailed thanks to those who had provided advice on owl finding.

This morning I slept in, because of the need to be well rested for the upcoming pelagic trip and because I could not think of anything else to chase. Then I had a leisurely Denny's breakfast and puttered about at Spanish Landing Park near my motel, not expecting, and not finding, any new birds.

N O V E M B E R

Mopping Up an Owl and a Couple of "Chickens"

NEW BIRD SPECIES SEEN THIS MONTH: 11
TOTAL BIRD SPECIES BY THE END OF THE MONTH: 715
PLACES BIRDED: California, Texas, New Mexico, Arizona, Colorado, Washington, Oregon

NOVEMBER 4

The two-day pelagic trip (November 1–3) was a first for me—two days at sea, going out about 150 miles, sleeping in bunks, and eating real food at sea. Amazingly, not only did I not get sick but I hardly thought about getting sick. I enjoyed it—except for having to stand most of the time since the boat did not have outside seats. Many people brought canvas deck chairs, which those of us from out of town and the others who had not brought chairs were allowed to squat on when unoccupied.

We left the San Diego dock a little after 7:00 A.M. on the *Grande,* which has bunks stacked four deep lining the walls of two parallel long chambers in the belly of the boat beneath the salon, which had indoor seating and tables. On a pelagic trip, of which this was my tenth for the year, while one can look and bird from inside the salon, it usually is not such a good idea for people who might be susceptible to seasickness to get too far from the fresh air. Inside it is also difficult to hear the birders outside calling out bird sightings.

As with most pelagic trips, this one had very long time periods when we saw absolutely no birds after the boat-following gulls drifted off. Probably because I so desperately wanted new birds, I got less bored than usual on pelagic trips. On our first day, November 1, we saw Brandt's Cormorants and miscellaneous land birds, plus many Black-vented, Sooty, Pink-footed, and Flesh-footed Shearwaters, Cassin's Auklets, Red and Red-necked Phalaropes, Pomarine Jaegers, Common Terns, and two Xantus's Murrelets on the way out. The latter species was the first new year bird of the pelagic trip. The Xantus's Murrelets were exciting even for the old hands on board because they were of the "hypoleucos" race, not usually found here.

On the afternoon of the first day out on the water, we saw very few birds but resolutely plowed farther out to sea on the not-really-substantiated hope for good things just beyond the next swell. As dusk approached, yummy baked chicken smells emerged from the little galley. I was glad that I had signed up for dinner. Although I was afraid that I was being reckless with my stomach, I was fine. Dinner was served after dark, since we could not bird anyway, and soon thereafter I went down to my bunk. The boat had very little storage space, except on my bunk, for all my cold-weather and rainy-weather clothing, including my rubber boots, but if I put very much on the 2-foot wide bunk, I did not fit. I made a little nest, putting my camera, telephoto lens, boots, and clothing down the side and foot area of the bunk and used my down coat for a very welcome supplemental pillow. I slept like a log at sea, not bothering to change clothes but just crawling in.

Before dawn, people began to emerge from their curtain-covered bunks to make their way outside. Soon after that, one of the guides started putting out on the water great amounts of oil, fish parts, and things I wasn't sure I wanted to know about, in the hope of attracting seabirds. The "tubenoses" have bills with horny plates and tubular nasal passages used for olfaction, which helps them locate patchily distributed prey at sea. Maybe some of them would

Brandt's Cormorants watch our boat depart on a two-day pelagic trip from San Diego on November 1.

A Red-billed Tropicbird was one of two new birds for the year on the second day of the San Diego pelagic trip.

come to our little offering of goodies. We did eventually get some birds, but the hoped-for shearwaters were not among them.

Although new shearwaters did not materialize, I got two new birds for the year—a Least Storm-Petrel and a Red-billed Tropicbird, which we saw well two different times (or of which there were two different birds). The second time the tropicbird came, it circled around our boat before it headed off. It's too bad more pelagic birds do not do that.

Other birds seen on day two of the pelagic trip as we worked our way west and north and then back toward San Diego were a flock of Brant, Long-tailed and Pomarine Jaegers, and more Red Phalaropes, hundreds, maybe thousands. A couple of times, the little bobbing phalarope groups turned toward the boat as the swells rose and fell beneath them, looking exactly like little white bowling pins balanced on the water.

Again, as dusk fell, food smells rose. I had put in an order to the cook for anything other than beef, the meat du jour, and I was delighted to find that I alone was served baked tuna, undoubtedly from the tuna caught that day. Very good. Our second dawn on the boat found us packing our gear and paying our food and beverage bills. We arrived in San Diego before 6:30 yesterday morning.

I could not resist this Burrowing Owl peering out near the Salton Sea in California on November 3.

I immediately drove toward the Salton Sea. After speeding past the sandy, sparsely vegetated expanses, my goal was Sonny Bono National Wildlife Refuge, where Ruddy Ground-Doves had been reported on the south side of the Salton Sea. All I found there were two Common Ground-Doves, even though I looked very thoroughly around the area, and saw a Burrowing Owl hiding in a haystack. After that I checked two other areas where Ruddy Ground-Doves are also supposed to occur. Hopefully someone will find them in Arizona just before I go there again, whenever that is. I'm at 707 and on my way home.

NOVEMBER 11

On Friday (November 7), after I had been home long enough for my husband to take my picture birding, I went to the Lower Rio Grande Valley (6:50 P.M.), where a Rose-throated Becard had been seen at Estero Llano Grande. This year there were none reported in Arizona and until a single report a few weeks ago, none had been reported from Texas either. I had crossed it off my list of species still possible to add this year.

I drove and drove and drove, just over 500 miles to Weslaco, where I parked myself at about 3:30 A.M. in a Wal-Mart parking lot and tried to doze.

On November 8 I first went over to Frontera Audubon, which opened at 7:00 A.M. and passed the time until Estero Llano Grande's morning tour at 8:30. The highlight at Frontera was a Clay-colored Thrush.

At 8:05 A.M. Jennifer Owen, then a naturalist at Estero Llano Grande, took me out on the trail where the becard had been seen and where a group from the Harlingen Rio Grande Valley Birding Festival was already watching a warbler flock. A White-tailed Kite sailed over, and an uncountable (undoubtedly an escapee) Black-throated Magpie-Jay put in a spectacular appearance.

Back to the goal. One of the people in the group pointed out a small bird flitting about a palm tree trunk, the size and big-headed shape and behavior of a becard, but I could not see any color or marking on the silhouetted bird. I believe the group members who saw the bird decided to count it as a becard, but I hoped for a better view. I kept vacillating between "yes, of course, what else would it be?" and "I've just got to stay around and get a better view." I wasn't even sure we had seen a becard. I stayed and wandered up and down the nearby trails, watching Couch's Kingbirds, Orange-crowned Warblers, Inca Doves, high-soaring American White Pelicans, many Great Kiskadees, a Black-throated Gray Warbler, and Ruby-crowned Kinglets, but did not find a becard.

I actually birded a bit in my yard on November 6. Photo by David Barber.

This Rose-throated Becard in Weslaco, Texas, was the first male I had seen (November 8).

While I was resting and sitting on a hunk of cement, Benton Basham drove slowly by. He is an early leader in the ABA organization, who did an ABA big year in 1983 and got 711 species. He told me that I was welcome to sit on a chair in the backyard of his trailer where the magpie-jay had been feeding. I thanked him, but I didn't "need" the magpie-jay. Eventually though, I wandered over and sat in his yard. Nothing appeared, and I wandered off. About an hour later, the thought of sitting sounded very good and I went back. I saw the magpie-jay, but it skittered away and hid, an amazing feat for such a large blue, long-tailed bird.

About 2:15 amid the Great Kiskadees and Couch's Kingbirds, a smaller flycatcher moved into view above the trailer, the Rose-throated Becard.

Although when I first saw it, I thought it was a female, my pictures showed that it had a faint pink on its throat and was a young male.

When my excitement died down, I realized again how exhausted I was, with essentially no sleep the night before. I decided to find a motel somewhere near Anzalduas County Park where I planned to bird the next day. Once I started driving, however, I could not resist returning to Frontera Audubon, hoping a Crimson-collared Grosbeak would repeat the performance of the winter of 2004–2005, but no, not yet, just the usual birds.

I found a motel in McAllen and slept over 11 hours. On the morning of November 9, somewhat refreshed, I went to Anzalduas County Park. The Border Patrol was out in force and had closed off a portion of the park. I was able to stand on the levee, however, where I had seen Hook-billed Kites in 2005 and from which I hoped to see one this year. It was my third time there this year. About 9:10 I spotted the first Turkey Vulture, with which Hook-billed Kites often ascend in the morning. Soon 50–70 Turkey Vultures floated by. It was quite cloudy with stratus-type clouds, less favorable for kettle formation, and most of the Turkey Vultures drifted by rather than forming

Buff-bellied Hummingbirds are common year-round in the Lower Rio Grande Valley, Texas (November 8).

kettles. (When the air is warmed from below, upward-moving thermals are created, providing support for groups of circling birds.) About 9:40 a Zone-tailed Hawk appeared low over the trees, surprising me with a tail stripe on what I thought was a Turkey Vulture. At 9:50 some Black Vultures joined the parade, and then at 9:54 a single Hook-billed Kite passed over the levee and into and through some trees and disappeared from view. I wandered around the park hoping for another view, but the birds had disappeared.

I headed north to Quintana jetty, some 300-plus indirect miles, where Ron Weeks (then president of the Texas Ornithological Society) had found a possibly countable Kelp Gull. A Kelp Gull was not even on my list of possible birds for the year. In 2007 I had checked to find out if Kelp Gulls, once on the Chandeleur Islands, Louisiana, were still there and had learned that hurricanes had demolished the colony. Kelp Gulls normally found breeding on coasts and islands in the Southern Hemisphere periodically venture to the United States. I had seen the one on the East Coast when I lived in North Carolina. It would be awhile until the Texas Bird Records Committee would rule on this gull; so many gulls are hybrids and not countable.

The route to Quintana was slow and winding, but I made as good a time as possible, slowed down somewhat when I was stopped by a very nice traffic police officer, who gave me a verbal warning about my speeding. I arrived at the Quintana jetty at dusk, in time to see a huge flock of Laughing Gulls take off toward the Gulf and disappear. The wind was picking up. I found a motel in the Freeport–Lake Jackson area and called Ron Weeks, who gave me suggestions for the morning search.

Before 6:30 A.M. on November 10 I was at the jetty scanning the large gull flock, again mostly Laughing Gulls with a few Ring-billed Gulls. Soon many of them headed off in the howling wind to wherever they were going for the day. At 7:13, a single large black-backed gull flew by fighting the wind; the gull had a very white face, little white on its wing tips, and a bit of uneven wing edge due to molt. I watched it carefully, forgetting to try for a picture as it worked its way down the beach to the fishing pier and disappeared behind it. I waited, expecting it to return, but it did not. I walked that way and found Herring Gulls and a single Lesser Black-backed Gull, clearly grayer (lighter colored) and sootier faced than the bird that I had seen. I wanted a picture of the Kelp Gull, but the rain had started in earnest, blowing nearly horizontally from the northeast, drenching me, my scope, and my camera.

In a distinctly uncheerful mood, I slogged back to the car. Although my heart was not in it, I made myself stay around, checking the Surfside area and then going back to Quintana before I gave up on getting a better view and drove north toward home. But I did not go directly home. McCown's Longspurs were back for the winter in the Granger area, and they were not yet on my big year list. I had to check, even though it was windy, somewhat rainy, and late afternoon when I got there. I did not see a longspur. Some birds have to be nemesis birds or life would just be too simple, and everyone would do a big year. I have tried to find McCown's Longspurs five times this year, so far. A morning with little or no wind would help in finding them.

NOVEMBER 14

I went back to Granger yesterday, leaving home about 3:35 A.M. and spending about six hours wandering every road that's ever seen a longspur, and a few others. I listened and scanned the fields but did not find a longspur of any kind. Plenty of American Pipits were walking around and flying over the fields, and I now am an expert at knowing them and their many flight sounds.

Today three North Texas birding friends and I piled into a car to go down to Lake Jackson so that they could get the Kelp Gull for their lists and I could try to get a picture of it. It's fun to bird with friends instead of alone or with strangers. Tomorrow we'll go to Quintana and see what we can see.

NOVEMBER 15

Today we did see the Kelp Gull and I got much better views of it flying and standing on the beach. We first saw it at the base of the Quintana jetty at about 8:40 A.M. Shortly after that it flew over to sit at the edge of a flock of Laughing Gulls quite near us but did not stay long and took off across the water to Surfside. We could see it sitting on the distant rocky shore. We drove to Surfside, winding our way over bridges and down residential streets. When we got there, we could not see the Kelp Gull anywhere. While we were discussing what to do next, the Kelp Gull suddenly materialized right where we were looking. It was clearly magic. No one saw it fly in. We saw it fly away, shortly after everyone took photographs.

Before we headed back to Fort Worth, we saw the other usual gulls, including a Lesser Black-backed Gull, many Killdeer flying low across the beach in the strong winds (or the same 25 going by again and again), and the usual pipits, waders, and terns. We took an indirect route home and saw a beautiful bright yellow Pine Warbler at a roadside park in Brazoria County.

I finally got a picture of the Kelp Gull on the Texas coast on November 15.

NOVEMBER 21

On November 19 I headed west from home to Bosque del Apache National Wildlife Refuge in central New Mexico where, astoundingly, a Sungrebe had been seen in one of the canals. A zillion e-mails bounced around the birding community—was the Sungrebe countable, or was it a zoo escapee? No zoos admitted to ever having one. I decided to go for it. When I arrived there in the middle of the afternoon, 20 birders with downcast faces and unoccupied telescopes where the bird had last been seen told the whole story. The bird's last witnessed flight was into an off-limits refuge area the day before. If it's refound and I can possibly go for it, I will. Unfortunately, it is turning colder, and the Sungrebe is a subtropical bird.

I left Bosque del Apache as it got dark and drove the 150 miles to Deming for a day total of 771 miles. The next morning (November 20), I headed west at 5:45 with my goal being the Portal, Arizona, area to look once again for Bendire's Thrasher. Everyone with whom I had discussed this hole in my year list had said that I needed to go to Rodeo and/or Stateline Road between Portal and Rodeo for Bendire's Thrasher, where I had already traveled multiple times. One more try, and if that failed again, I would try northwest of Tucson.

I assiduously checked each vacant lot and clump of brush in Rodeo to see if a thrasher would materialize and looked at every bird-shaped dark area in every bush, but found nothing close except a pair of Curve-billed Thrashers. I worked my way over to Stateline Road via Gin Road, another reportedly good spot. I went up and down Stateline Road, back onto Gin Road, and back on to Stateline Road.

On Stateline Road, south of the Gin Road intersection across from one of the few occupied houses, I saw a good-sized thrasher-shaped bird on top of a bush above a brush pile. I was nearly certain that it was a Curve-billed Thrasher and not a Bendire's Thrasher, but I thought it would be even more convincingly not a Bendire's Thrasher if it did not respond to the (very brief) playing of a Bendire's Thrasher on my iPod. It did not respond, as expected. But the surprising thing was that out of nowhere behind the brush pile a clearly smaller thrasher popped up into the bush with the Curve-billed Thrasher. The smaller thrasher then flew directly toward me over my head to the trees by the house, and then back over my head to a tree where I was able to see it well. I am convinced: Bendire's Thrashers can still be found on Stateline Road, or at least one of them can.

In a euphoric state of mind, I headed farther east through Douglas and Bisbee, went past Sonoita and on to Paton's in Patagonia where a few weeks ago a Ruddy Ground-Dove had been seen. All I saw were Inca Doves and White-crowned Sparrows.

About 2:45 I went to the San Rafael Grasslands, hoping for a Baird's Sparrow or maybe a McCown's Longspur. Horned Larks were perched on the fence line and in the vacant corral was a flock containing Yellow-headed and Brewer's Blackbirds, Brown-headed Cowbirds, Savannah and Vesper Sparrows, and a molting male Chestnut-collared Longspur, but no Baird's Sparrow or McCown's Longspur.

After dark, I drove to Sonoita to spend the night. This morning I was up bright and early to go to the grasslands before dawn because I love owls and hoped for a Short-eared Owl. What I saw was a Northern Harrier and a White-tailed Kite.

Sparrows were slow to emerge from their hiding places into the below-freezing air, but eventually Vesper, Savannah, Field, and Grasshopper Sparrows popped up to fence wires and then fled into the billowing dust when cars got too close. On my third pass down the road, in a very sparrowy area about one-third mile east of the cattle guard that separates the all-private land from the public lands, a very buffy-faced, buffy, striped-breasted/necklaced sparrow was just visible in the grasses, perched about 8 inches above the ground, a Baird's Sparrow. A truck chose to barrel by then, and all the sparrows vanished. A couple of drive-bys later I saw what was probably the same sparrow, even closer to the road, but so deeply immersed in the grasses that it was only visible in snatches.

A Chestnut-collared Longspur showed up briefly about 9:30 when the Horned Larks also appeared. Also along the fence were meadowlarks, at least some of which were the southwestern version of Eastern Meadowlark (Lilian's), which recently has been recommended for separate species status. It could add a bird to my year list (and mess up all my numbering, which of course I could handle). I left the grasslands about 10:30 and briefly stopped at Paton's again, hoping for Ruddy Ground-Dove, but I saw very few birds.

I headed to Red Rock, northwest of Tucson, where Ruddy Ground-Doves once were a sure thing. On the way I was treated to the exciting chase of a Red-tailed Hawk by a very persistent Prairie Falcon. At Red Rock, except for a large flock of blackbirds, including many Yellow-headed Blackbirds, I saw nothing of note—just wall-to-wall cattle and an overwhelming barnyard stench. My car's interior probably still reeks of it, and I think there's still a fly caught in my car that calls Red Rock home. (Actually, my car probably contains quite a zoo of critters from my big year.) I saw no little doves at all, even though I drove around to the other nearby spots that were also supposed to be good.

As darkness approached, I could not decide where to spend the night and where to go the next day. Should I stay near Tucson and try again at Red Rock, should I go somewhere else in Arizona, or should I just leave and head for Colorado, where Guanella Pass, the best place for White-tailed Ptarmigan, was closing soon for the year? I decided to start for Colorado. As far as I could tell, the birds that I needed in Arizona were not there.

NOVEMBER 24

After a night in Deming, New Mexico, on the morning of November 22 I drove north. It was a beautiful morning, with flocks of flying Sandhill Cranes making it even brighter. I kept checking e-mail messages, hoping that the Sungrebe would have magically reappeared and I could just pop into the refuge on my way north, but it appears to be a gone bird.

I only birded at one site on the trip to Colorado. I had read that a turf farm east of Albuquerque routinely had a wintering flock of mostly McCown's Longspurs but was no longer open to birders driving its roads. What did I have to lose? Maybe the turf farm could be scoped from the surrounding roads. I found it and began to drive slowly along looking for flocks of flying little birds. The first portion of the farm had very short green grass, and the second portion had very short dried grass, good places for longspurs.

The first drive past revealed only a Red-tailed Hawk sitting way out on the green sod. Immediately after I turned around, a small flock of Horned Larks on the dry grass cheered me up. When I got back to the green area, I stopped and got out my scope. To my delight I discovered a flock of birds so far off that they were barely visible in binoculars. The birds' behavior, reminding me of multidirectional goldfinches vaguely moving together, bouncing over the ground and then high into the air, then down to disappear behind a distant rise and up again, was longspur behavior. I waited for them to move closer. Every now and then the flock, or a portion of the flock, would veer in my direction, allowing me to pick up some plumage information. I heard a couple of them, too, the dry short rattle of McCown's Longspur over the almost unceasing truck noise off the highway behind me. Eventually, the overall drab buffiness, the brown or very white tails, the sound, and the habitat convinced me that all of them, or at least many of them, were my goal McCown's Longspurs.

I got back on task then and headed farther east and then north, getting back to I-25 after a pleasant drive on a tiny road connecting it to I-40. The drive through northern New Mexico was beautiful—golden grasses with dots of green junipers and a few groups of grazing antelopes. I reached Denver not long after dark, a 676-mile-drive from Deming.

Early on Sunday morning, November 23, I picked up Rich Stevens of Cobirders, who was going to help me find a White-tailed Ptarmigan. Three days earlier he had reported 14 of them at the soon-to-close Guanella Pass. We drove up the narrow, winding, under-construction road, arriving at the ptarmigan hill before dawn. We first realized the strength of the wind, which beat upon my car and noticeably rocked it, when we stopped toward the top of the road. Although my car thermometer showed it as being slightly above freezing outside, when we stepped out into the nearly 50-mile-per-hour winds, it felt very arctic.

Slowly, with me suffering from the over 12,000-foot elevation, we made our way up the nearly three football fields of slope. The upward walking around the rocks and through the grass would have been simple if not for the lack of oxygen and the stinging, forceful winds. We could not find any ptarmigans. As I miserably toiled on, my wind-beaten face seeming to lose all feeling, and my eyes and nose running, it seemed certain that this trip would conclude as my last effort at looking for White-tailed Ptarmigans had concluded.

Gradually we worked our way to where the wind was a little less violent on both us (and on the poor huddled ptarmigans, which presumably were up the mountain somewhere). We meandered around and sometimes through deep drifts that punctuated the mostly grassy brown slope, trying always to face downwind, not always possible.

Then, it happened. Less than 10 feet ahead of me were not one, but two, ptarmigans, slowly walking away from me. They had been invisible until I nearly stepped on them. I let out a shout, not wanting to take the time to dig out my radio to call Rich, who was upslope out of sight, to tell him of my find. He of course thought my shout meant that I had fallen and broken a leg, so I radioed him fast to tell him that I was very much okay and that I was looking at two wonderful ptarmigans. He also had spotted distant ptarmigans where he was, but mine were closer, so he joined me. By then the original two had wandered away from me, but I found two more even closer. I took pictures until my camera stopped functioning, which was not, I learned later, because it was too frozen but because the autofocus on my camera quit working.

The White-tailed Ptarmigans at Guanella Pass, Colorado, had been long sought and were spectacular (November 23).

We raced downhill to the car into the wind. Since I faced another 750 miles in addition to the 150 already on the car for that day, we left the mountain. After lunch in Denver, I began the homeward trek. Along the way at one of my stops, I changed from my snow-melt sopping wet socks and shoes to dry footwear. At Childress, Texas, I decided that I could not bear to drive anymore, so I stayed over and finished the trip today.

NOVEMBER 25

The day is beginning with a trip to Oregon, on the way to Spokane, Washington, my first trip as a gold member of American Airlines. We are flying over some humongous lake in the mountains, apparently Salt Lake. I have spent the last one and one-half hours trying to figure out the best spots for Gray Partridge, Dusky Grouse, and Boreal Owl in eastern Washington. I would not be taking this trip if I did not figure that the Gray Partridge was possible, but the other two are probably not. It's too early for lowland snow to make Gray Partridges less difficult to find, and it's too late in the year for the higher-altitude Boreal Owl and Dusky Grouse. I'll be searching for Gray Partridge until I find it or until this trip is over.

Nine-Tenths

The end is so near, but really it's not.
And where I am now, I would never have thought
That I would now be at seven fourteen
Species, that is. An awful lot seen!
But will I stop now? No, of course not because
When I look back someday at the big year that was,
I don't want to regret not trying to find
Some possible bird. Of course, losing my mind
Is a real risk as well. Perhaps it's too late
To worry 'bout that. But whatever my fate,
I'm exceedingly glad I embarked on this year.
Thirty-six days remain. The end is so near!

NOVEMBER 28

On November 25, I had about an hour of daylight to bird in Washington after my arrival. I raced out and birded north of the area between Reardon and Davenport, one of the areas where Gray Partridges are supposed to be. All I saw were a Northern Harrier and Rough-legged Hawk. I headed out the next morning in heavy fog and birded the area south of where I had birded the day before, adding a flock of California Quail that temporarily got me all excited until I identified them, plus Horned Larks, Eurasian Collared-Doves, an

American Kestrel, Northern Flickers, American Tree Sparrows, Black-billed Magpies, a Ring-necked Pheasant, and a Northern Shrike. I did not see or hear any partridges. In the evening, at about 4:30, which was already after sunset, as I drove back to Spokane, a large dark lump out in a field was a hunting Great Horned Owl. I hoped that it had not gotten the last Gray Partridge.

I retired early, planning the next morning (Thanksgiving) to try Turnbull NWR, where partridges were also supposed to be. John Puschock called to let me know of an Idaho sighting of a Whooper Swan, however, which caused me to get up again and turn on my computer to see where the bird was (520 miles away). I theoretically had sufficient time to do that before my noontime flight on the day after Thanksgiving, and I decided to try, though it was tiring to think of going 1,000 miles in the next one and a half days.

When I got up on Thanksgiving, it was extremely foggy and just below freezing. I started driving and got about 60 miles along on my trip, going 55 miles per hour or less because of the fog and the fear that the road might be slippery. It was still dark and very hard to see when I stopped for a breakfast biscuit. As I walked into the fast-food place, I realized how very slippery it was—I could barely keep from falling down on the slick pavement in the parking lot. As I sat in my car munching on my biscuit, I was torn between reluctance at the thought of slow driving for so long in crummy weather and my desire to see the swan. I reluctantly decided to go back to my original plan and headed to Turnbull NWR.

I had a nice walk at Turnbull, staying off to the side of the icy paved paths, but I saw no sign of partridges. At the closed visitor center, I saw a flock of California Quail and Black-capped Chickadees at the feeders. Also at the refuge were Red-tailed Hawks, a couple of Great Blue Herons (what do they eat in such a frozen world?), Black-billed Magpies, a Common Raven, and a Bald Eagle, as well as noisy Pygmy Nuthatches on the wildlife drive. No partridges.

I still had hours until I could check into a motel (I had checked out that morning, thinking I was going to Idaho), the roads were getting even more slippery, snow was lightly falling, and I had concluded that no partridges existed in eastern Washington. What should I do with my time? I began working my way back to my now-familiar stomping grounds between Reardon and Davenport. I retraced my routes, avoiding slippery paved roads if possible, and wound up on Euclid Road, which parallels U.S. 2 to the north, is gravel, and has many vegetated areas along it where a partridge might hide.

As the afternoon wore on, it periodically snowed, which eventually lightly

A new light dusting of snow made Gray Partridges magically appear west of Spokane, Washington, when nothing had previously been visible (November 27).

whitened some of the dirt fields between the plant stubble. It is this whitening that on my third pass down Euclid allowed me to notice a grouping of dark clumps in a field of cut-off thick stalks (perhaps corn stalks). These clumps were alive, finally, after I had stopped to check out what seemed like hundreds of other clumps that were dead. They were not California Quail—they were Gray Partridge. Number 715. I was laughing and crying and exclaiming and, of course, taking pictures, even though the birds were out quite a distance and it was getting dark. I got out of the car to get a bit closer to the partridges, which allowed better pictures but spooked the birds. I refound them in another field and then called my husband and a couple of birding friends so they could rejoice with me in my good fortune.

Before the grouse, I had been about to entitle this trip my "first unsuccessful flying trip of my big year." Of course, although I am now looking at it as a glass half full, I could look at it as a glass half empty since I did not get the swan. Maybe the swan will stay around awhile. I'm heading out a couple of hours early on standby and hopefully can also fly standby out of Portland to Texas. A unique part of this Horizon Air flight is that one of the stewardesses asked everyone's first name as we boarded, and as she serves our beverages and ginger cookies, she's remembering and addressing us by first name.

DECEMBER

Ending the Year with a Bit of a Whimper and a Big Cheer!

NEW BIRD SPECIES SEEN THIS MONTH: 8
TOTAL BIRD SPECIES BY THE END OF THE MONTH: 723
PLACES BIRDED: Texas, Newfoundland, Washington, Ontario, New Mexico, Arizona

DECEMBER 6

I arrived in Newfoundland about 10:30 yesterday morning. John Puschock has organized this trip to St. John's, and Debra and I will be rooming together. It was a wonderful cold, crisp day today, cloudy and very birdy. Although I had seen Iceland Gulls in the harbor outside last night after we got to the hotel, I did not count them until today when I could see something more than a moving pale blur. We had 20 Iceland Gulls, or more, some very close, both adults and immature, on the lake edge scrounging for bread crumbs from the passersby.

The next new year bird was close to the hotel and was also one I expected to find here, Black-headed Gulls sitting on low rocks near the shore. We saw many Herring Gulls and Great Black-backed Gulls and a couple of Lesser Black-backed Gulls, but we were looking for a Yellow-legged Gull. The ball field where one Yellow-legged Gull had been previously seen with many other gulls was empty today. Gradually, however, gulls began to arrive. We drove nearer. Gulls kept coming. Where was the mostly whiter-headed Yellow-legged Gull, in-between the gray of a Herring Gull and the slate color of a Lesser Black-backed Gull?

Then John saw it arrive. We studied it and took pictures. It had to be a Yellow-legged Gull by size and color (and the fact that this gull was different from all of the other gulls there both in size and color, with its "medium gray"–colored back). In addition to the three new gull species, we also had a surprise

The first of four new birds for St. John's, Newfoundland, was Iceland Gull (December 7).

Black-headed Gulls are regularly only found in the ABA area in winter on the upper east coast of North America. These were in St. John's, Newfoundland, on December 7.

Franklin's Gull (young of the year) and a Mew (Common) Gull, a Greater Scaup, Dark-eyed Juncos, and a couple of Glaucous and Ring-billed Gulls.

About 10:00 A.M., we headed out toward Portugal Cove South, where we hoped to find a Northern Lapwing that had been reported. On the way we saw Common Ravens, a glowing flock of Evening Grosbeaks hanging from the tree branches, two Blue Jays, flocks of American Goldfinches, and a pair of Pine Grosbeaks.

When we got to the exact lawn where the lapwing was being seen, usually with a single Killdeer, the Killdeer was there—but no lapwing. John went to talk with the owner of the lawn, who said, "Oh, you mean the bird with hair sticking up on its head—it was here this morning." The man did not mind if we wandered around his lawn. John checked out the whole lawn, and still we could not find the lapwing. We drove around the neighborhood, and still no lapwing. As we came back to the original yard, Debra looked over first and saw the silhouetted bird with its "hair" sticking up, where the Killdeer had been. We crept up on it a few times and got some pictures. It seemed very like a Killdeer in its tameness and was quite a beauty.

The Yellow-legged Gull (sitting) was our main goal in Newfoundland (December 7).

A carful of birders stopped by and told us that they had seen a Snowy Owl farther down the road toward the water, so we headed out that way. Not only was there one Snowy Owl but we saw six or seven spread out along the road, all perched on the ground or on low rocky piles, all very photogenic. There's no such thing as a plain or an ugly Snowy Owl.

For today, four new birds, and I'm at 719 for the year.

DECEMBER 7

We are still in Newfoundland. It was a snowy day at first, with about an inch of extremely clingy, wet, big flakes that stayed on and soaked through our clothing and piled up on the ducks' backs. We found no new year birds for me, but we had many duck and gull close-ups, as we tossed them food to entertain ourselves. The visibility was awful, with the snow turning to driving rain. We went back to the Battery Hotel to change to dry clothing and have lunch and then did a bit more pond jumping in the afternoon after giving up on the sea watch—no sea to see in the blinding rain.

One of many Snowy Owls near St. John's, Newfoundland, watches us (December 6).

The Northern Lapwing was a last-minute surprise addition to my year list on December 6.

St. John's, Newfoundland is a very scenic place (December 6).

DECEMBER 9

We are on the plane from Newfoundland headed home. I am so
glad that I came on this trip—an
unexpected, last-minute trip with
wonderful results. While John
Puschock reminds me that the gull
we are calling a Yellow-legged Gull
has at least a small chance of being
a hybrid (because of a bit of darker marking on its neck), there is great vari-
ability in the species, which apparently includes birds that are just like "our"
gull. If so, I'll still be at 719 species, as we did not find any rarities after the
big day on Saturday. We have seen 45 bird species on the trip, which is pretty
good for that far north and for such a short time and limited amount of
wandering.

Newfoundland

The Lapwing's "hair" sticks up in the air,
The Tufted Duck's "hair" is almost not there,
The gulls fill the sky, and the ball field's nearby.
A Newfoundland trip with which none can
    compare.

DECEMBER 13

My most recent trip was an
unsuccessful one in which I spent
a full day (December 11) not seeing
the reported Blue Bunting at Frontera Audubon in Weslaco, Texas. It
was a lovely, crisply cold day, and
nonbunting birds were plentiful. I
saw six species of warbler (Orange-
crowned, Yellow-rumped, Wilson's,
Black-throated Green, Black-
and-white, and Ovenbird), Ruby-
crowned Kinglets, a male Rose-
breasted Grosbeak, a Blue-headed
Vireo, and a fly-over flock of Green
Parakeets. I met Father Tom Pincelli, a nearly legendary birder in the
Valley, whom I somehow had not
managed to meet before.

Bunting

Little brown Blue Bunting;
I spent a full day hunting.
Where it is—a mystery.
Probably, it's history.

Written *after* a fruitless day of searching for
the Blue Bunting in Weslaco, Texas, in spite
of not finding it:

Thinking about My Big Year

I drive along, and I quiver with laughter.
It's all about now and not about after.
It's the love of the chase; I can't help it, I'm
    beaming.
It's hard to believe. It seems like I'm dreaming.
The effort's been great, but the joy has been
    greater;
And as for the cost, I'll think of it later.

On the way home, the bird highlight was about 30 Sandhill Cranes in a field south of San Antonio.

I was originally scheduled to be on my way to Seattle today, but a huge blizzard there delayed things for 24 hours. John Puschock may join me in the swan chase to Idaho. There's a problem though because the lake where the Whooper Swan has been is freezing over. It may be a wild-goose/swan chase. The likelihood of success for the rest of this year is low, because essentially all of the birds that I have not yet seen this year have not been seen all year for a reason—they are hard to see.

DECEMBER 14

I am to depart for Seattle at 10:10, facing blizzards present and future, and a possible iced-over Idaho lake without the Whooper Swan. John Puschock will meet me at the car rental place at the Seattle airport, and we'll head east to Idaho. If I had known that the previously reported Black-tailed Gull would disappear from the Vancouver area, I would have scheduled myself to fly directly to Idaho. But if I could accurately predict what birds were going to do, I would probably have 745 birds on my list right now.

DECEMBER 16

No Whooper Swan. None. I am heading back to Texas, tired but again hopeful. The swan chase all began with a 558-mile drive from Seattle to Mountain Home, Idaho. It was a companionable trip with John Puschock, but so long and icy and windy and snowy and dark. We arrived in Mountain Home at 3:00 A.M. yesterday. After only three hours of sleep, we met again for the motel's continental breakfast, bleary eyed, but awake enough for the icy drive to Hagerman Wildlife Management Area where the Whooper Swan had been seen, 60 miles away.

When we arrived, we looked and looked at every unfrozen pond and at the Snake River, seeing many ducks and geese and six Trumpeter Swans, but we did not find any Tundra Swans and definitely no Whooper Swan, which had been hanging out with the Tundra Swans. Resignedly (without jumping in the river in extreme agony, as befits seasoned birders), we turned toward Seattle for the long trip back. Of course, there were more snow, more icy roads, and more driving in the dark. We arrived at John's home just after midnight. The trip was especially long due to a nearly hour-long delay in the

Blue Mountains because of a huge truck's having pivoted somehow to face backward at the icy edge of the road.

I was scheduled to be in Washington for a couple more days, but I decided to try to leave Seattle early, with no birds to chase there, and changed my flight to today. Astoundingly, on Sunday a female Crimson-collared Grosbeak, a species that I have been thinking would be the best possible bird to cap off my big year, was reported at Frontera Audubon in Weslaco. Yesterday, I feared it had left because there were no immediate reports of it being seen again. Then Debra Corpora called to report that not only was the Crimson-collared Grosbeak still there but the Blue Bunting was back at Frontera Audubon. After I do another marathon day of driving today, I could (fingers crossed so tight, it may be hard to drive) get them both. Meanwhile, I'm stuck here on the plane, literally cooling my heels (the plane was not heated when we got on it). I'm scheduled to arrive at DFW a little after 1:00 P.M. today, pick up my car, which is handily in an airport parking lot, and race (through more ice) to the Lower Rio Grande Valley.

Meanwhile, I'm still holding at 719 species.

DECEMBER 18

It was a miracle. Not the driving of course, unless you count making it alive for the fifth 500-mile day of driving in less than a week. I drove from the DFW airport, on seven hours of sleep in two days, arriving in Pharr in South Texas just before midnight on December 16. After six hours sleep I went to Frontera Audubon to let myself in the locked gate (having obtained permission) and wandered around in the misty morning, checking all the spots that the female Blue Bunting had previously been seen and checking the potato tree for the Crimson-collared Grosbeak. (When Crimson-collared Grosbeaks are found in Texas, they are usually eating the leaves of potato trees that grow in the Valley.) It was birdy, but not with the birds I sought.

I tried a trail off to the south that I had not been on recently and, when checking out a couple of perched birds, found a mockingbird and what turned out to be the mockingbird's constant companion, the female Crimson-collared Grosbeak. They headed back from the trail, but about 20 minutes later, I found them again, still together, working their way across the central area of the sanctuary. Their path and my path intersected with a hackberry tree where a contented Clay-colored Thrush was munching berries.

I was elated, but I still wanted the female Blue Bunting. I walked all the

A female Crimson-collared Grosbeak, while not as bright as a male, still counts as a very welcome new year bird (Weslaco, Texas, December 17).

usual trails again at Frontera Audubon, and all the other trails, again and again, slowly, listening and looking for any kind of movement. I did not see the Crimson-collared Grosbeak again, but I was mostly looking in the lower levels of vegetation and on the ground.

A little after noon, I began to work the trails again. My meandering led me to the back of the refuge along the fence separating the refuge from a cemetery, where there is a water-filled ditch bordered by grasses, weeds, and a few small trees. Father Tom had told me when I was looking for Blue Bunting the week before that they had a call somewhat like a softer phoebe's call. When I heard a gentle phoebe sound coming toward me along the ditch, I paid attention. A very rusty brown fat little bird with a fat blackish beak was working its way through the brush—a well-seen and photographed female Blue Bunting.

These two very desirable birds brought me to 721 species for the year.

Last night I decided to ask local expert birders Scarlet and George Colley to take me out to find a Mangrove Warbler. It's not countable now, because it's currently classified as a subspecies of Yellow Warbler, but maybe someday. Scarlet was able to take me out last night, but her boat motor died when we were near a nesting area for the Mangrove Warblers. For a while, it looked like we would need to be towed in. We did hear the chip of a Mangrove Warbler before we left into the growing fog, and I could have counted it for my "in the bank" list, but when we went out again today, we did see a couple of Mangrove Warblers and I got a photo of a distant young male.

Predicting How a Big Year Will End

I thought it would end with the red, white, and
   blue:
A Grosbeak, a Bunting, a lovely swan too.
But swans have big wings and apparently fly,
And the Bunting was brown and exceedingly shy.
The Grosbeak was green—not a smidgen of red,
So when it was all debated and said:
I was clueless, not knowing, blindly running a race,
So I guess if there's red—it is found in my face.

DECEMBER 21

On December 18, I raced around doing client work and home chores, and then about 2:15, I drove to Nacogdoches, in the Piney Woods of Northeast Texas. There I joined Debra Corpora, who with me was scheduled to participate with Mimi Wolf in the Nacogdoches Christmas Bird Count (CBC) the

The female Blue Bunting at Frontera Audubon in Weslaco, Texas, was shy and took awhile to find (December 17).

next day. For a number of years, the Texas Ornithological Society had run a field trip in Northeast Texas in late winter, which included Henslow's Sparrow among its goal birds. I remembered that Mimi, one of the leaders, had remarked that the places we looked for and found these elusive little birds on the TOS trip in February were places where she had found them on the CBC the previous December.

I decided to participate in the Nacogdoches CBC with Mimi in one last try to add Henslow's Sparrows to my year list. Mimi met us at 6:00 A.M., and we headed out to listen to Eastern Screech-Owls and other nighttime birds before beginning the exhaustive and exhausting canvassing of large grassy areas set in the Piney Woods. The prime sparrow spots, especially for Henslow's and Le Conte's Sparrows, were the rusty brown little bluestem patches (or that's what I understand that the best plant areas are), but we also crossed through other brush habitat, counting whatever birds we could find, mostly Savannah Sparrows throughout the field and Chipping Sparrows near the edges and trees.

Almost immediately after entering the field (a private field, requiring permission) near Nacogdoches, a very, very welcome Henslow's Sparrow popped up from nearly under our feet, flew a short distance, and quickly went down again and disappeared. We saw it well when we rushed to where it had landed. We worked the large field another three hours or so, finding three more Henslow's Sparrows, a couple of Le Conte's Sparrows, a single Grasshopper Sparrow, about five Vesper Sparrows, and zillions of Chipping and Savannah Sparrows. We then wandered along some Piney Woods roads, adding common woodpeckers, Brown-headed Nuthatches, Brown Creepers, various wrens, Hermit Thrushes, both kinglets, and other woodland birds to the CBC count. We birded until it was dark, and then Debra and I drove off to our respective homes. I unpacked and then repacked for today's trip to Toronto, the goal in Toronto being Boreal Owl. Unfortunately, snow is forecast for today in Ontario.

I am now at 722 species. This is close to Sandy Komito's first record that he later broke by getting about 745 species. Those two records are the only two that are (to the best of my knowledge) above where I am now, and those two records were done when it was possible to fly into Attu to bird, where he undoubtedly got birds not present elsewhere during his big years.

Whether or not I get the Boreal Owl in Ontario, I plan to go to Arizona at Christmas to seek Rufous-capped Warblers, which have recently been reported in Florida Wash, and then to wander around all the possible areas for Ruddy Ground-Doves or any other rarities. I have given up on Dusky Grouse.

Although the plane that I am on began its flight to Ontario, we returned to DFW. The plane had some kind of de-icer problem. Makes me want to get my car and go home, crawl under the covers, and wait for 2009. But instead, American Airlines has found a plane for all of us to board, and we wait for it to arrive at our gate. At 5:00 we try again to begin the trip to Toronto. Thank goodness I did not check any luggage and thank goodness it is a direct flight. Hopefully not directly back to DFW.

DECEMBER 23

I did *not* find a Boreal Owl in Ontario. I tried my best yesterday, but in spite of tromping down an unplowed road through 2–3-foot drifts for over a mile, in spite of a lovely long snowy walk through deciduous and pine woods, and in spite of an ice-water-filled boot, I did not find any little owls at all. My hips still ache from the leg lifting, snow crunching, and balancing.

Big Year

I search and I search and I search some more.
But the sighting I want is just not in store.
"It's only one bird," I say, and that's so,
But one thing more I want to know,
Why does it seem that this bird's worth a lot,
Worth more in fact than some birds that I've got?
I guess it's a matter of view and perspective,
And nothing I do, neither prayer nor invective,
Will change the result or yield me a bird.
So I guess that "acceptance" will be the last word.

Hairy and Downy Woodpeckers can be compared when they are on the same feeder in Ontario (December 22).

A Short-eared Owl sat on a post in Ontario (December 22).

But I made the walk, saw a Downy and a Hairy Woodpecker feeding together, and on the walk back to my rental car had a Short-eared Owl perch on a low post about 50 feet from me, and then fly off carrying a small mammal. After that I saw two Snowy Owls and two more hunting Short-eared Owls. No Boreal Owl on my year list. Disappointments are sadly an integral part of birding, especially a big year of birding.

I sit in a plane that is not going anywhere. I can see a light covering of new snow on the ground, but why that should be holding things up, I do not know. What if I spend Christmas in Toronto? I just hope I don't have to spend Christmas in this plane.

Fear

Oft during this year I've had low-level dread,
That made me just need to curl up in my bed.
The fears of more snow, or road-slippery ice,
Of scary plane rides that were not very nice,
Of rushing wild rivers and rough-tossing seas,
Of crashing my car or losing my keys,
Of losing the trail or losing my dream,
And so when it ends, it surely should seem
That life is more gentle, and days have less stress,
Except I will surely still need to address
My need to go birding, to chase, and to find,
And somehow to harness my bird-obsessed mind.

An announcement was just made that some of us must get off the plane—it's too heavy, and there is too little fuel. This is truly bizarre. Meanwhile, we wait and wait. This whole trip from the first long-delayed flight to the terrible walk up the snowy road, to the lack of Boreal Owls, to this mess with this flight, are all helping me be glad this big year is ending and that I have absolutely *no plans* to fly again anywhere. It is helping me not regret that this huge effort will indeed be done in eight days. Other hassles will surely accompany the new year, but air travel isn't likely to be part of it—at least for the foreseeable future.

We just sit here. Whenever I pause to realize that we are essentially locked into a plane that isn't going anywhere, my heart starts to race and my claustrophobia nearly overwhelms me. I think the airline is trying to wait us out, forcing some people to just give up and stay here in Toronto. I wonder if the plane will leave here at all. Maybe I'll be required to relocate to Toronto. We have now boarded a different plane and have to wait for de-icing before heading home.

Solitary

Doing a big year is a solitary quest,
Even if that's not what you really like best.
The planning, the reading, the learning, the
    worry,
The decisions on when to go slow, when to
    hurry,
The places you go, the places you skip,
The decisions you make on timing each trip.
Though some of the birding is done with your
    friends,
The success of the year really depends
On being able, alone, to bear your mistakes,
To keep going alone, with whatever it takes
Through days of no birds, and days when they're
    found,
To keep on keeping on when there's no one
    around.

This big year is over, though three days remain,
I guess I could go out birding again
But I really can't fathom just what I could find,
There is no possibility that comes to my mind.
There are birds that I should have gotten, no
    doubt,
Still I'm really quite happy with how it turned
    out.

DECEMBER 28

So, how did it turn out?

Yesterday I arrived in Arizona after spending the night in New Mexico awaiting precipitation and freezing temperatures. The road from Deming to Tucson had dry tire tracks through the snow and only a few areas that looked dangerous.

I arrived at the Florida Canyon work station where the trail begins leading to the site where two Rufous-capped Warblers had been. I was concerned that they were gone because they had not been reported on the recent Christmas Bird Count. I was very delighted to learn from one of the people coming down the trail toward me that not only were the Rufous-capped Warblers still there but now there were three of them. I hurried up the trail and then the streambed, crossing back and forth over the stream on rocks when it became difficult or impossible to walk on one side or the other.

The birds had been reported as being some distance beyond a large sycamore along the stream-bed, beyond a dam over which water trickled cheerily. "Cheerily" because within 10 minutes of my getting past the dam, I saw two of the Rufous-capped Warblers. Number 723. The last bird species for my big year. Such a feeling of relieved thankfulness that the year was so

B   is for Big Year, one of which I've just done.
I   is for Incredible and Interesting (and fun)
G   is for Going out birding, nonstop.
    Obsessive, compulsive, and over the top.
Y   is for Yes to each chase, to each trip.
E   is for Each helpful person and tip.
A   is for All of the people I met
R   is for Repaying on mountains of debt.
    A Big Year it has been in so many ways:
    The birds, the miles, the fullness of days.

A hunting Short-eared Owl in Ontario (December 22).

The last bird of my big year was Rufous-capped Warbler in southeastern Arizona on December 28.

wonderful, mixed with regret and anguish over birds and opportunities missed.

When I checked out Paton's yesterday afternoon and this morning, I could not even find any small doves, much less a Ruddy Ground-Dove, nor did I see the Sinaloa Wren again. I did see and photograph a Northern Goshawk up the road from the Patagonia Sonoita preserve. That pleased me very much, because my only other sighting of a Northern Goshawk this year had been a quick fly-by in Maine. I then went back to photograph my last big year bird. Two of the Rufous-capped Warblers were casually hopping along 6–15 feet from the streambed, one of them

Summary of ABA Big Year

SPECIES SEEN IN ABA AREA: 723
SPECIES PHOTOGRAPHED: 503
SPECIES SEEN IN LOWER 48: 670
SPECIES SEEN IN TEXAS: 416

STATES BIRDED: 25
PROVINCES BIRDED: 3

MILES DRIVEN: 65,456
MILES WALKED: 1,071
MILES FLOWN *(estimate)*: 110,306
FLIGHTS TAKEN: 92
PELAGIC TRIPS: 10

DAYS BIRDING AWAY FROM HOME: 272
DAYS BIRDING AWAY FROM TEXAS: 195
DAYS NOT BIRDING *(except at home)*: 94

coming within about 5 feet of me as I stood still, snapping pictures. The warblers paid absolutely no attention to me.

That was it, apart from a little tumble that I took down the bank on my walk out, skewering my leg with a century plant and embedding a couple of sharp thorny things in one of my fingers—souvenirs of my big year.

Now I am headed home and have just crossed into New Mexico. I probably have 15–16 hours left on this drive before I get home. I'll probably stop somewhere in West Texas tonight, and then home on Monday to work before joining Dave in Rockport, coming full circle at the end of my big year and joining my birding friends there.

EPILOGUE

AFTER THE BIG YEAR

JANUARY 1, 2009

I birded again today to start the New Year, in spite of the miles and hours spent last year. While it was hard to slow down and get out of the big year mentality, it was great to know that I could enjoy the birds that I saw without needing to race around to get a big list.

MARCH 31, 2009

I am at home in Fort Worth. It's a cool morning after a night of thunderstorms and some hail three months after my big year's end. Outside the back window I can see two White-crowned Sparrows, at least three Lincoln's Sparrows, and a few Chipping Sparrows skittering about onto the ground to find birdseed that I just threw out for them, braving the way-too-many House Sparrows, Brown-headed Cowbirds, and Common Grackles. Two Blue Jays are fighting with the White-winged Doves for sunflower seeds on the bird table, as two Northern Cardinals chirp at it all from a bush nearby and a lingering American Goldfinch flits over to the birdbath for a morning sip. Somewhere a Mourning Dove is sitting and sending forth its owl-like hoots. Earlier, Rufie, my Rufous Hummingbird, was talking to me from the cover of a dense *Eleagnus* along the back fence. If she's got any thoughts at all, she's probably thinking about the long journey north that she will start any day now.

And me, I'm thinking about how wonderful it was to do my big year chasing birds from shore to shore, and also how wonderful it is that birds will come to me (or my yard) when my big year is over and I am no longer chasing them. In my mind, the images of the birds seen last year mingle with the images that I see in my yard now. Maybe that's one reason I love birding so much—it can be enjoyed minute by minute wherever I am and wherever there might be birds, and it can be enjoyed in my memory anytime that I wish.

Barber's Companions
A Lone Quest with Lots of Company

When we read about people climbing Mt. Everest without oxygen or Yosemite's cliffs without a rope, we do not see ourselves in their place, but driving and flying around the country looking for birds—well, we could do that. Nonbirders, though, will quickly ask, "Who would want to?" Surprisingly, many people. A survey by the U.S. Fish and Wildlife Service found some 46 million of us go birding, making it the country's most popular outdoor recreation. Although few actually do a big year, many think or dream about it, and we all recognize the urge to fulfill a dream like the one that drove Barber. And while the big year depends on such features of modern life as inexpensive airline travel, sophisticated field and finding guides, and a community of enthusiasts united by the Internet, the idea goes back to the days when genteel ladies went out with opera glasses to look at birds in the park, as do Barber's concerns about not disturbing birds and what could be counted and her reliance on friends and fellow birders. She followed a trail blazed by several generations of birders and maintained by a community.

Women started the hobby of birding, then called bird-watching, in the late nineteenth century, largely as a way to encourage conservation. Women who were interested in their bird neighbors, the thought ran, would become interested in bird protection, and the best way to interest them was to get them out to look. Identifying and listing were both genteel and humane. Bird protection was a women's issue in those days because many of the birds were being slaughtered for feathers to decorate dresses and hats. Federal and state laws soon ended the slaughter, but birding continued, supported by a national network of Audubon societies, and the hobby now has a century-long history of conservation achievements, and lists. Lists were the easiest way to measure knowledge and field craft and to organize competition and self-competition; besides, many people like making lists. Frank Chapman, founder and editor of the Audubon magazine *Bird-Lore* (now *Audubon*) said he did not believe "the making of a big list for the day or the season should be the one ambition of the field-glass student, yet an occasional effort of this kind, stimulated, perhaps, by friendly rivalry, may be a profitable as well as enjoyable pastime." You can see where that led! He encouraged the practice by starting the Audubon

Christmas Bird Count (still an annual event) and printing personal lists and the results of competitions in the magazine.

In 1908 Kate P. and E. W. Vietor found 93 species in Brooklyn's Prospect Park during 135 visits; E. Fleischer made 169 visits, found all but 3 of the Vietors' species, and brought the total up to 106. In 1913 Annie W. Cobb had the highest total in the Massachusetts Audubon Society, 197 species, followed by Anna Kingman Barry at 169. The next year Barry led with 186 species to Cobb's 181. These seem like modest achievements, but remember, these women had opera glasses, field guides that did not even identify all the species, much less juveniles and variants, and they had no cars, planes, or rare bird hotlines and Web sites. Most were enthusiastic; there were only a few dissenters, people like Eugene Swope, manager of the Audubon nature reserve at Oyster Bay, who in the early 1920s grumbled that listers "were almost as great a nuisance on the sanctuary as cats, and he hoped that their pastime was a fad that would soon run its course."

No such luck. Besides year lists, the kind that drove Barber, there were day lists, another form she mentions. In 1913 Chapman reported a record count, "that of Prof Lynds Jones, who, with two assistants, recorded in Northern Ohio, on May 13, 1907, 144 species." His own best effort, he said, stood at 95, but he thought it possible to see 100 inland species in the Atlantic states. With cars and better methods of identification, it was. On May 17, 1931, Ludlow Griscom, whom Roger Tory Peterson called the dean of the bird-watchers, set off with his friends at 3 A.M., had 104 species by 7:30 in the morning, and at the end of the day, as his ornithological journal triumphantly recorded, "a *world record* list of 163." Two years later Griscom and New Jersey expert Charles Urner drove 300 miles on May 14 to run up another record, 173 species. Peterson recalled these expeditions, meeting with Griscom "before dawn at the cafeteria in Harvard Square. Like a commanding general, Ludlow took charge." They checked tide tables and weather maps, plotted each hour, and "invaded the realm of the birds with military thoroughness. . . . Fast travel between strategic areas with a tankful of gas and good brakes was part of our tactics." They relied, as well, on Griscom's "statewide grapevine the like of which has not been equaled anywhere else in North America," to keep them up to date.

Better transportation made a big year practical, and in 1939, Guy Emerson, a longtime Audubon director, made the first recorded one, when his business travels (by train) aligned with the birds' migrations. He checked off 674 species and subspecies (in those days ornithologists thought subspecies important, and birders kept track of them). In his article in *Bird-Lore,* "The Lure of the List," he presented the project as a gentlemanly, even community, activity, "a cooperative venture" in which some 20 people had generously guided him around land they knew well, and he said the total was of no real importance, though it was "of some interest to know how many varieties of birds can be seen in this country in a year." The total apparently was important enough for him to speculate that it should be possible with good timing and help from local experts to notch up some 700 or 750 of the continent's 1,088 species and subspecies.

Roger Tory Peterson and an English friend, James Fisher, set the next record in 1953 on a summer tour of America's natural wonders. They found the "crucial bird"—Number 498 [now counting only species, not subspecies]—shortly after we reached Anchorage. Flying overhead near the airport was a short-billed gull . . . and [we] sent Guy Emerson a telegram informing him that he had lost his throne as champ of the bird-listers." By the end of the year Peterson had "572 species (not counting an additional 65 Mexican birds)" and Fisher "536, plus the 65 Mexican species, plus 117 others seen in Europe, a total of 718." A year after publication of *Wild America,* their book about the trip, Stuart Keith and his brother Anthony retraced the route, and Stuart notched up 598 species—though Peterson and Fisher still had, with their Mexican detour, a higher year total for the continent, 701. Kenn Kaufman, who left school at 16 to hitchhike around the country in pursuit of birds and in 1973 made his own run at the record (described in *Kingbird Highway: The Story of a Natural Obsession That Got a Little out of Hand*), said that in his early teens his "'bible' had been *Wild America.* Coauthored by my hero, Roger Tory Peterson" it showed that lists "could turn bird-watching into birding, an active game, even a competitive sport." On his own big year he found 666 species—but another enthusiast, Floyd Murdoch, had 669.

Kaufman said that when he made his run, a birder with little money could still compete, but emphasis soon shifted "away from knowledge and planning and experience, toward contacts and hotlines and money. . . . In 1979 a Mississippi businessman [who] admitted that he was a novice . . . hired experts to plan his trips and show him the birds, and he ended the year with a list of 699 species." Other things changed as well. In the early 1970s birders had kept track of their friends' big year journeys; at the end of the decade the journal of the American Birding Association, *Birding,* covered Benton Basham's attempt to eclipse the Mississippi businessman's record from start to finish. Twenty years later mass-market publishing took up the big year when the Free Press brought out Mark Obmascik's *The Big Year,* the tale of three men's pursuit of a new North American record in 1998. One spent $31,000, flew 87,000 miles, and drove another 36,000; a second ran through $60,000 and logged 135,000 miles on United Airlines (besides what he accumulated on other lines); while the winner, Sandy Komito, racked up 270,000 miles, amassing a record list of 745 species. By then, setting a new record depended on seeing all the residents and many strays. Basham's 711 was already 36 more than the breeding species of North America, and Komito benefited from an exceptional El Niño and a Siberian storm that pushed flocks of rarities onto Attu Island.

Here we reach Barber's realm, a year of long drives and longer flights, scheduled trips and unplanned dashes, a frantic, exhilarating quest, organized around birders' knowledge and enabled by businesses, hotlines, and Web sites. Some things, though, did not change. Like the Vietors out in Brooklyn's Prospect Park, Barber followed rules laid down in early field guides and the early volumes of *Bird-Lore.* What counted was an individual of what the American Ornithological Union counted as a "good" species. Escaped cage birds did not count, unless, like the budgies she saw in October, they had established breeding populations, which made them part of the country's bird life. They also had to be seen in the AOU's study area, roughly North America north of Mexico and the seas adjoining. Peterson, remember, had his separate total for Mexico. Mexican birds, of course, counted if they came across the Rio Grande and Asian and European ones if they strayed into our country. That accounted for Barber's trips to the Arizona border, to the Aleutians, and out to sea (this last, for her, a case of suffering for her fun). Birders relied on science, but, it should be said, contributed to it. Barber noted both the Audubon Christmas Bird Count, which ornithologists mined for historical data, and the Fish and Wildlife Service's Breeding Bird Survey, started almost 30 years ago by an ornithologist/birder, Chandler Robbins (author of the popular *Birds of North America,* known as the Golden Guide from its first publisher). Science set the rules of the game, but friends and community made it fun. Barber was always looking for the next bird and thinking about the next trip, but she had many connections to people. She belonged to bird clubs, knew ornithologists, and shared cars and motel rooms with her friends on trips they arranged for birds and companionship. She consulted Internet sites for local conditions and the latest rarities, the modern analog of Griscom's statewide grapevine, and in the field got tips from other birders about some species just down the trail. Her big year was a lone adventure in friendly company.

From the outside it must seem odd that she spent all this time when there was no prize money, no trophy, not even the chance to set a new record waiting for her, but the big year has always been about other things—outdoor skills, a personal best, memories, and something deeper. People went birding, ultimately, because birds fascinated them. The early field guides spoke of the beauties to be found in the birds' world, and Roger Tory Peterson found in his all-absorbing interest in birds a way to deal with the "strait jacket of a world which I did not comprehend" and make "some sort of peace with society. The birds, which started as an escape from the unreal, bridged the gap to reality and became a key whereby I might unlock eternal things." Kenn Kaufman, recounting his teenage big year, told of a California birding guru who worked on his list but felt it was unimportant, who believed birds were "magical, and . . . searching after them was a Great Adventure, . . . [with the list] just a frivolous incentive for birding." Millions of birders would echo these sentiments. Records, lists, and the fine points of field identification organized the search for wonder that made people into passionate birders.

—THOMAS R. DUNLAP

ABA BIRDS SEEN IN TAXONOMIC ORDER

The species name is followed by species' ABA code, date first seen, and place first seen.

Black-bellied Whistling-Duck 1 (Jan. 1, Aransas Co., TX)

Fulvous Whistling-Duck 1 (Jan. 30, Kleberg Co., TX)

Tundra Bean-Goose 3 (May 11, Adak Island, AK)

Pink-footed Goose 4 (Feb. 23, NY)

Greater White-fronted Goose 1 (Jan. 2, Kleberg Co., TX)

Emperor Goose 2 (June 8, Nome, AK)

Snow Goose 1 (Jan. 1, Aransas Co., TX)

Ross's Goose 1 (Jan. 2, Kleberg Co., TX)

Brant 1 (Jan. 18, CA)

Barnacle Goose 5 (Feb. 24, NJ)

Cackling Goose 1 (Jan. 20, CA)

Canada Goose 1 (Jan. 18, CA)

Mute Swan 1 (Feb. 23, NY)

Trumpeter Swan 1 (Mar. 1, OR)

Tundra Swan 1 (Feb. 17, NC)

Muscovy Duck 3 (Sept. 26, Starr Co., TX)

Wood Duck 1 (Jan. 25, Hartley Co., TX)

Gadwall 1 (Jan. 1, Aransas Co., TX)

Eurasian Wigeon 3 (Jan. 21, CA)

American Wigeon 1 (Jan. 1, Aransas Co., TX)

American Black Duck 1 (Feb. 15, NC)

Mallard 1 (Jan. 1, Aransas Co., TX)

Mottled Duck 1 (Jan. 1, Aransas Co., TX)

Blue-winged Teal 1 (Jan. 1, Aransas Co., TX)

Cinnamon Teal 1 (Jan. 1, Nueces Co., TX)

Northern Shoveler 1 (Jan. 1, Aransas Co., TX)

Northern Pintail 1 (Jan. 1, Aransas Co., TX)

Green-winged Teal 1 (Jan. 1, Aransas Co., TX)

Canvasback 1 (Jan. 1, Aransas Co., TX)

Redhead 1 (Jan. 1, Aransas Co., TX)

Ring-necked Duck 1 (Jan. 2, Kenedy Co., TX)

Tufted Duck 3 (May 11, Adak Island, AK)

Greater Scaup 1 (Jan. 18, CA)

Lesser Scaup 1 (Jan. 1, Aransas Co., TX)

Steller's Eider 2 (June 2, Gambell, AK)

Spectacled Eider 2 (June 11, Barrow, AK)

King Eider 1 (Feb. 23, NY)

Common Eider 1 (Feb. 23, NY)

Harlequin Duck 1 (Feb. 28, OR)

Surf Scoter 1 (Jan. 17, CA)

White-winged Scoter 1 (Feb. 23, NY)

Black Scoter 1 (Feb. 23, NY)

Long-tailed Duck 1 (Jan. 18, CA)

Bufflehead 1 (Jan. 1, Aransas Co., TX)

Common Goldeneye 1 (Jan. 1, Aransas Co., TX)

Barrow's Goldeneye 1 (Mar. 2, WA)

Hooded Merganser 1 (Jan. 1, Nueces Co., TX)

Common Merganser 1 (Jan. 9, MN)

Red-breasted Merganser 1 (Jan. 9, MN)

Masked Duck 3 (Jan. 30, Kleberg Co., TX)

Ruddy Duck 1 (Jan. 1, Aransas Co., TX)

Plain Chachalaca 2 (Jan. 2, Cameron Co., TX)

Chukar 2 (Oct. 3, WA)

Himalayan Snowcock 2 (Aug. 6, NV)

Gray Partridge 2 (Nov. 27, WA)

Ring-necked Pheasant 1 (Jan. 25, Hartley Co., TX)

Ruffed Grouse 1 (May 22, MI)

Greater Sage-Grouse 1 (Apr. 11, CO)

Gunnison Sage-Grouse 2 (Apr. 13, CO)

Spruce Grouse 2 (July 1, ME)

Willow Ptarmigan 1 (June 7, Nome, AK)

Rock Ptarmigan 1 (May 11, Adak Island, AK)

White-tailed Ptarmigan 2 (Nov. 23, CO)
Sooty Grouse 2 (Oct. 2, WA)
Sharp-tailed Grouse 2 (Jan. 10, MN)
Greater Prairie-Chicken 2 (Mar. 12, NE)
Lesser Prairie-Chicken 2 (Apr. 8, Lipscomb Co., TX)
Wild Turkey 1 (Jan. 5, Aransas Co., TX)
Mountain Quail 1 (Sept. 5, CA)
Scaled Quail 1 (Jan. 15, NM)
California Quail 1 (Jan. 17, CA)
Gambel's Quail 1 (Jan. 15, El Paso Co., TX)
Northern Bobwhite 1 (Jan. 4, Hidalgo Co., TX)
Montezuma Quail 2 (July 11, AZ)
Red-throated Loon 1 (Feb. 16, NC)
Arctic Loon 2 (May 16, Adak Island, AK)
Pacific Loon 1 (Jan. 19, CA)
Common Loon 1 (Jan. 1, Aransas Co., TX)
Yellow-billed Loon 2 (June 5, Gambell, AK)
Least Grebe 2 (Jan. 2, Cameron Co., TX)
Pied-billed Grebe 1 (Jan. 1, Aransas Co., TX)
Horned Grebe 1 (Jan. 7, Tarrant Co., TX)
Red-necked Grebe 1 (Feb. 28, OR)
Eared Grebe 1 (Jan. 1, Aransas Co., TX)
Western Grebe 1 (Jan. 18, CA)
Clark's Grebe 1 (July 17, NV)
Laysan Albatross 2 (Mar. 1, OR)
Black-footed Albatross 1 (Mar. 1, OR)
Black-capped Petrel 2 (Aug. 22, NC)
Cory's Shearwater 1 (Aug. 22, NC)
Pink-footed Shearwater 1 (Jan. 19, CA)
Flesh-footed Shearwater 3 (Sept. 13, CA)
Greater Shearwater 1 (Aug. 22, NC)
Buller's Shearwater 2 (Sept. 13, CA)
Sooty Shearwater 1 (Jan. 19, CA)
Short-tailed Shearwater 2 (Jan. 19, CA)
Manx Shearwater 2 (Feb. 16, NC)
Black-vented Shearwater 2 (Jan. 19, CA)
Audubon's Shearwater 1 (Apr. 22, FL)
Wilson's Storm-Petrel 1 (Aug. 22, NC)
Fork-tailed Storm-Petrel 2 (Sept. 13, CA)
Leach's Storm-Petrel 1 (Sept. 13, CA)
Ashy Storm-Petrel 2 (Sept. 13, CA)
Band-rumped Storm-Petrel 2 (Aug. 22, NC)

Black Storm-Petrel 2 (Sept. 13, CA)
Least Storm-Petrel 2 (Nov. 2, CA)
Red-billed Tropicbird 3 (Nov. 2, CA)
Masked Booby 3 (Apr. 22, FL)
Brown Booby 3 (Apr. 22, FL)
Northern Gannet 1 (Feb. 15, NC)
American White Pelican 1 (Jan. 1, Aransas Co., TX)
Brown Pelican 1 (Jan. 1, Aransas Co., TX)
Brandt's Cormorant 1 (Jan. 18, CA)
Neotropic Cormorant 1 (Jan. 4, Hidalgo Co., TX)
Double-crested Cormorant 1 (Jan. 1, Aransas Co., TX)
Great Cormorant 1 (Feb. 15, NC)
Red-faced Cormorant 2 (May 12, Adak, AK)
Pelagic Cormorant 1 (Jan. 18, CA)
Anhinga 1 (Jan. 3, Hidalgo Co., TX)
Magnificent Frigatebird 1 (Apr. 18, FL)
American Bittern 1 (Mar. 30, Chambers Co., TX)
Least Bittern 1 (Mar. 30, Chambers Co., TX)
Great Blue Heron 1 (Jan. 1, Aransas Co., TX)
Great Egret 1 (Jan. 1, Aransas Co., TX)
Snowy Egret 1 (Jan. 1, Aransas Co., TX)
Little Blue Heron 1 (Jan. 4, Hidalgo Co., TX)
Tricolored Heron 1 (Jan. 1, Aransas Co., TX)
Reddish Egret 1 (Jan. 1, Aransas Co., TX)
Cattle Egret 1 (Jan. 1, Aransas Co., TX)
Green Heron 1 (Jan. 30, Kleberg Co., TX)
Black-crowned Night-Heron 1 (Jan. 1, Aransas Co., TX)
Yellow-crowned Night-Heron 1 (Jan. 30, Nueces Co., TX)
White Ibis 1 (Jan. 1, Aransas Co., TX)
Glossy Ibis 1 (Feb. 19, FL)
White-faced Ibis 1 (Jan. 1, Aransas Co., TX)
Roseate Spoonbill 1 (Jan. 1, Aransas Co., TX)
Wood Stork 1 (Feb. 19, FL)
Black Vulture 1 (Jan. 1, Aransas Co., TX)
Turkey Vulture 1 (Jan. 1, Aransas Co., TX)
Greater Flamingo 3 (Oct. 24, FL)
Osprey 1 (Jan. 1, Aransas Co., TX)

Hook-billed Kite 3 (Nov. 9, Hidalgo Co., TX)

Swallow-tailed Kite 1 (Apr. 18, FL)

White-tailed Kite 1 (Jan. 2, Cameron Co., TX)

Snail Kite 2 (Feb. 19, FL)

Mississippi Kite 1 (Apr. 27, Jackson Co., TX)

Bald Eagle 1 (Jan. 8, MN)

Northern Harrier 1 (Jan. 1, Aransas Co., TX)

Sharp-shinned Hawk 1 (Jan. 1, Aransas Co., TX)

Cooper's Hawk 1 (Jan. 3, Hidalgo Co., TX)

Northern Goshawk 1 (July 3, ME)

Common Black-Hawk 2 (Apr. 2, Brewster Co., TX)

Harris's Hawk 1 (Jan. 2, Nueces Co., TX)

Red-shouldered Hawk 1 (Jan. 1, Aransas Co., TX)

Broad-winged Hawk 1 (Jan. 3, Cameron Co., TX)

Gray Hawk 2 (Jan. 3, Cameron Co., TX)

Short-tailed Hawk 2 (Feb. 19, FL)

Swainson's Hawk 1 (Mar. 20, Hidalgo Co., TX)

White-tailed Hawk 2 (Jan. 1, San Patricio Co., TX)

Zone-tailed Hawk 2 (Apr. 5, Jeff Davis Co., TX)

Red-tailed Hawk 1 (Jan. 1, Aransas Co., TX)

Ferruginous Hawk 1 (Jan. 5, Refugio Co., TX)

Rough-legged Hawk 1 (Jan. 8, MN)

Golden Eagle 1 (Jan. 20, CA)

Crested Caracara 1 (Jan. 1, Aransas Co., TX)

American Kestrel 1 (Jan. 1, Aransas Co., TX)

Merlin 1 (Jan. 7, Tarrant Co., TX)

Gyrfalcon 2 (June 7, Nome, AK)

Peregrine Falcon 1 (Jan. 1, Nueces Co., TX)

Prairie Falcon 1 (Jan. 20, CA)

Yellow Rail 2 (Mar. 30, Chambers Co., TX)

Black Rail 2 (Mar. 29, Calhoun Co., TX)

Clapper Rail 1 (Jan. 5, Aransas Co., TX)

King Rail 1 (Mar. 31, Jefferson Co., TX)

Virginia Rail 1 (Oct. 7, CA)

Sora 1 (Jan. 4, Cameron Co., TX)

Purple Gallinule 1 (Feb. 19, FL)

Common Moorhen 1 (Jan. 1, Aransas Co., TX)

American Coot 1 (Jan. 1, Aransas Co., TX)

Limpkin 2 (Feb. 19, FL)

Sandhill Crane 1 (Jan. 1, Aransas Co., TX)

Whooping Crane 2 (Jan. 5, Aransas Co., TX)

Northern Lapwing 4 (Dec. 6, NL)

Black-bellied Plover 1 (Jan. 1, Aransas Co., TX)

American Golden-Plover 1 (Mar. 17, Galveston Co., TX)

Pacific Golden-Plover 2 (May 15, Adak Island, AK)

Snowy Plover 1 (Mar. 20, Cameron Co., TX)

Wilson's Plover 1 (Mar. 17, Galveston Co., TX)

Common Ringed-Plover 2 (June 3, Gambell, AK)

Semipalmated Plover 1 (Jan. 1, Nueces Co., TX)

Piping Plover 2 (Mar. 17, Galveston Co., TX)

Killdeer 1 (Jan. 1, Aransas Co., TX)

Mountain Plover 2 (Jan. 20, CA)

American Oystercatcher 1 (Feb. 15, NC)

Black Oystercatcher 1 (Jan. 18, CA)

Black-necked Stilt 1 (Jan. 1, Refugio Co., TX)

American Avocet 1 (Jan. 1, Aransas Co., TX)

Northern Jacana 4 (Jan. 16, AZ)

Common Sandpiper 3 (May 26, St. Paul Island, AK)

Spotted Sandpiper 1 (Jan. 2, Cameron Co., TX)

Solitary Sandpiper 1 (Jan. 30, Kleberg Co., TX)

Gray-tailed Tattler 3 (June 5, Gambell, AK)

Wandering Tattler 1 (May 17, Adak Island, AK)

Greater Yellowlegs 1 (Jan. 1, Aransas Co., TX)

Willet 1 (Jan. 1, Aransas Co., TX)

Lesser Yellowlegs 1 (Jan. 1, Aransas Co., TX)

Wood Sandpiper 2 (Oct. 4, OR)

Upland Sandpiper 1 (Mar. 31, Ellis Co., TX)

Whimbrel 1 (Jan. 18, CA)

Bristle-thighed Curlew 2 (June 7, Nome, AK)

Long-billed Curlew 1 (Jan. 1, Aransas Co., TX)

Hudsonian Godwit 1 (May 1, Matagorda Co., TX)

Bar-tailed Godwit 2 (May 17, Adak Island, AK)

Marbled Godwit 1 (Jan. 18, CA)

Ruddy Turnstone 1 (Jan. 1, Nueces Co., TX)

Black Turnstone 1 (Jan. 18, CA)

Surfbird 1 (Jan. 18, CA)

Red Knot 1 (Mar. 31, Galveston Co., TX)

Sanderling 1 (Jan. 1, Nueces Co., TX)

Semipalmated Sandpiper 1 (Mar. 31, Galveston Co., TX)

Western Sandpiper 1 (Mar. 3, WA)

Red-necked Stint 3 (Aug. 25, St. Paul Island, AK)

Least Sandpiper 1 (Jan. 1, Aransas Co., TX)

White-rumped Sandpiper (Apr. 28, Kleberg Co., TX)

Baird's Sandpiper 1 (Apr. 15, Travis Co., TX)

Pectoral Sandpiper 1 (Mar. 29, Calhoun Co., TX)

Sharp-tailed Sandpiper 3 (Aug. 25, St. Paul Island, AK)

Purple Sandpiper 1 (Feb. 15, NC)

Rock Sandpiper 2 (May 12, Adak Island, AK)

Dunlin 1 (Jan. 1, Aransas Co., TX)

Stilt Sandpiper 1 (Feb. 12, Hidalgo Co., TX)

Buff-breasted Sandpiper 1 (May 1, Matagorda Co., TX)

Ruff 3 (Apr. 15, Travis Co., TX)

Short-billed Dowitcher 1 (Mar. 17, Galveston Co., TX)

Long-billed Dowitcher 1 (Jan. 1, Aransas Co., TX)

Jack Snipe 5 (June 4, Gambell, AK)

Wilson's Snipe 1 (Jan. 5, Aransas Co., TX)

Common Snipe 3 (May 16, Adak Island, AK)

American Woodcock 1 (Feb. 2, Tarrant Co., TX)

Wilson's Phalarope 1 (Apr. 15, Travis Co., TX)

Red-necked Phalarope 1 (May 16, Adak Island, AK)

Red Phalarope 1 (Feb. 16, NC)

Laughing Gull 1 (Jan. 1, Aransas Co., TX)

Franklin's Gull 1 (Apr. 10, CO)

Little Gull 3 (Mar. 6, Dallas Co., TX)

Black-headed Gull 3 (Dec. 6, Newfoundland)

Bonaparte's Gull 1 (Jan. 1, Nueces Co., TX)

Heerman's Gull 1 (Jan. 17, CA)

Mew Gull 1 (Jan. 18, CA)

Ring-billed Gull 1 (Jan. 1, Aransas Co., TX)

California Gull 1 (Jan. 17, CA)

Herring Gull 1 (Jan. 1, Aransas Co., TX)

Yellow-legged Gull 4 (Dec. 6, Newfoundland)

Thayer's Gull 2 (Jan. 18, CA)

Iceland Gull 2 (Dec. 6, Newfoundland)

Lesser Black-backed Gull 3 (Feb. 14, Harris Co., TX)

Slaty-backed Gull 3 (June 5, Gambell, AK)

Yellow-footed Gull 2 (Sept. 6, CA)

Western Gull 1 (Jan. 17, CA)

Glaucous-winged Gull 1 (Jan. 18, CA)

Glaucous Gull 1 (Jan. 9, MN)

Great Black-backed Gull 1 (Feb. 15, NC)

Kelp Gull 4 (Nov. 10, Brazoria Co., TX)

Sabine's Gull 1 (June 4, Gambell, AK)

Black-legged Kittiwake 1 (Jan. 19, CA)

Red-legged Kittiwake 2 (May 27, St. Paul Island, AK)

Ross's Gull 3 (Oct. 11, Barrow, AK)

Ivory Gull 3 (June 3, Gambell, AK)

Brown Noddy 2 (Apr. 22, FL)

Black Noddy 3 (Apr. 22, FL)

Sooty Tern 2 (Apr. 22, FL)

Bridled Tern 2 (Apr. 22, FL)

Aleutian Tern 2 (May 16, Adak Island, AK)

Least Tern 1 (Mar. 31, Galveston Co., TX)

Gull-billed Tern 1 (Jan. 1, Aransas Co., TX)

Caspian Tern 1 (Jan. 1, Aransas Co., TX)

Black Tern 1 (Mar. 31, Galveston Co., TX)

Roseate Tern 2 (July 1, ME)

Common Tern 1 (Jan. 1, Nueces Co., TX)

Arctic Tern 1 (May 16, Adak Island, AK)

Forster's Tern 1 (Jan. 1, Aransas Co., TX)

Royal Tern 1 (Jan. 1, Nueces Co., TX)

Sandwich Tern 1 (Mar 18, Nueces Co., TX)

Elegant Tern 1 (Sept. 2, CA)

Black Skimmer 1 (Jan. 30, Nueces Co, TX)

Great Skua 3 (Feb. 16, NC)
South Polar Skua 2 (Sept. 13, CA)
Pomarine Jaeger 1 (Jan. 19, CA)
Parasitic Jaeger 1 (May 11, Adak Island, AK)
Long-tailed Jaeger 1 (May 30, St. Paul Island, AK)
Dovekie 2 (Feb. 16, NC)
Common Murre 1 (Jan. 19, CA)
Thick-billed Murre 1 (May 27, St. Paul Island, AK)
Razorbill 1 (Feb. 16, NC)
Black Guillemot 1 (June 2, Gambell, AK)
Pigeon Guillemot 1 (Feb. 28, OR)
Marbled Murrelet 1 (Jan. 19, CA)
Kittlitz's Murrelet 2 (May 11, Adak Island, AK)
Xantus's Murrelet 2 (Nov. 1, CA)
Ancient Murrelet 2 (Mar. 3, WA)
Cassin's Auklet 1 (Mar. 1, OR)
Parakeet Auklet 2 (May 17, Adak Island, AK)
Least Auklet 2 (May 17, Adak Island, AK)
Whiskered Auklet 2 (May 17, Adak Island, AK)
Crested Auklet 2 (May 17, Adak Island, AK)
Rhinoceros Auklet 1 (Jan. 19, CA)
Atlantic Puffin 1 (July 2, ME)
Horned Puffin 1 (May 17, Adak Island, AK)
Tufted Puffin 1 (May 16, Adak Island, AK)
Rock Pigeon 1 (Jan. 1, San Patricio Co., TX)
White-crowned Pigeon 1 (Feb. 19, FL)
Red-billed Pigeon 3 (Feb. 11, Starr Co., TX)
Band-tailed Pigeon 1 (Jan. 20, CA)
Eurasian Collared-Dove 1 (Jan. 1, Aransas Co., TX)
Spotted Dove 1 (Sept. 3, CA)
White-winged Dove 1 (Jan. 1, Aransas Co., TX)
Mourning Dove 1 (Jan. 1, Aransas Co., TX)
Inca Dove 1 (Jan. 1, Nueces Co., TX)
Common Ground-Dove 1 (Jan. 30, Kleberg Co., TX)
White-tipped Dove 2 (Jan. 2, Cameron Co., TX)

Budgerigar 3 (Oct. 26, FL)
Monk Parakeet 2 (Jan. 12, Tarrant Co., TX)
Green Parakeet 2 (Jan. 2, Cameron Co., TX)
White-winged Parakeet 2 (Feb. 19, FL)
Red-crowned Parrot 2 (Mar. 18, Hidalgo Co., TX)
Yellow-billed Cuckoo 1 (Apr. 22, FL)
Mangrove Cuckoo 2 (Aug. 2, FL)
Black-billed Cuckoo 1 (Apr. 29, Hidalgo Co., TX)
Greater Roadrunner 1 (Jan. 15, El Paso Co., TX)
Smooth-billed Ani 3 (Oct. 24, FL) Number 700!
Groove-billed Ani 2 (Jan. 3, Cameron Co., TX)
Barn Owl 1 (Jan. 18, CA)
Flammulated Owl 2 (Apr. 3, Brewster Co., TX)
Western Screech-Owl 1 (Apr. 3, Brewster Co., TX)
Eastern Screech-Owl 1 (Feb. 5, Tarrant Co., TX)
Whiskered Screech-Owl 2 (July 13, AZ)
Great Horned Owl 1 (Jan. 3, Hidalgo Co., TX)
Snowy Owl 2 (Jan. 9, MN)
Northern Hawk Owl 2 (Jan. 9, MN)
Northern Pygmy-Owl 2 (July 13, AZ)
Ferruginous Pygmy-Owl 3 (Feb. 10, Hidalgo Co., TX)
Elf Owl 2 (Apr. 4, Brewster Co., TX)
Burrowing Owl 1 (Jan.15, El Paso Co., TX)
Spotted Owl 2 (Aug. 17, AZ)
Barred Owl 1 (Feb. 2, Tarrant Co., TX)
Great Gray Owl 2 (Jan. 10, MN)
Long-eared Owl 2 (Jan. 15, El Paso Co., TX)
Short-eared Owl 2 (Jan. 7, Tarrant Co., TX)
Northern Saw-whet Owl 2 (Oct. 30, CA)
Lesser Nighthawk 1 (Apr. 28, Hidalgo Co., TX)
Common Nighthawk 1 (Apr. 18, FL)
Antillean Nighthawk 3 (Aug. 1, FL)
Common Pauraque 2 (Jan. 3, Hidalgo Co., TX)
Common Poorwill 1 (Apr. 3, Brewster Co., TX)

Chuck-will's-widow 1 (Mar. 18, Hidalgo Co., TX)

Whip-poor-will 1 (May 1, Live Oak Co., TX)

Black Swift 2 (July 20, NM)

Chimney Swift 1 (Apr. 6, Tarrant Co., TX)

Vaux's Swift 1 (Oct. 3, WA)

White-throated Swift 1 (Apr. 3, Brewster Co., TX)

Green-breasted Mango 4 (Mar. 23, GA)

Broad-billed Hummingbird 2 (July 9, AZ)

White-eared Hummingbird 3 (July 9, AZ)

Berylline Hummingbird 3 (Aug. 15, AZ)

Buff-bellied Hummingbird 2 (Feb. 10, Cameron Co., TX)

Violet-crowned Hummingbird 2 (July 11, AZ)

Blue-throated Hummingbird 2 (Apr. 3, Brewster Co., TX)

Magnificent Hummingbird 2 (July 9, AZ)

Plain-capped Starthroat 4 (Sept. 22, AZ)

Lucifer Hummingbird 2 (July 10, AZ)

Ruby-throated Hummingbird 1 (Feb. 19, FL)

Black-chinned Hummingbird 1 (Apr. 4, Brewster Co., TX)

Anna's Hummingbird 1 (Jan. 16, AZ)

Costa's Hummingbird 1 (July 14, AZ)

Calliope Hummingbird 1 (Jan. 31, Harris Co., TX)

Broad-tailed Hummingbird 1 (July 9, AZ)

Rufous Hummingbird 1 (Jan. 4, Hidalgo Co., TX)

Allen's Hummingbird 1 (Jan. 31, Harris Co., TX)

Elegant Trogon 2 (July 13, AZ)

Ringed Kingfisher 2 (Jan. 3, Cameron Co., TX)

Belted Kingfisher 1 (Jan. 1, Nueces Co., TX)

Green Kingfisher 2 (Jan. 4, Hidalgo Co., TX)

Lewis's Woodpecker 1 (Jan. 20, CA)

Red-headed Woodpecker 1 (Feb. 6, Grayson Co., TX)

Acorn Woodpecker 1 (Jan. 16, AZ)

Gila Woodpecker 1 (Jan. 23, AZ)

Golden-fronted Woodpecker 1 (Jan. 2, Kenedy Co., TX)

Red-bellied Woodpecker 1 (Jan. 7, Tarrant Co., TX)

Williamson's Sapsucker 1 (July 18, NM)

Yellow-bellied Sapsucker 1 (Feb. 1, Parker Co., TX)

Red-naped Sapsucker 1 (Sept. 23, AZ)

Red-breasted Sapsucker 1 (Jan. 18, CA)

Ladder-backed Woodpecker 1 (Jan. 1, Nueces Co., TX)

Nuttall's Woodpecker 1 (Sept. 8, CA)

Downy Woodpecker 1 (Jan. 7, Tarrant Co., TX)

Hairy Woodpecker 1 (Jan. 9, MN)

Arizona Woodpecker 2 (Jan. 16, AZ)

Red-cockaded Woodpecker 2 (Mar. 24, GA)

White-headed Woodpecker 1 (Sept. 5, CA)

American Three-toed Woodpecker 2 (Jan. 9, MN)

Black-backed Woodpecker 2 (Jan. 9, MN)

Northern Flicker 1 (Jan. 7, Tarrant Co., TX)

Gilded Flicker 2 (July 14, AZ)

Pileated Woodpecker 1 (Jan. 8, MN)

Northern Beardless-Tyrannulet 2 (Jan. 3, Hidalgo Co., TX)

White-crested Elaenia 5 (Feb. 10, Cameron Co., TX)

Olive-sided Flycatcher 1 (May 3, Jefferson Co., TX)

Greater Pewee 2 (July 14, AZ)

Western Wood-Pewee 1 (July 10, AZ)

Eastern Wood-Pewee 1 (Apr. 29, Hidalgo Co., TX)

Yellow-bellied Flycatcher 1 (Apr. 29, Hidalgo Co., TX)

Acadian Flycatcher 1 (Apr. 29, Hidalgo Co., TX)

Alder Flycatcher 1 (May 31, Eagle River, AK)

Willow Flycatcher 1 (Apr. 29, Hidalgo Co., TX)

Least Flycatcher 1(Apr. 28, McMullen Co., TX)

Hammond's Flycatcher 1 (June 13, Fairbanks, AK)

Gray Flycatcher 1 (July 30, Culberson Co., TX)

Dusky Flycatcher 1 (July 15, NV)

Pacific-slope Flycatcher 1 (Sept. 3, CA)

Cordilleran Flycatcher 1 (July 10, AZ),

Buff-breasted Flycatcher 2 (July 10, AZ)

Black Phoebe 1 (Jan. 15, El Paso Co., TX)

Eastern Phoebe 1 (Jan. 1, Aransas Co., TX)

Say's Phoebe 1 (Jan. 15, NM)

Vermilion Flycatcher 1 (Jan. 1, Nueces Co., TX)

Dusky-capped Flycatcher 2 (Jan. 3, Cameron Co., TX)

Ash-throated Flycatcher 1 (Apr. 2, Brewster Co., TX)

Great Crested Flycatcher 1 (Mar. 25, GA)

Brown-crested Flycatcher 1 (Mar. 20, Hidalgo Co., TX)

Great Kiskadee 2 (Jan. 1, Nueces Co., TX)

Sulphur-bellied Flycatcher 2 (July 9, AZ)

Piratic Flycatcher 5 (May 4, Nueces Co., TX)

Tropical Kingbird 2 (Jan. 4, Hidalgo Co., TX)

Couch's Kingbird 2 (Jan. 2, Cameron Co., TX)

Cassin's Kingbird 1 (July 9, AZ)

Thick-billed Kingbird 2 (Aug. 16, AZ)

Western Kingbird 1 (Apr. 14, NM)

Eastern Kingbird 1 (Mar. 29, Calhoun Co., TX)

Gray Kingbird 2 (Apr. 18, FL)

Scissor-tailed Flycatcher 1 (Mar. 19, Zapata Co., TX)

Fork-tailed Flycatcher 4 (Mar. 16, Jefferson Co., TX)

Rose-throated Becard 3 (Nov. 8, Hidalgo Co., TX)

Loggerhead Shrike 1 (Jan. 1, Aransas Co., TX)

Northern Shrike 1 (Jan. 10, MN)

White-eyed Vireo 1 (Jan. 2, Cameron Co., TX)

Bell's Vireo 1 (Apr. 4, Brewster Co., TX)

Black-capped Vireo 2 (Mar. 28, Burnet Co., TX)

Gray Vireo 2 (Apr. 5, Brewster Co., TX)

Yellow-throated Vireo 1 (May 2, Jasper Co., TX)

Plumbeous Vireo 1 (July 10, AZ)

Cassin's Vireo 1 (Sept. 15, CA)

Blue-headed Vireo 1 (Jan. 3, Hidalgo Co., TX)

Hutton's Vireo 1 (Jan. 21, CA)

Warbling Vireo 1 (Apr. 29, Hidalgo Co., TX)

Philadelphia Vireo 1 (Apr. 29, Hidalgo Co., TX)

Red-eyed Vireo 1 (Apr. 19, FL)

Yellow-green Vireo 3 (Aug. 10, Cameron Co., TX)

Black-whiskered Vireo 2 (Apr. 21, FL)

Gray Jay 1 (Jan. 9, MN)

Steller's Jay 1 (Jan. 25, NM)

Blue Jay 1 (Jan. 7, Tarrant Co., TX)

Green Jay 2 (Jan. 2, Kenedy Co., TX)

Florida Scrub-Jay 2 (Apr. 17, FL)

Island Scrub-Jay 2 (Sept. 4, CA)

Western Scrub-Jay 1 (Jan. 17, CA)

Mexican Jay 2 (Jan. 16, AZ)

Pinyon Jay 1 (Apr. 11, CO)

Clark's Nutcracker 1 (Apr. 13, CO)

Black-billed Magpie 1 (Jan. 10, MN)

Yellow-billed Magpie 2 (Jan. 20, CA)

American Crow 1 (Jan. 6, Victoria Co., TX)

Northwestern Crow 1 (Mar. 3, BC)

Fish Crow 1 (Feb. 19, FL)

Chihuahuan Raven 1 (Jan. 2, Cameron Co., TX)

Common Raven 1 (Jan. 8, MN)

Sky Lark 2 (Mar. 3, BC)

Horned Lark 1 (Jan. 2, Cameron Co., TX)

Purple Martin 1 (Feb. 10, Hidalgo Co., TX)

Tree Swallow 1 (Jan. 31, Jefferson Co., TX)

Violet-green Swallow 1 (Apr. 5, Brewster Co., TX)

Northern Rough-winged Swallow 1 (Jan. 4, Hidalgo Co., TX)

Bank Swallow 1 (Apr. 22, FL)

Cliff Swallow 1 (Mar. 21, Refugio Co., TX)

Cave Swallow 1 (Jan. 3, Hidalgo Co., TX)

Barn Swallow 1 (Jan. 17, CA)

Carolina Chickadee 1 (Jan. 6, Williamson Co., TX)

Black-capped Chickadee 1 (Jan. 8, MN)

Mountain Chickadee 1 (Jan. 25, NM)

Mexican Chickadee 2 (Sept. 24, AZ)

Chestnut-backed Chickadee 1 (Jan. 17, CA)

Boreal Chickadee 1 (Jan. 9, MN)

Gray-headed Chickadee 3 (June 16, Arctic NWR, AK)

Bridled Titmouse 2 (Jan. 16, AZ)

Oak Titmouse 1 (Jan. 17, CA)

Juniper Titmouse 1 (July 12, AZ)

Tufted Titmouse 1 (Jan. 7, Tarrant Co., TX)

Black-crested Titmouse 2 (Jan. 2, Cameron Co., TX)

Verdin 1 (Jan. 3, Hidalgo Co., TX)

Bushtit 1 (Jan. 20, CA)

Red-breasted Nuthatch 1 (Jan. 8, MN)

White-breasted Nuthatch 1 (Jan. 9, MN)

Pygmy Nuthatch 1 (July 12, AZ)

Brown-headed Nuthatch 1 (Mar. 14, Smith Co., TX)

Brown Creeper 1 (Jan. 7, Tarrant Co., TX)

Cactus Wren 1 (Jan. 15, NM)

Rock Wren 1 (Apr. 2, Brewster Co., TX)

Canyon Wren 1 (Apr. 2, Brewster Co., TX)

Carolina Wren 1 (Jan. 2, Cameron Co., TX)

Bewick's Wren 1 (Jan. 7, Tarrant Co., TX)

House Wren 1 (Jan. 2, Cameron Co., TX)

Winter Wren 1 (Jan. 1, Aransas Co., TX)

Sedge Wren 1 (Mar. 29, Calhoun Co., TX)

Marsh Wren 1 (Jan. 15, El Paso Co., TX)

Sinaloa Wren 5 (Sept. 7, AZ)

American Dipper 1 (Feb. 29, OR)

Red-whiskered Bulbul 2 (Feb. 19, FL)

Golden-crowned Kinglet 1 (Feb. 28, OR)

Ruby-crowned Kinglet 1 (Jan. 1, Aransas Co., TX)

Arctic Warbler 2 (June 8, Nome, AK)

Blue-gray Gnatcatcher 1 (Jan. 1, Aransas Co., TX)

California Gnatcatcher 2 (Sept. 3, CA)

Black-tailed Gnatcatcher 1 (Apr. 5, Brewster Co., TX)

Black-capped Gnatcatcher 4 (Aug. 15, AZ)

Bluethroat 2 (June 2, Gambell, AK)

Northern Wheatear 2 (June 7, Nome, AK)

Eastern Bluebird 1 (Jan. 6, Refugio Co., TX)

Western Bluebird 1 (Jan. 18, CA)

Mountain Bluebird 1 (Jan. 20, CA)

Townsend's Solitaire 1 (May 31, Anchorage, AK)

Veery 1 (Apr. 29, Hidalgo Co., TX)

Gray-cheeked Thrush 1 (May 2, Galveston Co., TX)

Bicknell's Thrush 2 (July 1, ME)

Swainson's Thrush 1 (Apr. 22, FL)

Hermit Thrush 1 (Jan. 7, Tarrant Co., TX)

Wood Thrush 1 (Feb. 11, Zapata Co., TX)

Clay-colored Thrush 3 (Jan. 4, Hidalgo Co., TX)

White-throated Thrush 5 (Mar. 18, Hidalgo Co., TX)

Rufous-backed Robin 3 (Jan. 23, AZ)

American Robin 1 (Jan. 5, Nueces Co., TX)

Varied Thrush 1 (Jan. 9, MN)

Aztec Thrush 4 (Jan. 16, AZ)

Wrentit 1 (Jan. 21, CA)

Gray Catbird 1 (Jan. 5, Aransas Co., TX)

Northern Mockingbird 1 (Jan. 1, Aransas Co., TX)

Sage Thrasher 1 (Apr. 9, CO)

Brown Thrasher 1 (Feb. 2, Tarrant Co., TX)

Long-billed Thrasher 2 (Jan. 3, Cameron Co., TX)

Bendire's Thrasher 2 (Nov. 20, AZ)

Curve-billed Thrasher 1 (Jan. 2, Kenedy Co., TX)

California Thrasher 1 (Sept. 2, CA)

Crissal Thrasher 2 (Jan. 4, Ward Co., TX)

LeConte's Thrasher 2 (Sept. 5, CA)

European Starling 1 (Jan. 1, Aransas Co., TX)

Common Myna 1 (Oct. 24, FL) [newly countable]

Eastern Yellow Wagtail 1 (June 2, Gambell, AK)

White Wagtail 2 (June 2, Gambell, AK)

Red-throated Pipit 3 (June 2, Gambell, AK)

American Pipit 1 (Jan. 1, Aransas Co., TX)

Sprague's Pipit 2 (Jan. 30, Kleberg Co., TX)

Bohemian Waxwing 1 (Jan. 10, MN)

Cedar Waxwing 1 (Jan. 5, Nueces Co., TX)

Phainopepla 1 (Apr. 4, Brewster Co., TX)
Olive Warbler 2 (Aug. 17, AZ)
Blue-winged Warbler 1 (July 1, ME)
Golden-winged Warbler 2 (May 2, Jefferson Co., TX)
Tennessee Warbler 1 (Apr. 29, Hidalgo Co., TX)
Orange-crowned Warbler 1 (Jan. 1, Aransas Co., TX)
Nashville Warbler 1 (Jan. 3, Cameron Co., TX)
Virginia's Warbler 1 (Aug. 16, AZ)
Colima Warbler 2 (Apr. 3, Brewster Co., TX)
Lucy's Warbler 1 (Apr. 4, Brewster Co, TX)
Crescent-chested Warbler 5 (Jan. 24, AZ)
Northern Parula 1 (Feb. 20, FL)
Tropical Parula 3 (Jan. 4, Hidalgo Co., TX)
Yellow Warbler 1 (Feb. 12, Hidalgo Co., TX)
Chestnut-sided Warbler 1 (Apr. 29, Hidalgo Co., TX)
Magnolia Warbler 1 (Apr. 30, Cameron Co., TX)
Cape May Warbler 1 (Apr. 20, FL)
Black-throated Blue Warbler 1 (Apr. 19, FL)
Yellow-rumped Warbler 1 (Jan. 1, Nueces Co., TX)
Black-throated Gray Warbler 1 (July 11, AZ)
Golden-cheeked Warbler 2 (Mar. 28, Travis Co., TX)
Black-throated Green Warbler 1 (Jan. 3, Hidalgo Co., TX)
Townsend's Warbler 1 (Jan. 17, CA)
Hermit Warbler 1 (Sept. 24, AZ)
Blackburnian Warbler 1 (Apr. 29, Hidalgo Co., TX)
Yellow-throated Warbler 1 (Jan. 2, Cameron Co., TX)
Grace's Warbler 1 (July 18, NM)
Pine Warbler 1 (Jan. 6, Fayette Co., TX)
Kirtland's Warbler 3 (May 22, MI)
Prairie Warbler 1 (Feb. 20, FL)
Palm Warbler 1 (Feb. 17, NC)
Bay-breasted Warbler 1 (May 1, Nueces Co., TX)

Blackpoll Warbler 1 (Apr. 20, FL)
Cerulean Warbler 1 (May 1, Nueces Co., TX)
Black-and-white Warbler 1 (Feb. 12, Hidalgo Co., TX)
American Redstart 1 (Feb. 20, FL)
Prothonotary Warbler 1 (Mar. 25, GA)
Worm-eating Warbler 1 (Apr. 24, FL)
Swainson's Warbler 2 (May 2, Jasper Co., TX)
Ovenbird 1 (Jan. 3, Hidalgo Co., TX)
Northern Waterthrush 1 (Apr. 19, FL)
Louisiana Waterthrush 1 (Mar. 28, Nueces Co., TX)
Kentucky Warbler 1 (Apr. 29, Hidalgo Co., TX)
Mourning Warbler 1 (July 2, ME)
MacGillivray's Warbler 1 (July 17, NV)
Common Yellowthroat 1 (Jan. 1, Aransas Co., TX)
Hooded Warbler 1 (Mar. 30, Jefferson Co., TX)
Wilson's Warbler 1 (Jan. 2, Cameron Co., TX)
Canada Warbler 1 (May 1, Nueces Co., TX)
Red-faced Warbler 2 (July 10, AZ)
Painted Redstart 2 (Apr. 3, Brewster Co., TX)
Rufous-capped Warbler 4 (Dec. 27, AZ)
Yellow-breasted Chat 1 (Apr. 28, Live Oak Co., TX)
Bananaquit 4 (Feb. 18, FL)
Hepatic Tanager 2 (July 10, AZ)
Summer Tanager 1 (Apr. 30, Cameron Co., TX)
Scarlet Tanager 1 (Apr. 30, Hidalgo Co., TX)
Western Tanager 1 (Jan. 3, Hidalgo Co., TX)
Flame-colored Tanager 4 (July 13, AZ)
White-collared Seedeater 3 (Apr. 29, Zapata Co., TX)
Olive Sparrow 2 (Jan. 2, Cameron Co., TX)
Green-tailed Towhee 1 (Apr. 5, Brewster Co., TX)
Spotted Towhee 1 (Jan. 12, Tarrant Co., TX)
Eastern Towhee 1 (Feb. 17, NC)
Canyon Towhee 1 (Jan. 23, AZ)
California Towhee 1 (Jan. 17, CA)

Abert's Towhee 1 (Jan. 23, AZ)

Rufous-winged Sparrow 2 (July 14, AZ)

Cassin's Sparrow 1 (Apr. 2, Ward Co., TX)

Bachman's Sparrow 2 (May 2, Angelina Co., TX)

Botteri's Sparrow 2 (Apr. 29, Cameron Co., TX)

Rufous-crowned Sparrow 1 (Apr. 4, Brewster Co., TX)

Five-striped Sparrow 3 (July 13, AZ)

American Tree Sparrow 1 (Jan. 26, Dallam Co., TX)

Chipping Sparrow 1 (Jan. 3, Hidalgo Co., TX)

Clay-colored Sparrow 1 (Mar. 20, Cameron Co., TX)

Brewer's Sparrow 1 (Jan. 23, AZ)

Field Sparrow 1 (Jan. 7, Parker Co., TX)

Black-chinned Sparrow 1 (July 21, NM)

Vesper Sparrow 1 (Jan. 6, Williamson Co., TX)

Lark Sparrow 1 (Jan. 2, Kleberg Co., TX)

Black-throated Sparrow 1 (Jan. 15, NM)

Sage Sparrow 1 (Jan. 20, CA)

Lark Bunting 1 (Jan. 14, Ward Co., TX)

Savannah Sparrow 1 (Jan. 1, Aransas Co., TX)

Grasshopper Sparrow 1 (Jan. 5, Aransas Co., TX)

Baird's Sparrow 2 (Nov. 21, AZ)

Henslow's Sparrow 2 (Dec. 20, Nacogdoches Co., TX)

Le Conte's Sparrow 1 (Jan. 5, Aransas Co., TX)

Nelson's Sharp-tailed Sparrow 1 (Mar. 17, Galveston Co., TX)

Saltmarsh Sharp-tailed Sparrow 1 (July 1, ME)

Seaside Sparrow 1 (Mar. 17, Chambers Co., TX)

Fox Sparrow 1 (Jan. 7, Tarrant Co., TX)

Song Sparrow 1 (Jan. 15, El Paso Co., TX)

Lincoln's Sparrow 1 (Jan. 4, Hidalgo Co., TX)

Swamp Sparrow 1 (Jan. 4, Hidalgo Co., TX)

White-throated Sparrow 1 (Jan. 7, Tarrant Co., TX)

Harris's Sparrow 1 (Jan. 7, Tarrant Co., TX)

White-crowned Sparrow 1 (Jan. 2, Kleberg Co., TX)

Golden-crowned Sparrow 1 (Jan. 17, CA)

Dark-eyed Junco 1 (Jan. 10, MN)

Yellow-eyed Junco 2 (Jan. 16, AZ)

McCown's Longspur 2 (Nov. 22, NM)

Lapland Longspur 1 (May 11, Adak Island, AK)

Smith's Longspur 2 (Mar. 13, AR)

Chestnut-collared Longspur 1 (Jan. 23, AZ)

Little Bunting 4 (June 2, Gambell, AK)

Snow Bunting 1 (Jan. 9, MN)

McKay's Bunting 2 (June 2, Gambell, AK)

Crimson-collared Grosbeak 4 (Dec. 17, Hidalgo Co., TX)

Northern Cardinal 1 (Jan. 1, Aransas Co., TX)

Pyrrhuloxia 1 (Jan. 1, Aransas Co., TX)

Rose-breasted Grosbeak 1 (Jan. 3, Hidalgo Co., TX)

Black-headed Grosbeak 1 (July 10, AZ)

Blue Bunting 4 (Dec. 17, Hidalgo Co., TX)

Blue Grosbeak 1 (Apr. 21, FL)

Lazuli Bunting 1 (May 9, Tarrant Co., TX)

Indigo Bunting 1 (Apr. 20, FL)

Varied Bunting 2 (July 13, AZ)

Painted Bunting 1 (Feb. 19, FL)

Dickcissel 1 (Feb. 19, FL)

Bobolink 1 (Apr. 22, FL)

Red-winged Blackbird 1 (Jan. 1, Aransas Co., TX)

Tricolored Blackbird 2 (Jan. 20, CA)

Eastern Meadowlark 1 (Jan. 1, Aransas Co., TX)

Western Meadowlark 1 (Jan. 18, CA)

Yellow-headed Blackbird 1 (Jan. 23, AZ)

Rusty Blackbird 1 (Feb. 1, Johnson Co., TX)

Brewer's Blackbird 1 (Jan. 2, Kenedy Co., TX)

Common Grackle 1 (Jan. 1, Aransas Co., TX)

Boat-tailed Grackle 1 (Jan. 1, Aransas Co., TX)

Great-tailed Grackle 1 (Jan. 1, Aransas Co., TX)

Shiny Cowbird 2 (Feb. 19, FL)

Bronzed Cowbird 1 (Jan. 30, Kleberg Co., TX)

Brown-headed Cowbird 1 (Jan. 1, Aransas Co., TX)

Orchard Oriole 1 (Mar. 30, Jefferson Co., TX)

Hooded Oriole 1 (Feb. 11, Starr Co., TX)

Bullock's Oriole 1 (Apr. 27, McMullen Co., TX)

Spot-breasted Oriole 2 (Feb. 19, FL)

Altamira Oriole 2 (Jan. 4, Hidalgo Co., TX)

Audubon's Oriole 2 (Feb. 11, Starr Co., TX)

Baltimore Oriole 1 (Feb. 17, NC)

Scott's Oriole 1 (Apr. 4, Brewster Co., TX)

Gray-crowned Rosy-Finch 1 (Jan. 25, NM)

Black Rosy-Finch 2 (Jan. 25, NM)

Brown-capped Rosy-Finch 2 (Jan. 25, NM)

Pine Grosbeak 1 (Jan. 9, MN)

Purple Finch 1 (Feb. 6, Grayson Co., TX)

Cassin's Finch 1 (Jan. 24, AZ)

House Finch 1 (Jan. 11, MN)

Red Crossbill 1 (Jan. 10, MN)

White-winged Crossbill 2 (Jan. 11, MN)

Common Redpoll 1 (Jan. 9, MN)

Hoary Redpoll 2 (Jan. 9, MN)

Pine Siskin 1 (Jan. 24, AZ)

Lesser Goldfinch 1 (Jan. 3, Hidalgo Co., TX)

Lawrence's Goldfinch 2 (Oct. 8, CA)

American Goldfinch 1 (Jan. 3, Hidalgo Co., TX)

Evening Grosbeak 1 (Jan. 9, MN)

House Sparrow 1 (Jan. 1, San Patricio Co., TX)

Eurasian Tree Sparrow 2 (Oct. 19, MO)

USEFUL REFERENCES FOR PLANNING AND CARRYING OUT A BIG YEAR

These are the books that I used to varying degrees; the newer editions, as they become available, are recommended.

Adams, Mark T. 2003. *Chasing Birds across Texas: A Birding Big Year.* Louise Lindsey Merrick Natural Environment Series. College Station: Texas A&M University Press.

American Birding Association. 2002. *ABA Checklist—Birds of the Continental United States and Canada.* Colorado Springs: American Birding Association.

Cooper, Jerry A. 1995. *Bird Finder: A Birder's Guide to Planning North American Trips.* Colorado Springs: American Birding Association.

Dunn, Jon L., and Jonathan Alderfer, eds. 2006. *National Geographic Field Guide to the Birds of North America.* 5th ed. Washington, D.C.: National Geographic Society.

Dunn, Jon L., and Kimball L. Garrett. 1997. *Warblers.* Peterson Field Guides. Boston: Houghton Mifflin Harcourt.

Eckert, Kim R. 2002. *A Birder's Guide to Minnesota.* Duluth, Minn.: Gavian Guides.

Ehrlich, Paul R., David S. Dobkin, and Darryl Wheye. 1988. *The Birder's Handbook—A Field Guide to the Natural History of North American Birds.* New York: Simon and Schuster.

Fussell III, John O. 1994. *A Birder's Guide to Coastal North Carolina.* Chapel Hill: University of North Carolina Press.

Graham, Gary L. 1992. *Texas Wildlife Viewing Guide.* Helena, Mont.: Falcon Publishing.

Holt, Harold R. 1993. *A Birder's Guide to the Texas Coast.* Colorado Springs: American Birding Association.

Howell, Steve N. G., and Jon Dunn. 2007. *Gulls of the Americas.* Peterson Reference Guides. Boston: Houghton Mifflin Harcourt.

Howell, Steve N. G., and Sophie Webb. 1995. *A Guide to the Birds of Mexico and Northern Central America.* Oxford: Oxford University Press.

Kemper, John. 1999. *Birding Northern California.* Helena, Mont.: Falcon Publishing.

Komito, Sandy. 1999. *I Came, I Saw, I Counted.* Fairlawn, N.J.: Bergen Publishing.

Kutac, Edward A. 1998. *Birder's Guide to Texas.* 2nd ed. Houston: Gulf Publishing.

Lockwood, Mark W. 2001. *Birds of the Texas Hill Country.* Austin: University of Texas Press.

Lockwood, Mark W., and Brush Freeman. 2004. *The Texas Ornithological Society Handbook of Texas Birds.* Louise Lindsey Merrick Natural Environment Series. College Station: Texas A&M University Press.

Lockwood, Mark W., William B. McKinney, James N. Paton, and Barry R. Zimmer. 1999. *A Birder's Guide to the Rio Grande Valley.* Colorado Springs: American Birding Association.

NARBA (North American Rare Bird Alert) subscription. Available at http://www.narba.org.

Obmascik, Mark. 2004. *The Big Year: A Tale of Man, Nature and Fowl Obsession.* New York: Free Press.

Opperman, Hal. 2003. *A Birder's Guide to Washington.* Colorado Springs: American Birding Association.

Parmeter, John, Bruce Neville, and Doug Emkalns. 2002. *New Mexico Bird Finding Guide.* Albuquerque: New Mexico Ornithological Society.

Peterson, Jim, and Barry R. Zimmer. 1998. *Birds of the Trans Pecos.* Austin: University of Texas Press.

Pranty, Bill. 2005. *A Birder's Guide to Florida.* Colorado Springs: American Birding Association.

Rappole, John H., and Gene W. Blacklock. 1994. *Birds of Texas: A Field Guide.* College Station: Texas A&M University Press.

The Roads of Texas. 1999. Fredericksburg: Texas A&M University Cartographics Laboratory and Shearer Publishing.

Roberson, Don. 1985. *Monterey Birds.* Monterey, Calif.: Monterey Peninsula Audubon Society.

Rylander, Kent. 2002. *The Behavior of Texas Birds.* Austin: University of Texas Press.

Schram, Brad. 2007. *A Birder's Guide to Southern California.* Colorado Springs: American Birding Association.

Seyffert, Kenneth D. 2001. *Birds of the Texas Panhandle.* W. L. Moody Jr. Natural History Series. College Station: Texas A&M University Press.

Sibley, David A. 2000. *National Audubon Society: The Sibley Guide to Birds.* New York: Alfred A. Knopf.

Stevenson, Mark, ed. 2007. *Finding Birds in Southeast Arizona.* 7th ed. Tucson, Ariz.: Tucson Audubon Society.

Taylor, Richard Cachor. 2005. *A Birder's Guide to Southeastern Arizona.* Colorado Springs: American Birding Association.

Texas Parks & Wildlife Department. Great Texas Wildlife Trails, Wildlife Trail Maps. Available at www.tpwd.state.tx.us.

Texbirds listserv subscription and archives. Available at http://lists.texbirds. org/texbirds.html.

Wauer, Roland. 1996. *A Field Guide to Birds of the Big Bend.* 2nd ed. Houston: Gulf Publishing.

Wauer, Roland H., and Mark Elwonger. 1998. Helena, Mont.: Falcon Publishing.

West, George C. 2002. *A Birder's Guide to Alaska.* Colorado Springs: American Birding Association.

Westrich, LoLo, and Jim Westrich. 1991. *Birder's Guide to Northern California.* Houston: Gulf Publishing.

BIRDING AREAS THROUGH MY BIG YEAR

Time frame	Place	Birds sought and/or found
Jan. 1–4	South Texas, Valley	South Texas residents and winter specialties
Jan. 8–11	Minnesota	Northern owls, woodpeckers, specialties
Jan. 14–27	New Mexico, Arizona, California	Winter southwestern specialties, Aztec Thrush
Jan. 30	Texas—King Ranch	Masked Duck
Feb. 5–6	North Texas	Rusty Blackbird, Purple Finch
Feb. 10	Texas—Valley	Elaenia
Feb. 15–18	North Carolina—land/pelagic	Eastern coastal/ocean birds
Feb. 19–21	Florida	Parrots, Short-tailed Hawk
Feb. 21–24	New Jersey, New York	Rare geese, eastern waterbirds
Feb. 27–Mar. 4	Oregon, Washington, British Columbia	Oregon pelagic birds, Northwestern Crow, Sky Lark
Mar. 10–12	Nebraska	Try for Common Crane, Greater Prairie-Chicken
Mar. 16–21	Texas coast	Fork-tailed Flycatcher, coastal birds, Valley birds
Mar. 23–25	Georgia	Green-breasted Mango
Mar. 28	Texas Hill Country	Golden-cheeked Warbler, Black-capped Vireo
Mar. 31–Apr. 1	Texas upper coast	Warblers, rails
Apr. 2–5	Texas—Big Bend	Colima Warbler, Zone-tailed Hawks, Common Black-Hawks
Apr. 8–14	Texas Panhandle, Colorado	Lek birds (Sage-Grouse, Lesser Prairie-Chicken)
Apr. 17–25	Florida	Everglades, Dry Tortugas specialties
Apr. 29–May 4	Texas coast	Great Texas Birding Classic—spring migrants
May 10–19	Alaska—Adak Island	Wandering Asian birds, Common Snipe, bean-geese
May 21–22	Michigan	Kirtland's Warbler, Ruffed Grouse
May 25–30	Alaska—St. Paul Island	Cliff birds, Red-legged Kittiwake
June 2–6	Alaska—Gambell	Seabirds, rarities
June 6–9	Alaska—Nome	Bristle-thighed Curlew, western Alaska specialties
June 10–13	Alaska—Barrow	Eiders, shorebirds
June 14–21	Alaska—Arctic NWR	Gray-headed Chickadee
June 30–July 3	Maine	Bicknell's Thrush, Spruce Grouse, Atlantic Puffin
July 9–15	Arizona	Hummingbirds, Montezuma Quail
July 15–19	Nevada	Try for Himalayan Snowcock
July 19–21	New Mexico	Black Swifts, mountain birds
July 28–30	Texas—Guadalupe Mountains	Try for Spotted Owl

Time frame	Place	Birds sought and/or found
July 30–Aug. 2	Florida	Antillean Nighthawk, Mangrove Cuckoo
Aug. 4–8	Nebraska	Himalayan Snowcock
Aug. 10	Texas—Valley	Yellow-green Vireo
Aug. 14–18	Arizona	Berylline Hummingbird, Thick-billed Kingbird, Spotted Owl
Aug. 21–24	North Carolina	Two pelagic trips
Aug. 24–31	Alaska—St. Paul Island	Sharp-tailed Sandpiper, Red-necked Stint
Sept. 2–8	California, Arizona	Land and pelagic birds, Island Scrub-Jay, Le Conte's Thrasher
Sept. 12–17	California	Two pelagic trips plus land birds
Sept. 22–25	Arizona	Plain-capped Starthroat
Sept. 25–26	Texas—Valley	Muscovy Duck
Oct. 1–5	Washington, Oregon	Sooty Grouse, Chukar, Vaux's Swift, Wood Sandpiper
Oct. 7–10	California	Virginia Rail, Lawrence's Goldfinch
Oct. 10–13	Alaska—Barrow	Ross's and Ivory Gull
Oct. 19–20	Missouri	Eurasian Tree-Sparrow
Oct. 23–27	Florida	Smooth-billed Ani, Flamingo, Budgerigar
Oct. 30–Nov. 4	California	Two-day pelagic, Northern Saw-whet Owl
Nov. 7–10	Texas—Valley, coast	Rose-throated Becard, Northern Saw-whet Owl
Nov. 20–22	New Mexico, Arizona	Bendire's Thrasher, Baird's Sparrow
Nov. 22–24	New Mexico, Colorado	White-tailed Ptarmigan, McCown's Longspur
Nov. 25–28	Washington	Gray Partridge
Dec. 5–9	Newfoundland	Yellow-legged, Black-headed, and Iceland Gulls, Northern Lapwing
Dec. 11–12	Texas—Valley	Nothing (Blue Bunting disappeared)
Dec. 14–16	Washington, Idaho	Nothing (Black-tailed Gull and Whooper Swan had been there)
Dec. 16–17	Texas—Valley	Crimson-collared Grosbeak, Blue Bunting
Dec. 18	Texas—Nacogdoches	Henslow's Sparrow
Dec. 21–23	Ontario	Nothing (Boreal Owl not found)
Dec. 27–28	Arizona	Rufous-capped Warbler

INDEX